Acclaim for Joan Didion's

Political Fictions

"It is Didion's cool perspective on hot issues that has made her work some of the most powerful writing of our time." —*Interview*

"Perceptive. . . . Didion has written one of the best outsider works on the insider game of politics." —*Business Week*

"Powerful. . . . Consistently intriguing and provocative." —*Seattle Post-Intelligencer*

"Didion is saying that staying informed is like being a good English student, a never-ending assignment to spot unreliable narrators, practice close reading and intuit what lurks between the lines." —*Salon*

"The insistent, inexorable rhythms of Didion's prose . . . are like a surgeon's strokes. No one else practices quite so precise dissection on the page." —*The Boston Globe*

"Blindingly brilliant." —*Kirkus Reviews*

"Didion's prose is as beautifully terse as ever; her observations as precise and deadly." —*W* magazine

Joan Didion

Political Fictions

Joan Didion was born in California and lives in New York. She is the author of five novels and five previous books of nonfiction: *After Henry*, *Miami*, *Salvador*, *The White Album*, and *Slouching Towards Bethlehem*.

ALSO BY JOAN DIDION

The Last Thing He Wanted

After Henry

Miami

Democracy

Salvador

The White Album

A Book of Common Prayer

Play It As It Lays

Slouching Towards Bethlehem

Run River

Political Fictions

Political Fictions

Joan Didion

Vintage International
Vintage Books
A Division of Random House, Inc.
New York

FIRST VINTAGE INTERNATIONAL EDITION, SEPTEMBER 2002

 Published in the United States by Vintage Books, a division of Random House, Inc., New York, and simultaneously in Canada by Random House of Canada Limited, Toronto. Originally published in hardcover in the United States by Alfred A. Knopf, a division of Random House, Inc., New York, in 2001.

Vintage is a registered trademark and Vintage International and colophon are trademarks of Random House, Inc.

The following essays, some retitled and in somewhat different form, first appeared in *The New York Review of Books* and are reprinted here by kind permission:

"Eye on the Prize" (retitled "Eyes on the Prize"), " 'Something Horrible' in El Salvador" and "The Lion King" (portions of the essay titled "The West Wing of Oz"), "The Teachings of Speaker Newt Gingrich" (retitled "Newt Gingrich, Superstar"), "The Deferential Spirit" (retitled "Political Pornography"), "Clinton Agonistes," "Uncovered Washington" (retitled "Vichy Washington"), "God's Country"; copyright © 1992, 1994, 1995, 1996, 1997, 1998, 1999, 2000 by NYREV, Inc. Reprinted by permission of *The New York Review of Books*. "Insider Baseball" and "Shooters Inc." (a portion of the essay titled "The West Wing of Oz") were first published in the *The New York Review of Books* in 1988, and are adapted by permission of Simon & Schuster, Inc., from *After Henry* by Joan Didion, copyright © 1992 by Joan Didion.

The Library of Congress has cataloged the Knopf edition as follows:
Didion, Joan.
Political fictions / Joan Didion.
New York : A. A. Knopf, 2001.
p. cm.
1. Political culture—United States—History—20th century. 2. Presidents—United States—Election—History—20th century. 3. Presidents —United States—Election—2000. 4. Political campaigns—United States—History—20th century. 5. United States—Politics and government—1989– .
E839.5 . D52 2001
973.929—dc21
2001093172
CIP

Vintage ISBN: 0-375-71890-7

Book design by Iris Weinstein

www.vintagebooks.com

Printed in the United States of America
10 9 8 7 6 5 4 3 2 1

This book is for Robert Silvers.
It is also for John Gregory Dunne, who lived through my discovering what he already knew.

Contents

Political Fictions

A Foreword

Early in 1988, Robert Silvers of *The New York Review of Books* asked me if I would do some pieces or a piece about the presidential campaign just then getting underway in New Hampshire. He would arrange credentials. All I had to do was show up, see what there was to see, and write something. I was flattered (a presidential election was a "serious" story, and no one had before solicited my opinions on one), and yet I kept putting off the only essential moment, which was showing up, giving the thing the required focus. In January and February I was selling a house in California, an easy excuse. In March and April I was buying an apartment in New York, another easy excuse. I had packing to do, then unpacking, painting to arrange, many household negotiations and renegotiations. Clippings and books and campaign schedules kept arriving, and I would stack them on shelves unread. I kept getting new deadlines from *The New York Review,* but there remained about domestic politics something resistant, recondite, some occult irreconcilability that kept all news of it just below my attention level. The events of the campaign as reported seemed to have taken place in a language I did not recognize. The stakes of the election as presented seemed not to compute. At the very point when I had in my mind successfully abandoned this project to which I could clearly bring no access, no knowledge, no understanding, I got another, more urgent call from *The New York Review.* The California primary was only days away. The Democratic and Republican national conventions were only weeks away. The office could put me on a campaign charter the next day, Jesse Jackson was flying out of Newark to California, the office could connect me in Los Angeles with the other campaigns. It so happened that my husband was leaving that day to do some research in Ireland. It so happened that our daughter was leaving that day to spend the summer in Guatemala and Nicaragua. There seemed, finally, no real excuse for me not to watch the California primary (and even to vote in it, since I was still registered in Los Angeles County), and so I went to Newark, and got on the plane. From the notes I typed at three the next morning in a room at the Hyatt Wilshire in Los Angeles, after a rally in South Central and a fundraiser at the Hollywood Palace and a meet-and-greet at the housing project where the candidate was to spend what remained of the night ("Would you call this Watts," the reporters kept saying, and "Who knows about guns? Who makes an AK?"), my introduction to American politics:

> I was told the campaign would be leaving Newark at 11:30 and to be at the Butler Aviation terminal no later than 10:30. Delmarie Cobb was to be the contact. At Butler Aviation the man on the gate knew nothing about the Jackson campaign but agreed to make a phone call, and was told to send me to Hangar 14. Hangar 14, a United hangar, was locked up except for a corrugated fire door open about two feet off the ground. Some men who approached knew nothing about any Jackson plane, they were "just telephone," but they limboed under the fire door and I followed them.
>
> The empty hangar. I walked around Malcolm Forbes's green 727, "Capitalist Tool," looked around the tarmac, and found no one. Finally a mechanic walked through and told me to try the office upstairs. I did. The metal door to the stairs was locked. I ran after the mechanic. He said he would pick the lock for me, and did. Upstairs, I found someone who told me to go to "Post J."
>
> At "Post J," an unmarked gate to the tarmac, I found a van open in back and four young men waiting. They said they were Jackson campaign, they were waiting for the Secret Service and then

the traveling campaign. I sat down on my bag and asked them to point out Delmarie Cobb when she came. Delmarie, one of them said, was already in California, but he was Delmarie's nephew, Stephen Gaines.

"Who's she," the Secret Service agents kept saying after they arrived. "She hasn't been cleared by the campaign, what's she doing here." "All I know is, she's got the right names in Chicago," Stephen Gaines kept saying. In any case the agents were absorbed in sweeping the bags. Finally one said he might as well sweep mine. Once he had done this he seemed confused. It seemed he had no place to put me. I wasn't supposed to be on the tarmac with the swept bags, but I wasn't supposed to be on the plane either. "Look," he said finally. "Just wait on the plane."

I waited, alone on the plane. Periodically an agent appeared and said, "You aren't supposed to be here, see, if there were someplace else to put you we'd put you there." The pilot appeared from the cockpit. "Give me a guesstimate how many people are flying," he said to me. I said I had no idea. "Fifty-five?" the pilot said. I shrugged. "Let's say fifty-five," the pilot said, "and get the fuel guys off the hook." None of this seemed promising.

The piece I finally did on the 1988 campaign, "Insider Baseball," was the first of a number of pieces I eventually did about various aspects of American politics, most of which had to do, I came to realize, with the ways in which the political process did not reflect but increasingly proceeded from a series of fables about American experience. As the pieces began to accumulate, I was asked with somewhat puzzling frequency about my own politics, what they "were," or "where they came from," as if they were eccentric, opaque, somehow unreadable. They are not. They are the logical product of a childhood largely spent among conservative California Republicans (this was before the meaning of "conservative" changed) in a postwar boom economy. The people with whom I grew up were interested in low taxes, a balanced budget, and a limited government. They believed above all that a limited government had no business tinkering with the private or cultural life of its citizens. In 1964, in accord with these interests and beliefs, I voted, ardently, for Barry Goldwater. Had Goldwater remained the same age and continued running, I would have voted for him in every election thereafter. Instead, shocked and to a curious extent personally offended by the enthusiasm with which California Republicans who had jettisoned an authentic conservative (Goldwater) were rushing to embrace Ronald Reagan, I registered as a Democrat, the first member of my family (and perhaps in my generation still the only member) to do so. That this did not involve taking a markedly different view on any issue was a novel discovery, and one that led me to view "America's two-party system" with—and this was my real introduction to American politics—a somewhat doubtful eye.

At a point quite soon during the dozen-some years that followed getting on that charter at Newark, it came to my attention that there was to writing about politics a certain Sisyphean aspect. Broad patterns could be defined, specific inconsistencies documented, but no amount of definition or documentation seemed sufficient to stop the stone that was our apprehension of politics from hurtling back downhill. The romance of New Hampshire would again be with us. The crucible event in the candidate's "character" would again be explored. Even that which seemed ineluctably clear would again vanish from collective memory, sink traceless into the stream of collapsing news and comment cycles that had become our national River Lethe. It was clear for example in 1988 that the political process had already become perilously remote from the electorate it was meant to represent. It was also clear in 1988 that the decision of the two major parties to obscure any possible perceived distinction between themselves, and by so doing to narrow the contested ground to a handful of selected "target" voters, had already imposed considerable strain on the basic principle of the democratic exercise, that of assuring the nation's citizens a voice in its affairs. It was also clear in 1988 that the rhetorical manipulation of resentment and anger designed to attract these target voters had reduced the nation's political dialogue to a level so dispiritingly low that its highest expression had come to be a pernicious nostalgia. Perhaps most strikingly of all, it was clear in 1988 that those inside the process had congealed into a permanent political class, the defining characteristic of which was its readiness to abandon those not inside the process. All of this was known. Yet by the time of the November 2000 presidential election and the onset of the thirty-six days that came to be known as "Florida," every aspect of what had been known in 1988 would again need to be rediscovered, the stone pushed up the hill one more time.

Perhaps the most persistent of the fables from which the political process proceeds has to do with the "choice" it affords the nation's citizens, who are seen to remain unappreciative. On the Saturday morning before the November 2000 presidential election, *The Washington Post* ran on its front page a piece by Richard Morin and Claudia Deane headlined "As Turnout Falls, Apathy Emerges As Driving Force." The thrust of this piece, which was based on polls of voter and nonvoter attitudes conducted both by the *Post* and by the Joan Shorenstein Center's "Vanishing Voter Project" at Harvard, was reinforced by a takeout about a Missouri citizen named Mike McClusky, a thirty-seven-year-old Army veteran who, despite "the 21-foot flagpole with the Stars and Stripes in the middle of the front yard," had never voted and did not now intend to vote. His wife, Danielle

McClusky, did vote, and the *Post* noted the readiness with which she discussed "her take on Social Security, and health care, and health maintenance organizations, and what she heard on Larry King, and what she heard on Chris Matthews, and what George W. Bush would do, and what Al Gore would do." Meanwhile, the *Post* added, making it fairly clear which McClusky merited the approval of its Washington readers, "Mike McClusky pets the dogs and half-listens because he doesn't really have to sift through any of this." Accompanying the main story were graphs, purporting to show why Americans did not vote, and the *Post*'s analysis of its own graphs was this: "Apathy is the single biggest reason why an estimated 100 million Americans will not vote on Tuesday."

The graphs themselves, however, told a somewhat more complicated story: only thirty-five percent of nonvoters, or about seventeen percent of all adult Americans, fell into the "apathetic" category, which, according to a director of the Shorenstein study, included those who "have no sense of civic duty," "aren't interested in politics," and "have no commitment in keeping up with public affairs." Another fourteen percent of nonvoters were classified as "disconnected," a group including both those "who can't get to the polls because of advanced age or disability" and those "who recently changed addresses and are not yet registered"—in other words, people functionally unable to vote. The remaining fifty-one percent of these nonvoters, meaning roughly a quarter of all adult Americans, were classified as either "alienated" ("the angry men and women of U.S. politics . . . so disgusted with politicians and the political process that they've opted out") or "disenchanted" ("these non-voters aren't so much repelled by politics as they are by the way politics is practiced"), in either case pretty much the polar opposite of "apathetic." According to the graphs, more than seventy percent of all nonvoters were in fact registered, a figure that cast some ambiguity on the degree of "apathy" even among the thirty-five percent categorized as "apathetic."

Study of the actual Shorenstein results clouded the *Post*'s "apathy" assessment still further. According to the Shorenstein Center's release dated the same Saturday as the *Post* story, its polling had shown that the attitudes toward politicians and the political process held by those who intended to vote differed—up to an interesting point—only narrowly from the attitudes held by those who did not intend to vote. Eighty-nine percent of nonvoters and seventy-six percent of voters agreed with the statement "most political candidates will say almost anything in order to get themselves elected." Seventy-eight percent of nonvoters and seventy percent of voters agreed with the statement "candidates are more concerned with fighting each other than with solving the nation's problems." Almost seventy percent of nonvoters and voters alike agreed with the statement "campaigns seem more like theater or entertainment than something to be taken seriously." The interesting point at which the attitudes of voters and nonvoters did diverge was that revealed by questioning about specific policies. Voters, for example, tended to believe that the federal budget surplus should go to a tax cut. Nonvoters, who on the whole had less education and lower income, more often said that the surplus should be spent on health, welfare, and education. "Nonvoters have different needs," is the way the *Post* summarized this. "But why should politicians listen?"

This notion of voting as a consumer transaction (the voter "pays" with his or her vote to obtain the ear of his or her professional politician, or his or her "leader," or by logical extension his or her "superior") might seem a spiritless social contract, although not—if it actually delivered on the deal—an intrinsically unworkable one. But of course the contract does not deliver: only sentimentally does "the vote" give "the voter" an empathetic listener in the political class, let alone any leverage on the workings of that class. When the chairman of Michael Dukakis's 1988 New York Finance Council stood barefoot on a table at the Atlanta Hyatt during that summer's Democratic convention (see page 48) and said "I've been around this process a while and one thing I've noticed, it's the people who write the checks who get treated as if they have a certain amount of power," she had a clear enough understanding of how the contract worked and did not work. When the only prominent Democrat on the west side of Los Angeles to raise money in 1988 for Jesse Jackson (see page 55) said "When I want something, I'll have a hard time getting people to pick up the phone, I recognize that, I made the choice," he had a clear enough understanding of how the contract worked and did not work.

When the same Democrat, Stanley Sheinbaum, said, in 1992 (see page 151), "I mean it's no longer a thousand dollars, to get into the act now you've got to give a hundred thousand," he had a clear enough understanding of how the contract worked and did not work. When Jerry Brown, who after eight years as governor of California had become the state party chairman who significantly raised the bar for Democratic fundraising in California, said at the 1992 Democratic convention in Madison Square Garden (see page 120) that the time had arrived to listen to "the people who fight our wars but never come to our receptions," he had a clear enough understanding of how the contract worked and did not work. When one of George W. Bush's lawyers told *The Los Angeles Times* in December 2000 that "if you were in this game, you had to be in Florida," he too had a clear enough understanding of how the contract worked and did not work. "Almost every lobbyist, political organizer, consulting group with ties to the Republicans was represented," a Republican official was quoted by Robert B. Reich, writing on the op-ed page of *The New York Times,* as having said to the same point. "If you ever were or wanted to be a Republican, you were down there."

Such clear understandings among the professionals of both major parties notwithstanding, the fact that the 2000 presidential election in Florida could come down to only a handful of votes would still be popularly presented as evidence that "every vote counts," conclusive proof of the absolute power of the American voter. "Whatever else one might conclude about the events of the past two weeks, they have awakened young people to election politics, to the daily news, and to the importance of the vote," a director of the Vanishing Voter project rather mysteriously concluded from data showing that although the attention level of younger respondents rose during the events in Florida, seventy percent of all Americans, young and old, reported themselves to be "discouraged" by those events and fifty percent to believe that the election had been "unfair to voters." Two weeks after the election, according to the Shorenstein Center's comparison of polling conducted just before the election and that conducted in its immediate aftermath, the number of Americans who answered "None" to the question "How much influence do you think people like you have on what the government does?" had increased from one in ten to one in four.

This "civics lesson" aspect of the thirty-six days that followed the election was much stressed, yet what those days actually demonstrated, from the morning on Day One when the candidate whose brother happened to be governor of Florida lined up the critical Tallahassee law firms until the evening on Day Thirty-five when the Supreme Court decided *Bush v. Gore* for the same candidate, was the immateriality of the voter against the raw power of being inside the process. "The Republicans didn't have to hire the big firms, or tie them up," a Gore strategist told *The Washington Post* about what happened on the morning of Day One. "Jeb Bush didn't need to send a note for them to know." About what happened on the evening of Day Thirty-five, Cokie Roberts, on *This Week,* made the case of the permanent political class for order, for continuity, for the perpetuation of the contract that delivered only to itself: "I think people do think it's political but they think that's okay. They expect the court to be political and—and they wanted this election to be over." In the absence of actual evidence to back up this arrestingly constructive reading of what "people" expected or wanted, she offered the rationale then common among those inside the process: "At least now, we are beginning to have that post-election coming together. Period."

The events that followed the November 2000 election were widely interpreted by those inside the process as aberrant, a source of outrage or education (the civics-lesson benefit again) but in any case an improbable random sequence thrown up by chance, in no way predictable and therefore dangerous: a "disaster," a "debacle," a disruption that could lead, in the absence of "closure," or of "that post-election coming together" longed for by Mrs. Roberts and by many others, only to "chaos." Yet the events in question were in many ways not only entirely predictable but entirely familiar: the reactive angers that drove this post-election period were not different in kind from the reactive angers that had driven American politics since the 1960s. Now as before, "the rule of law" was repeatedly invoked, although how a matter as demonstrably lawyered up as the Florida recount could be seen to threaten the rule of law was unclear. Now as before, the principal threat to "the rule of law" was construed to be the court system, which Robert H. Bork had described in *Slouching Towards Gomorrah* as the "enforcement arm" of what he called "the 'intellectual' class," the branch of government "responsible in no small measure for the spread of both radical individualism and radical egalitarianism." Now as before, the prevailing tone, on all sides, was self-righteous, victimized, grandiose; a quite florid instance of what Richard Hofstadter had identified in 1965 as the paranoid style in American politics.

This was all familiar, but the events that followed the 2000 presidential election represented something more than another airing of popular resentments to advance one or another element within the political process. The Democrats had lost that election, according to Al From of the Democratic Leadership Council, because their candidate's "populist" message had failed to resonate with the Democratic target voter, who was "affluent, educated, diverse, suburban, 'wired,' and moderate." That the same adjectives described the Republican target voter was, according to Mr. From, the point itself: the "true story" of the 2000 campaign was that the Republican and Democratic parties had at last achieved "parity," which meant that they were now positioned to split the remaining electorate, those "middle- and upper-middle-class Americans" who would be "the dominant voters of the Information Age." In other words we had reached the zero-sum point toward which the process had been moving, the moment in which the determination of the Republican Party to maximize its traditional low-turnout advantage was perfectly matched by the determination of the Democratic Party to shed any association with its traditional low-income base. "Who cares what every adult thinks," as one Republican strategist had presciently said to *The Washington Post* (see page 248) in 1998. "It's totally not germane to this election."

"Florida," in this light, could be seen as a perfectly legible ideogram of the process itself, and of where that process had taken us: the reduction of a national presidential election to a few hundred voters over which both parties could fight for thirty-six days was the logical imaginative representation of a process that had relentlessly worked, to the end of eliminating known risk factors, to restrict the contest to the smallest possible electorate. Fifty-three percent of voters in the 2000 election, Mr. From noted with what seemed genuine enthusiasm, had ("for the first time in our history") incomes above $50,000. Forty-three percent were suburban.

Seventy-four percent had some higher education; forty-two percent had actual college degrees. Seventy percent said that they invested in the stock market. That this was not a demographic profile of the country at large, that half the nation's citizens had only a vassal relationship to the government under which they lived, that the democracy we spoke of spreading throughout the world was now in our own country only an ideality, had come to be seen, against the higher priority of keeping the process in the hands of those who already held it, as facts without application.

Insider Baseball

October 27, 1988

1.

It occurred to me during the summer of 1988, in California and Atlanta and New Orleans, in the course of watching first the California primary and then the Democratic and Republican national conventions, that it had not been by accident that the people with whom I had preferred to spend time in high school had, on the whole, hung out in gas stations. They had not run for student body office. They had not gone to Yale or Swarthmore or DePauw, nor had they even applied. They had gotten drafted, gone through basic at Fort Ord. They had knocked up girls, and married them, had begun what they called the first night of the rest of their lives with a midnight drive to Carson City and a five-dollar ceremony performed by a justice of the peace still in his pajamas. They got jobs at the places that had laid off their uncles. They paid their bills or did not pay their bills, made down payments on tract houses, led lives on that social and economic edge referred to, in Washington and among those whose preferred locus is Washington, as "out there." They were never destined to be, in other words, communicants in what we have come to call, when we want to indicate the traditional ways in which power is exchanged and the status quo maintained in the United States, "the process."

"The process today gives everyone a chance to participate," Tom Hayden, by way of explaining "the difference" between 1968 and 1988, said to Bryant Gumbel on NBC at 7:50 A.M. on the day after Jesse Jackson spoke at the 1988 Democratic convention in Atlanta. This was, at a convention that had as its controlling principle the notably nonparticipatory goal of "unity," demonstrably not true, but people inside the process, constituting as they do a self-created and self-referring class, a new kind of managerial elite, tend to speak of the world not necessarily as it is but as they want people out there to believe it is. They tend to prefer the theoretical to the observable, and to dismiss that which might be learned empirically as "anecdotal." They tend to speak a language common in Washington but not specifically shared by the rest of us. They talk about "programs," and "policy," and how to "implement" them or it, about "tradeoffs" and constituencies and positioning the candidate and distancing the candidate, about the "story," and how it will "play."

They speak of a candidate's "performance," by which they usually mean his skill at circumventing questions, not as citizens but as professional insiders, attuned to signals pitched beyond the range of normal hearing. "I hear he did all right this afternoon," they were saying to one another in the press section of the Louisiana Superdome in New Orleans on the evening in August 1988 when Dan Quayle was to be nominated for the vice presidency. "I hear he did all right with Brinkley." By the time the balloons fell that night the narrative had changed: "Quayle, zip," the professionals were saying as they brushed the confetti off their laptops. These were people who spoke of the process as an end in itself, connected only nominally, and vestigially, to the electorate and its possible concerns. "She used to be an issues person but now she's involved in the process," a prominent conservative said to me in New Orleans by way of suggesting why an acquaintance who believed Jack Kemp to be "speaking directly to what people out there want" had nonetheless backed George Bush. "Anything that brings the process closer to the people is all to the good," George Bush had declared in his 1987 autobiography, *Looking Forward,* accepting as given this relatively recent notion that the people and the process need not automatically be on convergent tracks.

When we talk about the process, then, we are talking, increasingly, not about "the democratic process," or the general mechanism affording the citizens of a state a voice in its affairs, but the reverse: a mechanism seen as so specialized that access to it is correctly limited to its own professionals, to those who manage policy and those who report on it, to those who run the polls and those who quote them, to those who ask and those who answer the questions on the Sunday shows, to the media consultants, to the columnists, to the issues advisers, to those who give the off-the-record breakfasts and those who attend them; to that handful of insiders who invent, year in and year out, the narrative of public life. "I didn't realize you were a political junkie," Martin Kaplan, the former *Washington Post* reporter and Mondale speechwriter who was married to Susan Estrich, the manager of the Dukakis campaign, said when I mentioned that I planned to write about the campaign; the assumption here, that the narrative should be not just written only by its own specialists but also legible only to its own specialists, is why, finally, an American presidential campaign raises questions that go so vertiginously to the heart of the structure.

2.

What strikes one most vividly about such a campaign is precisely its remoteness from the real life of the country. The figures are well known, and suggest a national indifference usually construed, by those inside the process, as ignorance, or "apathy," in any case a defect not in themselves but in the clay they have been given to mold. Only slightly more than half of those eligible to vote in the United States did vote in the 1984 presidential election. An average 18.5 percent of what Nielsen Media Research calls the "television households" in the United States tuned into network coverage of the 1988 Republican convention in New Orleans, meaning that 81.5 percent did not. An average 20.2 percent of those "television households" tuned into network coverage of the 1988 Democratic convention in Atlanta, meaning that 79.8 percent did not. The decision to tune in or out ran along predictable lines: "The demography is good even if the households are low," a programming executive at Bozell, Jacobs, Kenyon & Eckhardt told *The New York Times* in July 1988 about the agency's decision to buy "campaign event" time for Merrill Lynch on both CBS and CNN. "The ratings are about nine percent off 1984," an NBC marketing executive allowed, again to *The New York Times,* "but the upscale target audience is there."

When I read this piece I recalled standing, the day before the 1988 California primary, in a dusty central California schoolyard to which the leading Democratic candidate had come to speak one more time about what kind of president he wanted to be. The crowd was listless, restless. There were gray thunderclouds overhead. A little rain fell. "We welcome you to Silicon Valley," an official had said by way of greeting the candidate, but this was not in fact Silicon Valley: this was San Jose, and a part of San Jose particularly untouched by technological prosperity, a neighborhood in which the lowering of two-toned Impalas remained a central activity. "I want to be a candidate who brings people together," the candidate was saying at the exact moment a man began shouldering his way past me and through a group of women with children in their arms. This was not a solid citizen, not a member of the upscale target audience. This was a man wearing a down vest and a camouflage hat, a man with a definite little glitter in his eyes, a member not of the 18.5 percent and not of the 20.2 percent but of the 81.5 percent, the 79.8. "I've got to see the next president," he muttered repeatedly. "I've got something to tell him."

". . . Because that's what this party is all about," the candidate said.

"Where is he?" the man said, confused. "Who is he?"

"Get lost," someone said.

". . . Because that's what this country is all about," the candidate said.

Here we had the last true conflict of cultures in America, that between the empirical and the theoretical. On the empirical evidence this country was about two-toned Impalas and people with camouflage hats and a little glitter in their eyes, but this had not been, among people inclined to the theoretical, the preferred assessment. Nor had it even been, despite the fact that we had all stood together on the same dusty asphalt, under the same plane trees, the general assessment: this was how Joe Klein, writing a few weeks later in *New York* magazine, had described those last days before the California primary:

> Breezing across California on his way to the nomination last week, Michael Dukakis crossed a curious American threshold. . . . The crowds were larger, more excited now; they seemed to be searching for reasons to love him. They cheered eagerly, almost without provocation. People reached out to touch him—not to shake hands, just to touch him. . . . Dukakis seemed to be making an almost subliminal passage in the public mind: he was becoming presidential.

Those June days in 1988 during which Michael Dukakis did or did not cross a curious American threshold had in fact been instructive. The day that ended in the schoolyard in San Jose had at first seemed, given that it was the day before the California primary, underscheduled, pointless, three essentially meaningless events separated by plane flights. At Taft High School in Woodland Hills that morning there had been little girls waving red and gold pom-poms in front of the cameras. "Hold that tiger," the band had played. "Dream . . . maker," the choir had crooned. "Governor Dukakis . . . this is . . . Taft High," the student body president had said. "I understand that this is the first time a presidential candidate has come to Taft High," Governor Dukakis had said. "Is there any doubt . . .

under those circumstances . . . who you should support?"

"Jackson," a group of Chicano boys on the back sidewalk shouted in unison.

"That's what it's all about," Governor Dukakis had said, and "health care," and "good teachers and good teaching."

This event had been abandoned, and another materialized: a lunchtime "rally" in a downtown San Diego office plaza through which many people were passing on their way to lunch, a borrowed crowd but a less than attentive one. The cameras focused on the balloons. The sound techs picked up "La Bamba." "We're going to take child-support enforcement seriously in this country," Governor Dukakis had said, and "tough drug enforcement here and abroad." "Tough choices," he had said, and "we're going to make teaching a valued profession in this country."

Nothing said in any venue that day had seemed to have much connection with anybody listening ("I want to work with you and with working people all over this country," the candidate had said in the downtown San Diego office plaza, but people who work in offices in downtown San Diego do not think of themselves as "working people"), and late that afternoon, on the bus to the San Jose airport, I had asked a reporter who had traveled through the spring with the various campaigns (among those who moved from plane to plane it was agreed, by June, that the Bush plane had the worst access to the candidate and the best food, that the Dukakis plane had average access and average food, and that the Jackson plane had full access and no time to eat) if the candidate's appearances that day did not seem a little off the point.

"Not really," the reporter said. "He covered three major markets."

Among those who traveled regularly with the campaigns, in other words, it was taken for granted that these "events" they were covering, and on which they were in fact filing, were not merely meaningless but deliberately so: occasions in which film could be shot and no mistakes made ("They hope he won't make any mistakes," the NBC correspondent covering George Bush kept saying the evening of the September 25, 1988, debate at Wake Forest College, and, an hour and a half later, "He didn't make any big mistakes"), events designed only to provide settings for those unpaid television spots which in this case were appearing, even as we spoke, on the local news in California's three major media markets. "On the fishing trip, there was no way for the television crews to get videotapes out," *The Los Angeles Times* noted a few weeks later in a piece about how "poorly designed and executed events" had interfered with coverage of a Bush campaign "environmental" swing through the Pacific Northwest. "At the lumber mill, Bush's advance team arranged camera angles so poorly that in one setup only his legs could get on camera." A Bush adviser had been quoted: "There is no reason for camera angles not being provided for.

We're going to sit down and talk about these things at length."

Any traveling campaign, then, was a set, moved at considerable expense from location to location. The employer of each reporter on the Dukakis plane the day before the California primary was billed, for a total flying time of under three hours, $1,129.51; the billing to each reporter who happened, on the morning during the Democratic convention in Atlanta when Michael Dukakis and Lloyd Bentsen met with Jesse Jackson, to ride along on the Dukakis bus from the Hyatt Regency to the World Congress Center, a distance of perhaps ten blocks, was $217.18. There was the hierarchy of the set: there were actors, there were directors, there were script supervisors, there were grips. There was the isolation of the set, and the arrogance, the contempt for outsiders. I recall pink-cheeked young aides on the Dukakis campaign referring to themselves, innocent of irony and so of history, as "the best and the brightest." On the morning after the Wake Forest debate, Michael Oreskes of *The New York Times* gave us this memorable account of Bush aides crossing the Wake Forest campus:

> The Bush campaign measured exactly how long it would take its spokesmen to walk briskly from the room in which they were watching the debate to the center where reporters were filing their articles. The answer was three and a half minutes—too long for Mr. Bush's strategists, Lee Atwater, Robert Teeter, and Mr. Darman. They

> ran the course instead as young aides cleared students and other onlookers from their path.

There was also the tedium of the set: the time spent waiting for the shots to be set up, the time spent waiting for the bus to join the motorcade, the time spent waiting for telephones on which to file, the time spent waiting for the Secret Service ("the agents," they were called on the traveling campaigns, never the Secret Service, just "the agents," or "this detail," or "this rotation") to sweep the plane. It was a routine that encouraged a certain passivity. There was the plane, or the bus, and one got on it. There was the schedule, and one followed it. There was time to file, or there was not. "We should have had a page-one story," a *Boston Globe* reporter complained to *The Los Angeles Times* after the Bush campaign had failed to provide the advance text of a Seattle "environment" speech scheduled to end only twenty minutes before the departure of the plane for California. "There are times when you sit up and moan, 'Where is Michael Deaver when you need him,'" an ABC producer said to the *Times* on this point.

A final victory, for the staff and the press on a traveling campaign, would mean not a new production but only a new location: the particular setups and shots of the campaign day (the walk on the beach, the meet-and-greet at the housing project) would dissolve imperceptibly, isolation and arrogance and tedium intact, into the South Lawns, the Oval Office signings, the arrivals and departures of the administration day. There would still be the "young aides." There would still be the "onlookers" to be cleared from the path. Another location, another stand-up: "We already shot a tarmac departure," they say on the campaign planes. "This schedule has two Rose Gardens," they say in the White House press room. Ronald Reagan, when asked by David Frost how his life in the Oval Office had differed from his expectation of it, said this: "I was surprised at how familiar the whole routine was—the fact that the night before I would get a schedule telling me what I'm going to do all day the next day and so forth."

3.

American reporters "like" covering a presidential campaign (it gets them out on the road, it has balloons, it has music, it is viewed as a big story, one that leads to the respect of one's peers, to the Sunday shows, to lecture fees and often to Washington), which is why there has developed among those who do it so arresting an enthusiasm for overlooking the contradictions inherent in reporting that which occurs only in order to be reported. They are willing, in exchange for "access," to transmit the images their sources wish transmitted. They are even willing, in exchange for certain colorful details around which a "reconstruction" can be built (the "kitchen table" at which the Dukakis campaign was said to have conferred on the night Lloyd Bentsen was added to the 1988 Democratic ticket, the "slips of paper" on which key members of the 1988 Bush campaign, aboard Air Force Two on their way to the Republican convention in New Orleans, were said to have written their choices for vice president), to present these images not as a story the campaign wants told but as fact. This was *Time,* reporting from New Orleans on George Bush's reaction to criticism of Dan Quayle, his chosen running mate:

> Bush never wavered in support of the man he had lifted so high. "How's Danny doing," he asked several times. But the Vice President never felt the compulsion to question Quayle face-to-face. The awkward interrogation was left to Baker. Around noon, Quayle grew restive about answering further questions. "Let's go," he urged, but Baker pressed to know more. By early afternoon, the mood began to brighten in the Bush bunker. There were no new revelations: the media hurricane had for the moment blown over.

"Appeal to the media by exposing the [Bush campaign's] heavy-handed spin-doctoring," William Safire advised the Dukakis campaign. "We hate to be seen being manipulated." This was Sandy Grady, reporting from Atlanta and the Dukakis campaign:

> Ten minutes before he was to face the biggest audience of his life, Michael Dukakis got a hug

from his 84-year-old mother, Euterpe, who chided him, "You'd better be good, Michael." Dukakis grinned and said, "I'll do my best, Ma."

"Periodically," *The New York Times* reported in March 1988, "Martin Plissner, the political editor of CBS News, and Susan Morrison, a television producer and former political aide, organize gatherings of the politically connected at their house in Washington. At such parties, they organize secret ballots asking the assembled experts who will win. . . . By November 1, 1987, the results of Mr. Dole's organizing efforts were clear in a new Plissner-Morrison poll." The symbiosis here was complete, and the only outsider was the increasingly hypothetical voter, who was seen as responsive not to actual issues but to their adroit presentation: "At the moment the Republican message is simpler and more clear than ours," the Democratic chairman for California, Peter Kelly, said to *The Los Angeles Times* in August 1988, complaining, on the matter of what was called the Pledge of Allegiance issue, not that it was a false issue but that Bush had seized the initiative, or "the symbolism."

"Bush Gaining in Battle of TV Images," *The Washington Post* headlined a front-page story in September 1988, and quoted Jeff Greenfield, the ABC News political reporter: "George Bush is almost always outdoors, coatless, sometimes with his sleeves rolled up, and looks ebullient and Happy Warrior-ish. Mike Dukakis is almost always indoors, with his jacket on, and almost always behind a lectern." According to the same week's issue of *Newsweek,* the Bush campaign, which had the superior gift for getting film shot in "dramatic settings—like Boston Harbor," was winning "the all-important battle of the backdrops." A CBS producer covering the Dukakis campaign was quoted complaining about an occasion when Governor Dukakis, speaking to students on a California beach, had faced the students instead of the camera. "The only reason Dukakis was on the beach was to get his picture taken," the producer had said. "So you might as well see his face." Pictures, *Newsweek* had concluded, "often speak louder than words."

This "battle of the backdrops" story appeared on page 24 of the *Newsweek* dated September 12, 1988. On page 23 of the same issue there appeared, as illustrations for the lead National Affairs story ("Getting Down and Dirty: As the mudslinging campaign moves into full gear, Bush stays on the offensive—and Dukakis calls back his main street-fighting man"), two half-page color photographs, one of each candidate, which seemed designed to address the very concerns expressed on page 24 and in the *Post.* The photograph of George Bush showed him indoors, behind a lectern, with his jacket on. That of Michael Dukakis showed him outdoors, coatless, sleeves rolled up, looking ebullient, about to throw a baseball on an airport tarmac: something had been learned from Jeff Greenfield, or something had been told to Jeff Greenfield. "We talk to the press, and things take on a life of their own," Mark Siegel, a Democratic political consultant, said to Elizabeth Drew.

About this baseball on the tarmac. On the day that Michael Dukakis appeared at the high school in Woodland Hills and at the office plaza in San Diego and in the schoolyard in San Jose, there was, although it did not appear on the schedule, a fourth event, what was referred to among the television crews as a "tarmac arrival with ball tossing." This event had taken place in late morning, on the tarmac at the San Diego airport, just after the campaign's chartered 737 had rolled to a stop and the candidate had emerged. There had been a moment of hesitation, or decision. Then baseball mitts had been produced, and Jack Weeks, the traveling press secretary, had tossed a ball to the candidate. The candidate had tossed the ball back. The rest of us had stood in the sun and given this our full attention: some forty adults standing on a tarmac watching a diminutive figure in shirtsleeves and a red tie toss a ball, undeflected even by the arrival of an Alaska Airlines 767, to his press secretary.

"Just a regular guy," one of the cameramen had said, his inflection that of the "union official" who confided, in an early Dukakis commercial aimed at blue-collar voters, that he had known "Mike" a long time, and backed him despite his not being "your shot-and-beer kind of guy."

"I'd say he was a regular guy," another cameraman had said. "Definitely."

"I'd sit around with him," the first cameraman said.

Kara Dukakis, one of the candidate's daughters, had at that moment emerged from the 737.

"You'd have a beer with him?"

Jack Weeks had tossed the ball to Kara Dukakis.

"I'd have a beer with him."

Kara Dukakis had tossed the ball to her father. Her father had caught the ball and tossed it back to her.

"OK," one of the cameramen had said. "We got the daughter. Nice. That's enough. Nice."

The CNN producer then on the campaign told me, later in the day, that the first recorded ball tossing on the Dukakis campaign had been outside a bowling alley somewhere in Ohio. CNN had shot it. When the campaign realized that only one camera had it, they restaged it.

"We have a lot of things like the ball tossing," the producer said. "We have the Greek dancing, for example."

I asked if she still bothered to shoot it.

"I get it," she said, "but I don't call in anymore and say, 'Hey, hold it, I've got him dancing.'"

This sounded about right (the candidate might, after all, bean a citizen during the ball tossing, and CNN would need film), and not until I read Joe Klein's version of those days in California did it occur to me that this eerily contrived moment on the tarmac at San Diego could become, at least provisionally, history. "The Duke seemed downright jaunty," Joe Klein reported. "He tossed a baseball with aides. He was flagrantly multilingual. He danced Greek dances. . . ." In the July 25, 1988, issue of *U.S. News & World Report,* Michael Kramer opened his cover story ("Is Dukakis Tough Enough?") with a more developed version of the ball tossing:

> The thermometer read 101 degrees, but the locals guessed 115 on the broiling airport tarmac in Phoenix. After all, it was under a noonday sun in the desert that Michael Dukakis was indulging his truly favorite campaign ritual—a game of catch with his aide Jack Weeks. "These days," he has said, "throwing the ball around when we land somewhere is about the only exercise I get." For 16 minutes, Dukakis shagged flies and threw strikes. Halfway through, he rolled up his sleeves, but he never loosened his tie. Finally, mercifully, it was over and time to pitch the obvious tongue-in-cheek question: "Governor, what does throwing a ball around in this heat say about your mental stability?" Without missing a beat, and without a trace of a smile, Dukakis echoed a sentiment he has articulated repeatedly in recent months: "What it means is that I'm tough."

Nor was this the last word. On July 31, 1988, in *The Washington Post,* David S. Broder, who had also been with the Dukakis campaign in Phoenix, gave us a third, and, by virtue of his seniority in the process, perhaps the official version of the ball tossing:

Dukakis called out to Jack Weeks, the handsome, curly-haired Welshman who goodnaturedly shepherds us wayward pressmen through the daily vagaries of the campaign schedule. Weeks dutifully produced two gloves and a baseball, and there on the tarmac, with its surface temperature just below the boiling point, the governor loosened up his arm and got the kinks out of his back by tossing a couple hundred 90-foot pegs to Weeks.

What we had in the tarmac arrival with ball tossing, then, was an understanding: a repeated moment witnessed by many people, all of whom believed it to be a setup and yet most of whom believed that only an outsider, only someone too "naive" to know the rules of the game, would so describe it.

4.

The narrative is made up of many such understandings, tacit agreements, small and large, to overlook the observable in the interests of obtaining a dramatic story line. It was understood, for example, that the first night of the 1988 Republican convention in New Orleans should be for Ronald Reagan "the last hurrah." "Reagan electrifies GOP" was the headline the next morning on the front page of *New York Newsday;* in fact the Reagan appearance, which was rhetorically pitched not to a live audience but to the more intimate demands of the camera, was, inside the Superdome, barely registered. It was understood, similarly, that Michael Dukakis's acceptance speech on the last night of the 1988 Democratic convention in Atlanta should be the occasion on which his "passion," or "leadership," emerged. "Could the no-nonsense nominee reach within himself to discover the language of leadership?" *Time* had asked. "Could he go beyond the pedestrian promise of 'good jobs at good wages' to give voice to a new Democratic vision?"

The correct answer, since the forward flow of the story here demanded the appearance of a genuine contender (a contender who could be seventeen points "up," so that George Bush could be seventeen points "down," a position from which he could rise to "claim" his own convention), was yes: "The best speech of his life," David S. Broder reported. Sandy Grady found it "superb," evoking "Kennedyesque echoes" and showing "unexpected craft and fire." *Newsweek* had witnessed Michael Dukakis "electrifying the convention with his intensely personal acceptance speech." In fact the convention that evening had been electrified, not by the speech, which was the same series of nonsequential clauses Governor Dukakis had employed during the primary campaign ("My friends . . . son of immigrants . . . good jobs at good wages . . . make teaching a valued and honored profession . . . it's what the Democratic Party is all about"), but because the floor had been darkened, swept with laser beams, and flooded with "Coming to America," played at concert volume with the bass turned up.

It is understood that this invented narrative will turn on certain familiar elements. There is the continuing story line of the "horse race," the reliable daily drama of one candidate falling behind as another pulls ahead. There is the surprise of the new poll, the glamour of the one-on-one colloquy on the midnight plane, a plot point (the nation sleeps while the candidate and his confidant hammer out its fate) pioneered by Theodore H. White. There is the abiding if unexamined faith in the campaign as personal odyssey, and in the spiritual benefits accruing to those who undertake it. There is, in the presented history of the candidate, the crucible event, the day that "changed the life." Robert Dole's life was understood to have changed when he was injured in Italy in 1945. George Bush's life is understood to have changed when he and his wife decided to "get out and make it on our own" (his words, or those of his speechwriter, Peggy Noonan, from the "lived the dream" acceptance speech at the 1988 convention, suggesting action, shirtsleeves, privilege cast aside) in west Texas. For Bruce Babbitt, "the dam just kind of broke" during a student summer in Bolivia. For Michael Dukakis, the dam was understood to have broken not during his own student summer in South America, in his case Peru, but after his 1978 defeat in Massachusetts: his tragic flaw, we read repeatedly during the 1988 campaign, was neither his evident sulkiness at losing that earlier election nor what many saw later as a rather dissociated self-satisfaction ("We're two people very proud of what we've done," he said on NBC in Atlanta, falling into a favorite speech pattern, "very proud of each other, actually . . . and very proud that a couple of guys named Dukakis and Jackson have come this far"), but the more attractive "hubris."

The narrative requires broad strokes. Michael Dukakis was physically small, and had associations with Harvard, which suggested that he could be cast as an "intellectual"; the "immigrant factor," on the other hand, could make him tough (as in "What it means is that I'm tough"), a "streetfighter." "He's cool, shrewd, and still trying to prove he's tough," the July 25, 1988, cover of *U.S. News & World Report* said about Dukakis. "Toughness is what it's all about," one of his advisers was quoted as having said. "People need to feel that a candidate is tough enough to be president. It is the threshold perception." George Bush had presented a more tortured narrative problem. The tellers of the story had not understood, or had not responded to, the essential Bush style, which was complex, ironic, the diffident edge of the Northeastern elite. This was what was at first identified as "the wimp factor," which was replaced not by a more complicated view of the personality but by its reverse: George Bush was by late August of 1988 no longer a "wimp" but someone who had "thrown it over," "struck out" to make his own way: no longer a product of the effete Northeast but someone who had thrived in Texas, and was therefore "tough enough to be president."

That George Bush might have thrived in Texas not in spite of being but precisely because he was a member of the Northeastern elite was a shading that had no part in the narrative: "He was considered back at that time one of the most charismatic people ever elected to public office in the history of Texas," Congressman Bill Archer of Houston said. "That charisma, people talked about it over and over again." People talked about it, probably, because Andover and Yale and the inheritable tax avoidance they suggested were, during the years George Bush lived in Texas, the exact ideals toward which the Houston and Dallas establishment aspired, but the narrative called for a less ambiguous version: "Lived in a little shotgun house, one room for the three of us," as Bush, or Peggy Noonan, had put it in the celebrated no-subject-pronoun cadences of the "lived the dream" acceptance speech. "Worked in the oil business, started my own. . . . Moved from the shotgun to a duplex apartment to a house. Lived the dream—high school football on Friday night, Little League, neighborhood barbecue . . . pushing into unknown territory with kids and a dog and a car. . . ."

All stories, of course, depend for their popular interest upon the invention of personality, or "character," but in the political narrative, designed as it is to maintain the illusion of consensus by obscuring rather than addressing actual issues, this invention served a further purpose. It was by 1988 generally if unspecifically agreed that the United States faced certain social and economic realities that, if not intractable, did not entirely lend themselves to the kinds of policy fixes that people who run for elected office, on whatever ticket, were likely to undertake. We had not yet accommodated the industrialization of parts of the third world. We had not yet adjusted to the economic realignment of a world in which the United States was no longer the principal catalyst for change. "We really are in an age of transition," Brent Scowcroft, Bush's leading foreign policy adviser, told Robert Scheer of *The Los Angeles Times* in the fall of 1988, "from a postwar world where the Soviets were the enemy, where the United States was a superpower and trying to build up both its allies and its former enemies and help the third world transition to independence. That whole world and all of those things are coming to an end or have ended, and we are now entering a new and different world that will be complex and much less unambiguous than the old one."

What continued to dominate the rhetoric of the 1988 campaign, however, was not this awareness of a new and different world but nostalgia for an old one, and coded assurance that any evidence of ambiguity or change, of what George Bush called the "deterioration of values," would be summarily dealt with by increased social control. It was not by accident that the word "enforcement," devoid of any apparent awareness that it had been tried before, played a large role in the language of both the Bush and Dukakis campaigns. Dukakis had promised, by way of achieving his goal of "no safe haven for dope dealers and drug profits anywhere on this earth," to "double the number" of Drug Enforcement Administration agents, not a promising approach. George Bush had repeatedly promised his support for the death penalty, and for both the Pledge of Allegiance and prayer, or "moments of silence," in public schools. "We've got to change this entire culture," he said in the Wake Forest debate; polling indicated that the electorate wanted "change," and this wish for change had been translated, by both campaigns, into the wish for a "change back," a regression to the "gentler America" of which George Bush repeatedly spoke.

To the extent that there was a "difference" between the candidates, the difference lay in just where on the time scale this "gentler America" could be found. The Dukakis campaign was oriented to "programs," and the programs it proposed were similar to those that had worked (the encouragement of private-sector involvement in low-cost housing, say) in the boom years after World War II. The Bush campaign was oriented to "values," and the values to which it referred were those not of a postwar but of a prewar America. In neither case did "ideas" play a part: "This election isn't about ideology, it's about competence," Michael Dukakis had said in Atlanta. "First and foremost, it's a choice between two persons," one of his senior advisers, Thomas Kiley, had told *The Wall Street Journal.* "What it comes down to, after all the shouting and the cheers, is the man at the desk," George Bush had said in New Orleans. In other words, what it "came down to," what it was "about," what was wrong or right with America, was not an historical shift largely unaffected by the actions of individual citizens but "character," and if "character" could be seen to count, then every citizen—since everyone was a judge of character, an expert in the field of personality—could be seen to count. This notion, that the citizen's choice among determinedly centrist candidates makes a "difference," is in fact the narrative's most central element, and its most fictive.

5.

The Democratic National Convention of 1968, during which the process was put to a popular vote on the streets of Chicago and after which it was decided that what had occurred could not be allowed to recur, is generally agreed to have prompted the increased emphasis on primaries, and the concomitant increased coverage of those primaries, that led to the end of the national party convention as a more than ceremonial occasion. Early in 1987, as the primary campaigns got underway for the 1988 election, David S. Broder, in *The Washington Post,* offered this compelling analysis of the power these "reforms" in the nominating procedure had vested not in the party leadership, which is where this power of choice ultimately resides, but in "the existing communications system," by which he meant the press, or the medium through which the party leadership sells its choice:

> Once the campaign explodes to 18 states, as it will the day after New Hampshire, when the focus shifts to a super-primary across the nation, the existing communications system simply will not accommodate more than two or three candidates in each party. Neither the television networks, nor the newspapers nor magazines, have the resources of people, space and time to describe and analyze the dynamics of two simultaneous half-national elections among Republicans and Democrats. That task is simply beyond us. Since we cannot reduce the number of states voting on Super Tuesday, we have to reduce the number of candidates treated as serious contenders. These news judgments will be arbitrary—but not subject to appeal. Those who finish first or second in Iowa and New Hampshire will get tickets from the mass media to play in the next big round. Those who don't, won't. A minor exception may be made for the two reverends, Jesse L. Jackson and Marion G. (Pat) Robertson, who have their own church-based communications and support networks and are less dependent on mass-media attention. But no one else.

By the time the existing communications network set itself up in July and August 1988 in

Atlanta and New Orleans, the priorities were clear. "NOTICE NOTICE NOTICE," read the typed note given to some print reporters when they picked up their credentials in Atlanta. "Because the Democratic National Convention Committee permitted the electronic media to exceed specifications for their broadcast booths, your assigned seat's sight line to the podium and the convention floor was obliterated." The network's skyboxes, in other words, had been built in front of the sections originally assigned to the periodical press. "This is a place that was chosen to be, for all intents and purposes, a large TV studio, to be able to project our message to the American people and a national audience," Paul Kirk, the chairman of the Democratic National Committee, said by way of explaining why the podium and the skyboxes had so reduced the size of the Omni Coliseum in Atlanta that some thousand delegates and alternates had been, on the evening Jesse Jackson spoke, locked out. Mayor Andrew Young of Atlanta apologized for the lock-out, but said that it would be the same on nights to follow: "The one hundred and fifty million people in the country who are going to vote have got to be our major target." Still, convention delegates were seen to have a real role: "The folks in the hall are so important to how it looks," Lane Venardos, senior producer in charge of convention coverage for CBS News, said to *The New York Times* about the Republican convention. The delegates, in other words, were the dress extras who could make the set seem authentic.

During those eight summer evenings in 1988, four in Atlanta and four in New Orleans, when roughly eighty percent of the television sets "out there" were tuned somewhere else, the entire attention of those inside the process was directed toward the invention of this story in which they themselves were the principal players, and for which they themselves were the principal audience. The great arenas in which the conventions were held became self-contained worlds, constantly transmitting their own images back to themselves, connected by skywalks to interchangeable structures composed not of floors but of "levels," mysteriously separated by fountains and glass elevators and escalators that did not quite connect. In the Louisiana Superdome in New Orleans as in the Omni Coliseum in Atlanta, the grids of lights blazed and dimmed hypnotically. Men with rifles patrolled the high catwalks. The nets packed with balloons swung gently overhead, poised for that instant known as "the money shot," the moment, or "window," when everything was working and no network had cut to a commercial. Minicams trawled the floor, fishing in Atlanta for Rob Lowe, in New Orleans for Donald Trump. In the NBC skybox Tom Brokaw floated over the floor, adjusting his tie, putting on his jacket, leaning to speak to John Chancellor. In the CNN skybox Mary Alice Williams sat bathed in white light, the blond madonna of the skyboxes. On the television screens in the press section the images reappeared, but from another angle: Tom Brokaw and Mary Alice Williams again, broadcasting not just above us but also to us, the circle closed.

At the end of prime time, when the skyboxes went dark, the action moved across the skywalks and into the levels, into the lobbies, into one or another Hyatt or Marriott or Hilton or Westin. In the portage from lobby to lobby, level to level, the same people kept materializing, in slightly altered roles. On a level of the Hyatt in Atlanta I saw Ann Lewis in her role as a Jackson adviser. On a level of the Hyatt in New Orleans I saw Ann Lewis in her role as a correspondent for *Ms.* Some pictures were vivid: "I've been around this process a while, and one thing I've noticed, it's the people who write the checks who get treated as if they have a certain amount of power," I recall Nadine Hack, the chairman of New York fundraising for Dukakis, saying in a suite at the Hyatt in Atlanta: here was a willowy woman with long blond hair standing barefoot on a table and explaining to those present how they could buy into the action. "The great thing about those evenings was you could even see Michael Harrington there," I recall Richard Viguerie saying to me at a party in New Orleans: here was the man who managed the action for the American right sounding wishful about evenings he and I had spent together in the early 1960s at the Washington Square apartment of a mutual friend, a woman whose evenings had been at the time a kind of salon for the political edges.

There was in Atlanta in 1988, according to the

Democratic National Committee, "twice the media presence" that there had been at the 1984 convention. There were in New Orleans "media workspaces" assigned not only to 117 newspapers and news services and to the American television and radio industry at full strength but to fifty-two foreign networks. On every corner one turned in the French Quarter someone was doing a standup. There were telephone numbers to be called for quotes: "Republican State and Local Officials," or "Pat Robertson Campaign," or "Richard Wirthlin, Reagan's Pollster." Newspapers came with teams of thirty, forty, fifty. In every lobby there were stacks of fresh newspapers, *The Atlanta Constitution, The New Orleans Times-Picayune, The Washington Post, The Miami Herald, The Los Angeles Times.* In Atlanta these papers were collected in bins and "recycled": made into thirty thousand posters, which were in turn distributed to the press in New Orleans.

This perfect recycling tended to present itself, in the narcosis of the event, as a model for the rest: like American political life itself, and like the printed and transmitted images on which that life depended, this was a world with no half-life. It was understood that what was said here would go on the wire and vanish. Garrison Keillor and his cute kids would vanish. Ann Richards and her peppery ripostes would vanish. Phyllis Schlafly and Olympia Snowe would vanish. All the opinions and all the rumors and all the housemaid Spanish spoken in both Atlanta and New Orleans would vanish, and all that would remain would be the huge arenas themselves, the arenas and the lobbies and the levels and the skywalks to which they connected, the agora, the symbolic marketplace in which the narrative was not only written but immediately, efficiently, entirely, consumed.

6.

A certain time lag exists between this world of the arenas and the world as we know it. One evening in New York between the Democratic and Republican conventions I happened to go down to Lafayette Street, to the Public Theater, to look at clips from documentaries on which the English-born filmmaker Richard Leacock had worked during his fifty years in America. We saw folk singers in Virginia in 1941 and oil riggers in Louisiana in 1946 (this was *Louisiana Story,* which Leacock had shot for Robert Flaherty) and tent performers in the Corn Belt in 1954; we saw Eddy Sachs preparing for the Indianapolis 500 in 1960 and Piri Thomas in Spanish Harlem in 1961. We saw parades, we saw baton twirlers. We saw quints in South Dakota in 1963. There on the screen in the Public Theater that night were images and attitudes from an America that had largely vanished, and what was striking was this: these were the very images and attitudes on which "the campaign" was predicated.

That "unknown territory" into which George Bush had pushed "with kids and a dog and a car" had existed in this vanished America, and had long since been subdivided, cut up for those tract houses on which the people who were not part of the process had made down payments. Michael Dukakis's "snowblower," and both the amusing frugality and the admirable husbandry of resources it was meant to suggest, derived from some half-remembered idea of what citizens of this vanished America had found amusing or admirable. "The Pledge" was an issue that referred back to that world. "A drug-free America" had perhaps seemed in that world an achievable ideal. I recall listening in Atlanta to Madeleine Albright, at that time Dukakis's foreign-policy adviser, as she conjured up, in the course of arguing against a "no first use" minority plank in the Democratic platform, a scenario in which "Soviet forces overrun Europe" and the United States has, by promising no first use of nuclear weapons, crippled its ability to act: she was talking about a world that had not turned since 1948. What was at work here seemed on the one hand a grave, although in many ways a comfortable, miscalculation of what people in America might have as their deepest concerns in 1988; it seemed on the other hand just another understanding, another of those agreements to overlook the observable.

It was into this sedative fantasy of a fixable imperial America that Jesse Jackson rode, on a Trailways bus. "You've never heard a sense of panic sweep the party as it has in the past few days," David Garth had told *The New York Times* during those perilous spring weeks in 1988 when there seemed a real possibility that a black candidate with no experience in elected office, a candidate believed to be so profoundly unelectable that he could take the entire Democratic Party down with him, might go to Atlanta with more delegates than any other Democratic candidate. "The party is up against an extraordinary endgame," the pollster Paul Maslin had said. "I don't know where this leaves us," Robert S. Strauss had said. One uncommitted superdelegate, *The New York Times* had reported, "said the Dukakis campaign changed its message since Mr. Dukakis lost the Illinois primary. Mr. Dukakis is no longer the candidate of 'inevitability' but the candidate of order, he said. 'They're not doing the train's leaving the station and you better be on it routine anymore,' this official said. 'They're now saying that the station's about to be blown up by terrorists and we're the only ones who can defuse the bomb.'"

The threat, or the possibility, presented by Jesse Jackson, the "historic" (as people liked to say after it became certain he would not have the numbers) part of his candidacy, derived from something other than the fact that he was black, a circumstance that had before been and could again be compartmentalized, segregated out. For example: "Next week, when we start doing our black media stuff, Jesse Jackson needs to be on the air in the black community on our behalf," Donna Brazile of the Dukakis campaign said to *The New York Times* in September 1988 by way of emphasizing how much the Dukakis campaign "sought to make peace" with Jackson. "Black," in other words, could be useful, and even a moral force, a way for white Americans to attain more perfect attitudes: "How moving it is, and how important, to see a black candidate meet and overcome the racism that lurks in virtually all of us white Americans," Anthony Lewis had noted in a March 1988 column explaining why the notion that Jesse Jackson could win was nonetheless "a romantic delusion" of the kind that had "repeatedly undermined" the Democratic Party. "You look at what Jesse Jackson has done, you have to wonder what a Tom Bradley of Los Angeles could have done, what an Andy Young of Atlanta could have done," I heard someone say on one of the Sunday shows after the Jackson campaign had entered its "historic," or in the candidate's word its "endless," phase.

"Black," by itself and in the right context—the right context being a reasonable constituency composed exclusively of blacks and supportive liberal whites—could be accommodated by the process. Something less traditional was at work in the 1988 Jackson candidacy. I recall having dinner, the weekend before the California primary, at the Pebble Beach house of the chairman of a large American corporation. There were sixteen people at the table, all white, all well off, all well dressed, all well educated, all socially conservative. During the course of the evening it came to my attention that six of the sixteen, or every one of the registered

Democrats present, intended to vote on Tuesday for Jesse Jackson. Their reasons were unspecific, but definite. "I heard him, he didn't sound like a politician," one said. "He's talking about right now," another said. "You get outside the gate here, take a look around, you have to know we've got some problems, and he's talking about them."

What made the 1988 Jackson candidacy a bomb that had to be defused, then, was not that blacks were supporting a black candidate, but that significant numbers of whites were supporting—not only supporting but in many cases overcoming deep emotional and economic conflicts of their own in order to support—a candidate who was attractive to them not because of but in spite of the fact that he was black, a candidate whose most potent attraction was that he "didn't sound like a politician." "Character" seemed not to be, among these voters, the point-of-sale issue the narrative made it out to be: a number of white Jackson supporters to whom I talked would quite serenely describe their candidate as "a con man," or even, in George Bush's phrase, as "a hustler." "And yet . . . ," they would say. What "and yet" turned out to mean, almost without variation, was that they were willing to walk off the edge of the known political map for a candidate who was running against, as he repeatedly said, "politics as usual," against what he called "consensualist centrist politics"; against what had come to be the very premise of the process, the notion that the winning and maintaining of public office warranted the invention of a public narrative based at no point on observable reality.

In other words they were not idealists, these white Jackson voters, but empiricists. By the time Jesse Jackson got to California, where he would eventually win twenty-five percent of the entire white vote and forty-nine percent of the total vote from voters between the demographically key ages of thirty to forty-four, the idealists had rallied behind the sole surviving alternative, who was, accordingly, just then being declared "presidential." In Los Angeles, during May and early June 1988, those Democrats who had not fallen into line behind Michael Dukakis were described as "self-indulgent," or as "immature"; they were even described, in a dispiriting phrase that prefigured the tenor of the campaign to come, as "issues wimps." I recall talking to a rich and politically well-connected Californian who had been, during the primary season there, virtually the only Democrat on the famously liberal west side of Los Angeles who was backing Jackson. He said that he could afford "the luxury of being more interested in issues than in process," but that he would pay for it: "When I want something, I'll have a hard time getting people to pick up the phone. I recognize that. I made the choice."

7.

On the June night in 1988 when Michael Dukakis was declared the winner of the California Democratic primary, and the bomb officially defused, there took place in the Crystal Room of the Biltmore Hotel in downtown Los Angeles a "victory party" that was less a celebration than a ratification by the professionals, a ritual convergence of those California Democrats for whom the phones would continue to get picked up. Charles Manatt was there. John Emerson and Charles Palmer were there. John Van de Kamp was there. Leo McCarthy was there. Robert Shrum was there. All the custom-made suits and monogrammed shirts in Los Angeles that night were there, met in the wide corridors of the Biltmore to murmur assurances to one another. The ballroom had been cordoned as if to repel late invaders, roped off in such a way that once the Secret Service, the traveling press, the local press, the visiting national press, the staff, and the candidate himself had assembled, there would be room for only a controllable handful of celebrants, over whom the cameras would dutifully pan.

In fact the actual "celebrants" that evening were not at the Biltmore at all, but a few blocks away at the Los Angeles Hilton, dancing under the mirrored ceiling of the ballroom in which the Jackson campaign had gathered, its energy level in defeat notably higher than that of other campaigns in victory. Jackson parties tended to spill out of ballrooms onto several levels of whatever hotel they were in, and to last until three or four in the morning: anyone who wanted to be at a Jackson party was welcome at a Jackson party, which was unusual among the campaigns, and tended to reinforce the populist spirit that had given this one its extraordinary animation. Of that evening at the Los Angeles Hilton I recall a pretty woman in a gold lamé dress, dancing with a baby in her arms. I recall empty beer bottles, Corona and Budweiser and Excalibur, sitting among the loops of television cable. I recall the candidate, dancing on the stage, and, on this June evening when the long shot had not come in, this evening when his campaign was effectively over, giving the women in the traveling press the little parody wave they liked to give him, "the press chicks' wave," the stiff-armed palm movement they called "the Nancy Reagan wave"; then taking off his tie and throwing it into the crowd, like a rock star. This was of course a narrative of its own, but a relatively current one, and one that had, because it seemed at some point grounded in the recognizable, a powerful glamour for those estranged from the purposeful nostalgia of the traditional narrative.

In the end the predictable decision was made to go with the process, with predictable, if equivocal, results. On the last afternoon of the 1988 Republican convention in New Orleans I walked from the hotel in the Quarter where I was staying over to Camp Street. I wanted to see 544 Camp, a local point of interest not noted on the points-of-interest maps distributed at the convention but one that figures large in the literature of American conspiracy. "544 Camp Street" was the address stamped on the leaflets Lee Harvey Oswald was distributing around New Orleans between May and September of 1963, the "Fair Play for Cuba Committee" leaflets that, in the years after Lee Harvey Oswald assassinated John Fitzgerald Kennedy, suggested to some that he had been acting for Fidel Castro and suggested to others that he had been set up to appear to have been acting for Fidel Castro. Guy Bannister had his detective agency at 544 Camp. David Ferrie and Jack Martin frequented the coffee shop on the ground floor at 544 Camp. The Cuban Revolutionary Council, the members of which would have made up the provisional government of Cuba had the 1961 invasion of Cuba not ended at the Bay of Pigs, rented an office at 544 Camp. People had taken the American political narrative seriously at 544 Camp. They had argued about it, fallen out over it, hit each other over the head with pistol butts because of it.

In fact I never found 544 Camp, because there was no more such address: the small building had been bought and torn down and replaced by a new federal courthouse. Across the street in Lafayette Square that afternoon there had been a loudspeaker, and a young man on a makeshift platform talking about abortion, and unwanted babies being put down the Disposall and "clogging the main sewer drains of New Orleans," but no one except me had been there to listen. *"Satan, you're the liar,"* the young woman with him on the platform had sung, lip-synching a tape originally made, she told me, by a woman who sang with an Alabama traveling ministry, the Ministry of the Happy Hunters.

"There's one thing you can't deny / You're the father of every lie. . . ." The young woman had been wearing a black cape, and was made up to portray Satan, or Death, I was unclear which and it had not seemed a distinction worth pursuing.

Still, there were clouds off the Gulf that day and the air was wet and there was about the melancholy of Camp Street a certain sense of abandoned historic moment, heightened, quite soon, by something unusual: the New Orleans police began lining Camp Street, blocking every intersection from Canal Street west. I noticed a man in uniform on a roof. Before long there were Secret Service agents, with wires in their ears. The candidates, it seemed, would be traveling east on Camp Street on their way from the Republican National Committee Finance Committee Gala (Invitation Only) at the Convention Center to the Ohio Caucus Rally (Media Invited) at the Hilton. I stood for a while on Camp Street, on this corner that might be construed as one of those occasional accidental intersections where the remote narrative had collided with the actual life of the country, and waited until the motorcade itself, entirely and perfectly insulated, a mechanism dedicated like the process for which it stood only to the maintenance of itself, had passed, and then I walked to the Superdome. "I hear he did OK with Brinkley," they said that night in the Superdome, and, then, as the confetti fell, "Quayle, zip."

The West Wing of Oz

1.

December 22, 1988

In August 1986, George Bush, traveling in his role as vice president of the United States and accompanied by his staff, the Secret Service, the traveling press, and a personal camera crew wearing baseball caps reading "Shooters, Inc." and working on a $10,000 retainer paid by a Bush PAC called the Fund for America's Future, spent several days in Israel and Jordan. The schedule in Israel included, according to reports in *The Los Angeles Times* and *The New York Times,* shoots at the Western Wall, at the Holocaust memorial, at David Ben-Gurion's tomb, and at thirty-two other locations chosen to produce camera footage illustrating that George Bush was, as Marlin Fitzwater, at that time the vice-presidential press secretary, put it, "familiar with the issues." The Shooters, Inc. crew did not go on to Jordan (there was, an official explained to *The Los Angeles Times,* "nothing to be gained from showing him schmoozing with Arabs"), but the Bush advance team in Amman had nonetheless directed considerable attention to improving visuals for the traveling press.

Members of the advance team had requested, for example, that the Jordanian army marching band change its uniforms from white to red. They had requested that the Jordanians, who did not have enough equipment to transport Bush's traveling press corps, borrow the necessary helicopters to do so from the Israeli air force. In an effort to assure the color of live military action as a backdrop for the vice president, they had asked the Jordanians to stage maneuvers at a sensitive location overlooking Israel and the Golan Heights. They had asked the Jordanians to raise, over the Jordanian base there, the American flag. They had asked that Bush be photographed studying, through binoculars, "enemy territory," a shot ultimately vetoed by the State Department, since the "enemy territory" at hand was Israel. They had also asked, possibly the most arresting detail, that, at every stop on the itinerary, camels be present.

Some months later I happened to be in Amman, and mentioned reading about this Bush trip to several officials at the American embassy there. They could have, it was agreed, "cordially killed" the reporters in question, particularly Charles P. Wallace from *The Los Angeles Times,* but the reports themselves had been accurate. "You didn't hear this, but they didn't write the half of it," one said.

This is in fact the kind of story we expect to hear about our elected officials. We not only expect them to use other nations as changeable scrims in the theater of domestic politics but encourage them to do so. After the April 1961 failure of the Bay of Pigs, John Kennedy's job approval rating was four points higher than it had been in March. After the 1965 intervention in the Dominican Republic, Lyndon Johnson's job approval rating rose six points. After the 1983 invasion of Grenada, Ronald Reagan's job approval rating rose four points, and what was that winter referred to in Washington as "Lebanon"—the sending of American marines into Beirut, the killing of the 241, and the subsequent pullout—was, in the afterglow of this certified success in the Caribbean, largely forgotten. "Gemayal could fall tonight and it would be a two-day story," I recall David Gergen saying a few months later. In May 1984, Francis X. Clines of *The New York Times* described the view taken by James Baker, who was routinely described during his years in the Reagan White House as a manager of almost supernatural executive ability, the "ultimate pragmatist": "In attempting action in Lebanon, Baker argues, President Reagan avoided another 'impotent' episode, such as the taking of American hostages in Iran, and in withdrawing the Marines, the President avoided another 'Vietnam' . . . 'Pulling the Marines out put the lie to the argument that the President's trigger-happy,' he [Baker] said." The "issue," in other words, was one of preserving faith in President Reagan at home, a task that, after the ultimate pragmatist left the White House, fell into the hands of the less adroit.

History is context. At a moment when the nation had seen control of its economy pass to its creditors and when the administration-elect had for political reasons severely limited its ability to regain that control, this extreme reliance on the efficacy of faith over works meant something different from what it might have meant in 1984 or 1980. On the night in New Orleans in August 1988 when George Bush accepted the Republican nomination and spoke of his intention to "speak for freedom, stand for freedom, and be a patient friend to anyone, east or west, who will fight for freedom," the word "patient" was construed by some in the Louisiana Superdome as an abandonment of the Reagan Doctrine, a suggestion that a Bush administration would play a passive rather than an active role in any further dreams of rollback.

This overlooked the real nature of the Reagan Doctrine, the usefulness of which to the Reagan administration had been essentially political. Administrations with little room to maneuver at home have historically looked for sideshows abroad, for the creation of what pollsters call "a dramatic event," an external crisis, preferably one so remote that it remains an abstraction. On the evening of the

November 1988 election and on several evenings that followed, I happened to sit at dinner next to men with considerable experience in the financial community. They were agreed that the foreign markets would allow the new Bush administration, which was seen to have limited its options by promising for political reasons not to raise taxes, only a limited time before calling in the markers; they disagreed only as to the length of that time and to the nature of the downturn. One thought perhaps two years, another six months. Some saw a blowout ("blowout" was a word used a good deal), others saw a gradual tightening, a slow transition to that era of limited expectations of which Jerry Brown had spoken when he was governor of California.

These men were, among themselves, uniformly pessimistic. They saw a situation in which the space available for domestic maneuvering had been reduced to zero. In this light it did not seem encouraging that George Bush, on the Thursday before he left for his post-election Florida vacation, found time to meet not with those investors around the world who were that week sending him a message (the dollar was again dropping against the yen, against the mark, and against the pound; the Dow was dropping 78.47 points), not with the Germans, not with the Japanese, not even with anyone from the American financial community, but with representatives of the Afghan resistance. "Once in a while I think about those things, but not much," the president-elect told the CBS News crew which asked him, a few days later in Florida, about the falling market.

2.

July 14, 1994

In December 1981 in El Salvador, twenty-one months after the murder of Archbishop Oscar Arnulfo Romero in San Salvador and twelve months after the murder of the four American Maryknoll women outside San Salvador and eleven months after the murder of the head of the Salvadoran land-reform agency and two of his American aides at the Sheraton Hotel in San Salvador, which is to say at a time when the Reagan administration had already demonstrated its ability to tolerate grave insults to its Central American policy, certain events occurred in certain remote villages north of the Torola River in Morazán province. In what has since become the most familiar of those villages, El Mozote, the events in question began late on a Thursday afternoon, December 10, at a time when the village was crowded with refugees from areas believed less safe, and were concluded at dawn on Saturday.

Later that day, in Los Toriles, two kilometers to the southeast, similar events occurred, as similar events had already occurred or would within a few hours occur in Arambala and La Joya and Jocote Amarillo and Cerro Pando and Joateca and La Rancheria. These events were later and variously described to the American writer Mark Danner by the two American embassy officials assigned to investigate them, Todd Greentree and Major John McKay, as "something bad," "something horrible," a case in which "there had probably been a massacre, that they had lined people up and shot them," a case in which "abuses against the civilian population probably took place"; a case that presented as its most urgent imperative the need to craft a report that would "have credibility among people who were far away and whose priorities were—you know, we're talking about people like Tom Enders—whose priorities were definitely not necessarily about getting at exactly what happened."

On December 10, 1992, eleven years to the day after the commencement of what has become known as the Mozote massacre (the largest number of those killed on that long December weekend were killed during the thirty-six hours spent in El Mozote by members of the Salvadoran army's Atlacatl Battalion), four American forensic experts submitted to the United Nations Truth Commission the results of their analysis of skeletal remains and artifacts recovered by a team of Argentinian forensic anthropologists originally assembled to reconstruct evidence of their own country's "dirty war." Working exclusively with material exhumed from what had been the sacristy of the Mozote church, the Americans were able to identify the bones of

143 human beings, 136 of whom were children and adolescents. Of the remaining seven adults, six were women, one in the third trimester of pregnancy. The average age of the children was six.

The report prepared for the United Nations noted that there may have been a greater number of deaths in the sacristy, which was one of several sites mentioned by survivors as places where bodies would be found, since "many young infants may have been entirely cremated" (much of the village had been burned before the Atlacatl left El Mozote) and "other children may not have been counted because of excessive fragmentation of body parts." Of the ten officers who commanded the units participating in the Morazán operation, according to the report prepared for the United Nations, three were by then dead, and four still serving in the Salvadoran army. None had been officially charged on any count related to the massacre. A year before, Tutela Legal, the human rights office of the Archbishopric of San Salvador, had compiled what may be the final and most comprehensive list of all those known or believed to have died in El Mozote and the surrounding villages. The Tutela Legal list numbered 767 men, women, and children, the youngest the two-day-old grandson of a day laborer named Miguel Marquez (the grandfather was also killed, as were his son, his daughter-in-law, two of his daughters, and seven of his other grandchildren), the oldest a man named Leoncio Diaz, who was said to be 105 years old and to have had a 100-year-old companion named Leoncia Marquez, who was also killed. Of the 767 victims cited on the Tutela Legal list, 358 were infants and children under the age of thirteen.

This was of course not a new story, and the fact that it was not a new story seems in many ways what moved Mark Danner to write his dispassionate, meticulously documented, and for these reasons conclusive *The Massacre at El Mozote: A Parable of the Cold War.* The essential facts of the Mozote massacre were published on January 27, 1982, on the front pages of both *The New York Times* and *The Washington Post,* accompanied by photographs taken by Susan Meiselas, who had walked into Morazán from Honduras with Raymond Bonner of the *Times.* Bonner reported seeing the charred skulls and bones of what appeared to him to be several dozen men, women, and children. Allowing that it was "not possible for an observer who was not present at the time of the massacre to determine independently how many people died or who killed them," he reported that the surviving relatives and friends of the victims believed the dead to number 733 and the killing to have been done "by uniformed soldiers" during an Atlacatl sweep of the region.

Alma Guillermoprieto, who was then a stringer for *The Washington Post* and who entered Mozote a few days after Bonner and Meiselas had left, also reported seeing bodies and body parts and quoted the same survivors, as well as the Salvadoran ambassador in Washington, Ernesto Rivas Gallont, who dismissed the reports from Morazán as the "type of story that leads us to believe there is a plan," the plan being either to derail the Salvadoran election scheduled for March 1982 or "to take credit away from the certification President Reagan must make to Congress." This "certification," during 1982 and 1983 a semiannual requirement for continued American aid to El Salvador, involved asserting that its government was "making a concerted and significant effort to comply with internationally recognized human rights" and was "achieving substantial control over all elements of its own armed forces, so as to bring to an end the indiscriminate torture and murder of Salvadoran citizens by those forces."

The Reagan administration made its certification to these points on January 28, 1982, one day after Bonner's and Alma Guillermoprieto's extensive reports from Morazán appeared in the *Times* and the *Post.* Mark Danner's true subject in *The Massacre at El Mozote,* then, was not the massacre itself but the way in which the story of the massacre, which was carried out by troops trained by the U.S. Special Forces and equipped with U.S.-manufactured M-16s and with ammunition manufactured for the U.S. government at Lake City, Missouri, came to be known and discounted in the United States, the way in which the story of El Mozote "was exposed to the light and then allowed to fall back into the dark."

Reports that something bad had happened in Morazán had begun to circulate almost immediately. The Reverend William L. Wipfler at the New York office of the National Council of Churches first heard the story from a contact at Socorro Juridico, which was then the legal aid office at the Archbishopric of San Salvador. Wipfler left a message for Raymond Bonner at the Mexico City bureau of the *Times,* and also sent a cable, dated December 15, 1981, asking Ambassador Deane Hinton in San Salvador for "confirmation or otherwise" of "reliable reports received here [indicating] that between December 10 and 13 a government joint military and security forces operation took place in Morazan Department which resulted in over 900 civilian deaths."

Hinton did not reply until January 8, by which time the guerrillas' Radio Venceremos was back in operation (to at least temporarily knock out the Venceremos transmitter had been one goal, perhaps the single successfully realized goal, of the Atlacatl's Morazán operation) and broadcasting a detailed account of the massacre from a survivor named Rufina Amaya. Rufina Amaya had witnessed the killing of her husband and four of her children, ages nine, five, three, and eight months, but in the confusion and terror of the event had herself been inadvertently overlooked as the soldiers corralled groups of struggling and screaming women, many of them torn from their infants and children, to be killed and then burned. "I do not know what your sources are but the only sources that I have seen alleging something like this are the clandestine Radio Venceremos reports," Hinton's January 8 cable to the National Council of Churches read in part. "Frankly, I do not consider Radio Venceremos to be a reliable source." Since Radio Venceremos did not restore its ability to broadcast until well after the National Council of Churches query was sent, that Hinton would devote ten of this cable's twelve paragraphs to illustrations of Radio Venceremos's unreliability seems in retrospect to suggest a certain crisis of confidence, if not a panic, at the embassy.

In fact, definitely before January 8 and probably closer to mid-December, Todd Greentree, then a junior reporting officer at the embassy in San Salvador and later a desk officer for Nicaragua at the State Department, had relayed to Hinton not only a report from his own sources on the left about a massacre in Morazán but also an offer from the FMLN to guide him there. "I knew the guerrillas would never have masqueraded something like this, would never have fabricated it, if they were offering safe-conduct," Greentree told Danner. "I was convinced that something had gone on, and that it was bad. I mean, it was pretty clear, if they were going to do this, that something must have happened." Hinton's decision was that Greentree could not go in under guerrilla protection. "I should emphasize that I never got the feeling that they just wanted this to go away," Greentree told Danner about the meeting in which this decision was taken. "But there were political and military restraints that we were operating under."

What discussion there may have been of an independent investigation (at least ten of the fifty-five

American military advisers Congress then allowed in El Salvador were assigned to the Atlacatl) is unknown, although Danner was told by one of the officers assigned to the Atlacatl that someone from the embassy Milgroup (Military Advisory Group) had called the Atlacatl base at La Libertad a few days after the massacre "and talked to the Special Forces people and told them they wanted Monterrosa [Lieutenant Colonel Domingo Monterrosa Barrios, the Atlacatl commander] to come in—they wanted to talk to him about something that had happened during the operation." Monterrosa had declined to come in, a suggestive illustration of the level of control the United States then had over the military forces it was funding. Whether or not the embassy decision to refuse the FMLN offer to guide Greentree to the site of the massacre was discussed with Washington also remains shrouded in the subjunctive. "However much we might have wanted more information, no one in State was going to make that call," Danner was told by Peter Romero, at the time of Mozote an El Salvador specialist at the State Department.

Most of the interested players, then, knew about Morazán, in outline if not in detail, well before January 6, when Raymond Bonner and Susan Meiselas, followed a few days later by Alma Guillermoprieto, first walked into El Mozote. Not until January 30, however, three days after the story had appeared on the front pages of the *Times* and the *Post,* did the embassy dispatch Todd Greentree and Major John McKay, who was then in the defense attaché's office at the embassy and was at the time Danner interviewed him a colonel attached to NATO in Brussels, to Morazán. Greentree and McKay did not exactly get to El Mozote, although they did fly over it. Greentree's impression from the air was that "El Mozote had been pretty much destroyed." Once on the ground in Morazán, although not in El Mozote, Greentree and McKay, accompanied by a squad of the Atlacatl, interviewed those residents of the northern villages who had reached the refugee camp outside San Francisco Gotera. Although the Americans later recalled being able to "observe and feel this tremendous fear," they did not elicit eyewitness accounts of a massacre, nor had they expected to.

"You had a bunch of very intimidated, scared people, and now the Army presence further intimidated them," McKay told Danner. "I mean, the Atlacatl had supposedly done something horrible, and now these gringos show up under this pretense of investigating it, but in the presence of these soldiers. It was probably the worst thing you could do. I mean, you didn't have to be a rocket scientist to know what the Army people were there for." Greentree and McKay then set out for El Mozote, and got to within an hour's walk of what had been the village when the Atlacatl soldiers accompanying them stopped, and refused to go further. "In the end, we went up there and we didn't want to find that anything horrible had happened," McKay told Danner. "And the fact that we didn't get to the site turned out to be very detrimental to our reporting—the Salvadorans, you know, were never very good about cleaning up their shell casings." That evening, back at the embassy in San Salvador, Greentree wrote a report, the overriding aim of which appears to have been "credibility," summarizing his and McKay's findings.

Here is the point at which El Mozote entered the thin air of Washington, where the official story was that El Salvador, with the inspiration of the Reagan administration, was at last "turning the corner" toward democracy. "The end of Bob White's tour, and the transition period before Hinton arrived [Robert White had preceded Hinton as ambassador], and the first six months of Hinton's tour—those were the absolute worst days, really out of control," Greentree told Danner by way of explaining why the conviction that what was known or suspected in country would not be "credible" in Washington had by then increased exponentially. "And the fact that Bob White and everybody in the embassy had been so thoroughly traumatized by the murders of the nuns, and the AFL-CIO guys [the two Americans who were killed with the head of the Salvadoran land-reform agency at the Sheraton in San Salvador], and just the general sort of out-of-control way the military was—it meant that everything we reported could be taken as suspect."

The following day, after review and revisions, Greentree's report went to the State Department over Hinton's name. This was the cable containing the careful and soon to be repeated assertions that it was "not possible to prove or disprove excesses of violence against the civilian population of El Mozote by government troops" and that "no evidence could be found to confirm that government forces systematically massacred civilians in the operation zone, nor that the number of civilians killed even remotely approached the number being cited in other reports circulating internationally." The Greentree cable also contained, deep in its text, a curious warning from one of the interviewees, the mayor of Jocoaitique, who according to the cable "intimated that he knew of violent fighting in El Mozote" but was "unwilling to discuss deportment of government troops" and who then made a comment so coded that it could stand as a veiled but exact expression of the embassy position on what did or did not take place in Morazán. What the cable quoted the mayor of Jocoaitique as having said to Todd Greentree and Major McKay was this: "This is something one should talk about in another time, in another country."

That part of the embassy cable did not appear in the statement made two days later to the House Subcommittee on Western Hemisphere Affairs by Assistant Secretary of State for Inter-American Affairs Thomas O. Enders. (Nor would it appear in the sanitized version of the cable released under the Freedom of Information Act to Raymond Bonner in 1983.) The Enders statement was arresting not only for what it said and did not say but for its tone, which suggested an extreme version of a kind of exaggerated hauteur commonly translated as entitlement in the northeastern United States. "Many of you have read," he said, addressing what he called "special pleading" in the matter of death and disappearance statistics, "about something called the Legal Aid Office of the Archbishopric—Socorro Judico [sic] is its Spanish name; it is often cited in the international media. It strangely lists no victims of guerrilla or terrorist violence. Apparently they do not commit violence."

This was a level of seigneurial dismissal often emulated but never quite mastered by Jeane Kirkpatrick and Elliott Abrams and other regular defenders of administration policy in Central America. "There is another organization, the Central American University, that collects statistics too," Enders continued, referring to UCA, the Jesuit-run José Simeón Cañas University of Central America. "Its bias may be apparent from the fact that it does include a category of persons killed by what I believe Congressman Bonker referred to as paramilitary organizations. And they are called in Spanish *ajusticiados,* referring to persons that have received justice at the hands of their executioners." Only then did Enders turn his attention to what he described as "allegations" of massacres, including Mozote. "We sent two embassy officers down to investigate the reports," Enders said, inadvertently illuminating the particular distance between Washington and Morazán, which in local usage is said to be not "down" but "up" from San Salvador. Enders continued:

> It is clear from the report they gave that there has been a confrontation between the guerrillas occupying Mozote and attacking Government forces last December. There is no evidence to confirm that Government forces systematically massacred civilians in the operations zone, or that the number of civilians remotely approached the 733 or 926 victims cited in the press. I note they asked how many people were in that canton and were told probably not more than 300 in December, and there are many survivors including refugees now.

Enders said this on February 2, 1982. On February 1, Deane Hinton, in response to what he apparently construed as careless use of his reply to the National Council of Churches, had sent a corrective cable to the State Department. This cable read in part:

> I would be grateful if department would use extreme care in describing my views on alleged massacre. Case in point is description in para 3 of *REFTEL* referring to my letter . . . as "denying the incident." My letter did not "deny" incident: it reported that at that time I had no confirmation and argued from available evidence from Radio Venceremos and from lack of other reports that I had no reason to believe Venceremos reports. I still don't believe Venceremos version but additional evidence strongly suggests that something happened that should not have happened and that it is quite possible Salvadoran military did commit

> excesses. Allegations that it was unit from Atlacatl battalion in El Mozote remain to be confirmed or discredited.

Several days later, this Hinton cable notwithstanding, Assistant Secretary of State for Human Rights and Humanitarian Affairs Elliott Abrams echoed Enders in his statement to the Senate Foreign Relations Committee. The Mozote case was, Abrams said, "a very interesting one in a sense." "Interesting" was at the time a word much in use, as were "strange" and "unusual." Enders, for example, had noted that Socorro Juridico "strangely lists no victims of guerrilla and terrorist violence." I recall watching Jeane Kirkpatrick during this period tease an audience to frenzy with little silken whips of innuendo as she described how "*interested,*" even "*bemused,*" she was by the "*unusual* standards," the "*extraordinarily,* even *uniquely* demanding standards" imposed by the certification requirement. The reason Elliott Abrams found El Mozote "interesting" was this: ". . . because we found, for example, that the numbers, first of all, were not credible, because as Secretary Enders notes, our information was that there were only three hundred people in the canton." Abrams went on to wonder why a massacre that had occurred in mid-December, if indeed it had occurred at all, had not been "publicized" until late January.

Ten years later, in an interview, Abrams was still asking the same question, to the same innuendo: "If it had really been a massacre and not a firefight, why didn't we hear about it right off from the FMLN? I mean, we didn't start hearing about it until a month later." Abrams, in other words, was still trying to negotiate what had become, with the exhumation of the sacristy, unnegotiable, still trying to return discussion to the familiar question of whether or not a massacre had occurred. Enders, when he talked to Danner, had transcended this now inoperative line of attack, ascending effortlessly to the big-picture argument against the existence of a massacre: "Coming on top of everything else, El Mozote, if true, might have destroyed the entire effort. Who knows? I certainly thought that when I first heard about it." In other words it had been necessary to deny the massacre because had there been a massacre the "effort" would have become, and this was the word Enders used, "unfundable."

The effort did not become unfundable. The effort instead became what was at that time the most expensive effort to support a foreign government threatened by an insurgency since Vietnam. Progressively cruder interpretations of what had been the surgically precise statements made by the embassy came to dominate, during the spring and summer of 1982, discussion of this country's role in Central America. By February 10 of that spring *The Wall Street Journal* was noting editorially that "extremists" in El Salvador had "learned long ago the trick of dressing in military uniforms to confuse their victims." (This appears to have been the source for Ronald Reagan's later assertion that "communist operatives" were dressing in "freedom fighter uniforms" to discredit the Nicaraguan contras.) Shrill excoriations of Raymond Bonner, who necessarily had to be cast as having what George Melloan of *The Wall Street Journal* called "a political orientation," became commonplace.

Bonner was a graduate of Stanford Law School, had been a prosecutor in the San Francisco district attorney's office, and had served as a marine officer in Vietnam. John McKay, the marine major who went up to Morazán with Todd Greentree, had been with Bonner in Vietnam, where McKay lost an eye. "We could not have said, 'My God, there's been a massacre,'" McKay told Danner about the cable the embassy sent to Washington as a report of his and Greentree's trip to Morazán. "But, truth be known, the ambiguity of the cable that went out— in my own conscience I began to question it. And then when I saw the *New York Times* piece, and the picture, that really got me thinking. Bonner and I had gone to Quantico together, went to Vietnam together." In the late summer of 1980, at a time when Bonner had spent time in Bolivia and Guatemala but had made only a few short visits to El Salvador, he had been asked his opinion of U.S. policy in El Salvador. "Ask me about Bolivia, or Guatemala, or any country, I'll probably have an opinion," Bonner recalled having said. "But El Salvador, boy, I just don't know. I guess we're doing the right thing."

Bonner, then, might have seemed an unlikely target for the campaign then being mounted against him in Washington and New York. For those waging this campaign, however, the question of "political orientation" was answered once and for all in August 1982, when the *Times* abruptly withdrew Bonner from Central America. According to A. M. Rosenthal, then the executive editor of the *Times,* Bonner was withdrawn because he "didn't know the techniques of weaving a story together. . . . I brought him back because it seemed terribly unfair to leave him there without training." Actually Bonner had spent a good part of 1981 on the Metro desk at the *Times,* but Rosenthal suggested that those who believed Bonner to have been withdrawn for reasons other than "training" did so because they resented Rosenthal himself. "I was an agent of change in the *Times,*" he said, "and a lot of people didn't like my politics."

This self-referential approach worked to blur the issue. Whatever reason or reasons Rosenthal may have had for withdrawing Bonner, it was the sheer fact of that withdrawal, the fact of that apparent failure to back up a reporter who had put the paper on the line with a story denied by the government, that spoke so eloquently to those who wanted to discredit the reporting on El Mozote. That the *Times* withdrew Bonner was seen, immediately and by larger numbers of people than were actually knowledgeable about El Salvador or administration policy, as "proof" that he had been wrong about El Mozote; as recently as a few years ago it was possible to hear it casually said about Bonner that the *Times* "had to pull him out," that he had "bought into a massacre."

"For more than a year now we've been following the campaign that we victimized former *New York Times* correspondent Raymond Bonner," *The Wall Street Journal* noted editorially in 1993. "The excavation of children's bones in El Mozote is supposed to vindicate Mr. Bonner and discredit what we said. . . . We did not fire Mr. Bonner in the first place. *The New York Times* did. Or, more precisely, after then Managing Editor A. M. Rosenthal undertook his own reporting visit to El Salvador, it pulled Mr. Bonner off the beat and back to New York, where he left the paper." In defense of its own reasonableness, the *Journal* noted that in its original 1982 attack on Bonner it had "offered not one word of criticism of Alma Guillermoprieto of *The Washington Post.*"

Among the documents reproduced at the end of *The Massacre at El Mozote,* Danner included the full text of both Bonner's and Alma Guillermoprieto's stories. There was no substantive difference between the two in either the reporting or the qualifying of what had been observed, but there were certain marginal distinctions on which critics of Bonner could seize. Guillermoprieto referred to herself as "this correspondent" and said that she had been taken into Morazán by "the Farabundo Martí Liberation Front." Bonner referred to himself as "a visitor who traveled through the area with those who are fighting the junta that now rules El

Salvador," i.e., the Farabundo Martí Liberation Front. Guillermoprieto began: "Several hundred civilians, including women and children, were taken from their homes in and around this village and killed by Salvadoran Army troops during a December offensive against leftist guerrillas, according to three survivors who say they witnessed the alleged massacres." She then proceeded to describe the bodies she herself had seen. Bonner began: "From interviews with people who live in this small mountain village and surrounding hamlets, it is clear that a massacre of major proportions occurred here last month." He then proceeded to describe the bodies he himself had seen. Bonner's statement is the less varnished of the two, but to call it different is to resort to a point of journalistic convention so narrowly defined as to be merely legalistic.

There seemed at the time at least two clear reasons that Bonner, not Guillermoprieto, became the target of choice. One reason was that Bonner, unlike Guillermoprieto, continued to report on a daily basis from El Salvador, and so, all through the spring and into the summer of 1982, remained a stubborn mote in Deane Hinton's ability to project the situation as the State Department wanted it projected. "I'm just afraid he's going to get himself killed," I recall an embassy official saying about Bonner during a lunch with Hinton in June of 1982; the tone here was the macho swagger never entirely absent from American embassies on hardship status. "That would be a tragedy." The other clear reason that Bonner was targeted, and Guillermoprieto was not, was this: Benjamin C. Bradlee and *The Washington Post* had backed up their reporter. A. M. Rosenthal and *The New York Times* had not.

The Mozote massacre occurred only six years after most of us watched the helicopters lift off the roof of the Saigon embassy and get pushed off the flight decks of the U.S. fleet into the South China Sea. There were by the time the bodies were exhumed from the sacristy of the Mozote church more than twice as many years between us and Mozote as there were between Mozote and those helicopters. This is not an insignificant time line, and suggests a third reason that Raymond Bonner's report from Morazán elicited an acrimony that Alma Guillermoprieto's did not. Bonner was an American. Alma Guillermoprieto had been born in and was then living in Mexico, a fact that was in some way understood to render her ineligible for casting as a member of what was sometimes called "the adversary culture," the culture that was construed as hostile to the interests of American business and the American government, the culture that had caused the United States to "lose" Vietnam, the culture that was even then drawing parallels between Vietnam and El Salvador.

Certain parallels were inescapable, since El Salvador was seen, by both the American military and the American policy community, as an opportunity to "apply the lesson" of Vietnam. The counterinsurgency doctrine that rationalized such operations as the 1981 sweep of Morazán was intended as a "revision" of the failed counterinsurgency effort in Vietnam (the "revision" for El Salvador emphasized a need to correct "root causes," or to win popular support by "democratizing" Salvadoran society), yet it had come to sound dispiritingly the same. The word "pacification" was in use, as was the phrase "third force," usually in reference to José Napoleón Duarte. "The only territory you want to hold is the six inches between the ears of the *campesino,*" Colonel John C. Waghelstein, who took command of the Milgroup not long after Mozote, said when he spoke at the American Enterprise Institute in 1985 on "LIC [Low-Intensity Conflict] in the Post-Vietnam Period." As late as 1986, in *The Wall Street Journal,* an American military adviser was quoted describing a community event sponsored by a Salvadoran army unit as "winning hearts and minds." The event in question involved clowns, mariachis, and speeches from army officers calling on peasants to reject the guerrillas. "This is low-intensity-conflict doctrine in action," the adviser said.

Again as in Vietnam, the doctrine was met with resistance on the part of those charged with carrying it out. "Attempts to address root causes during [this] period enjoyed less success than did efforts to stabilize the military situation," four American military officers observed in their 1988 *American Military Policy in Small Wars: The Case of El Salvador,* the so-called "colonels' report" prepared for the Institute for Foreign Policy Analysis. "American officers recognized . . . [that] the government had to transform itself into an institution perceived as effective, impartial, and committed to bringing about genuine reform. Meaningful implementation of this concept has eluded the Salvadorans and their American advisers." In a 1991 Rand Institute report prepared for the Department of Defense, Benjamin C. Schwarz noted that "the greed and apparent tactical incompetence of Salvadoran officers has so exhausted American experts posted to El Salvador that all the individuals interviewed for this report who have served there in the past two years believe that the Salvadoran military does not wish to win the war because in so doing it would lose the American aid that has enriched it for the past decade."

In San Salvador as in Saigon, this had long been accepted as one of the many taxing givens that made the posting so difficult to share with those who were planning the effort in Washington. Deane Hinton, who would not talk to Danner, emerges in *The Massacre at El Mozote* as the ultimate example of the career foreign service officer trying to execute an extremely doubtful policy in an even more doubtful situation. In this role as the good soldier of American foreign policy, Hinton left El Salvador in 1983 for Pakistan, a more remote but equally doubtful situation, and then returned to Central America to mop up the debris left by the contra and then the Panama efforts. Alma Guillermoprieto, whose work after El Mozote was especially acute on the immediacy with which Washington dreams became Central and South American responsibilities, noted in *The Heart That Bleeds* that, as late as 1992 in Hinton's Panama embassy, the preferred way to refer to the 1989 invasion was as "*la liberación.*"

"This is a suicide mission," an unidentified embassy official in San Salvador had said when Warren Hoge of *The New York Times* asked, not long after Mozote, if assignment to El Salvador could advance a foreign service career. "Someone's got to be nuts to be here. How many people do you think profited from having worked in Vietnam?" What made the San Salvador embassy a suicide mission was, of course, the certain knowledge that the facts of the situation would be less than welcome at the other end of the cable traffic. "There was no secret about who was doing the killing," Danner was told by Howard Lane, the public affairs officer at the embassy at the time of El Mozote. "I mean, you formed that view within forty-eight hours after arriving in the country, and there was no secret at all about it—except, maybe, in the White House."

What Mark Danner detailed in *The Massacre at El Mozote* was the process by which actual eyewitness accounts (Bonner, Guillermoprieto) and photographs (Meiselas) came to be discounted by large numbers of Americans for no other reason than that the government, presenting no evidence, referred to the accounts (the photographs seemed rather eerily not to exist in anyone's argument) as describing an event that was intrinsically unconfirmable, rendering the accounts by definition untrue. "Accurate information," Thomas Enders said as he began his February 2, 1982, statement on Capitol Hill. "I think we have all found out that is very hard to establish." He continued, first questioning the possibility of ever determining who had been responsible for the deaths—if indeed there had even been "deaths." Then he raised the ultimate question, the coup de grâce question, the question that had to do with the true interests or motives of those who reported such deaths: "The responsibility for the overwhelming number of deaths is never legally determined nor usually accounted for by clear or coherent evidence. Seventy percent of the political murders known to our embassy were committed by unknown assailants. And there is much special pleading going on also in this."

What is especially striking about Enders, as he presents himself in *The Massacre at El Mozote,* is his apparent inability to recognize any contradiction between what he said in 1982 to the House Subcommittee on Western Hemisphere Affairs and what he said a decade later to Danner. At one point Danner asked Enders about a rumor, believed by a number of prominent Salvadorans, that two American advisers had observed the Mozote operation from a base camp below the Torola River. This was the answer Enders gave: "Certainly, one of the issues I remember raising between us and the embassy was: Were there any American advisers on this sortie? The embassy made a great effort to talk to advisers who were with the Atlacatl to try to find out the truth." Any admission of knowledge, Enders conceded, "would have ruined those guys' careers—they would have been cashiered. So no one's going to volunteer, 'Hey, I was up there.'" The effect of such a disclosure on administration efforts to continue funding the war would have been "devastating," Enders said, and then: "American advisers with a unit that committed an atrocity? Can you imagine anything more corrosive of the entire military effort?"

Enders had recognized at the time, then, the existence of a "sortie." He had even recognized the possibility of an "atrocity." (The atrocity if not the sortie was in the subjunctive.) He had raised with the embassy the question of whether there had been "American advisers" present. Yet what Enders had said in 1982 was this: ". . . frankly, we do not have people who go out with the units as advisers, you know. These are military trainers. They stay behind." The idea that there was a difference between "advisers" and "trainers," another of the many legalistic distinctions at that time employed to rhetorical advantage, seems not to have been consistently held even by Enders.

Danner describes what happened to the story of El Mozote during the days and months after its disclosure as "a parable of the cold war." It was that, and as such a parable Mozote is irresistibly legible, but it was also something else. It was a parable of ideology, and of the apparently inconsolable anger it had become possible to feel toward those who were perceived as not sharing this ideology. "There have also been many fewer allegations of massacres during this reporting period than last," Thomas Enders was able to say in July 1982, when the question of certification once again came before the House Committee on Foreign Affairs. "This may be in part," he said, still the loyalist but still careful—*fewer* allegations, *may* be, *in part*—"because many earlier reports proved to be fabricated or exaggerated." At the same hearing, Nestor Sanchez, then deputy assistant secretary of defense for inter-American affairs, was able to single out "the first quick-reaction battalion trained by U.S. instructors in El Salvador" not only for "its tactical capability in fighting the guerrillas" but also for "its humane treatment of the people."

The "first quick-reaction battalion trained by U.S. instructors in El Salvador" was the Atlacatl. Just six years after Vietnam and in the face of what was beginning to seem a markedly similar American engagement, El Mozote, by which we have come to mean not exactly the massacre itself but the systematic obfuscation and prevarication that followed the disclosure of the massacre, was the first hard evidence that we had emerged a people again so yearning to accept the government version, or again so angry, as to buy into a revision of history in which those Americans who differed—those

Americans who for reasons of their "political orientation" would "fabricate" reports of a massacre carried out by a unit noted for its "humane treatment of the people"—were again our true, and only truly sinister, enemy.

3.

December 18, 1997

The aides gave us the details, retold now like runes. Promptly at nine o'clock on most mornings of the eight years he spent as president of the United States, Ronald Reagan arrived in the Oval Office to find on his desk his personal schedule, printed on green stationery and embossed in gold with the presidential seal. Between nine and ten he was briefed, first by his chief of staff and the vice president and then by his national security adviser. At ten, in the absence of a pressing conflict, he was scheduled for downtime, an hour in which he answered selected letters from citizens and clipped items that caught his eye in *Human Events* and *National Review.* Other meetings followed, for example with the congressional leadership. "I soon learned that these meetings lasted just one hour, no more, no less," Tony Coelho, at the time majority whip in the House, told us in *Recollections of Reagan: A Portrait of Ronald Reagan,* a 1997 collection of reminiscences edited by Peter Hannaford. "If the agenda—which he had written out on cards—wasn't completed at the end of the hour, he would excuse himself and leave. If it was finished short of an hour, he would fill the rest of the time with jokes (and he tells a good one)." During some meetings, according to his press secretary, Larry Speakes, the president filled the time by reciting Robert Service's "The Cremation of Sam McGee."

When the entry on the schedule was not a meeting but an appearance or a photo opportunity, the president was rehearsed. "You'll go out the door and down the steps," Michael Deaver or someone else would say, we were told by Donald Regan, secretary of the treasury from 1981 until 1985 and White House chief of staff from 1985 until 1987. "The podium is ten steps to the right and the audience will be in a semi-circle with the cameras at the right end of the half-moon; when you finish speaking take two steps back, but don't leave the podium, because they're going to present you with a patchwork quilt." It was Larry Speakes, in his 1988 *Speaking Out: The Reagan Presidency from Inside the White House,* who told us how, at the conclusion of each meeting or appearance, the president would draw on his schedule a vertical line downward and an arrow pointing to the next event. "It gives me a feeling that I am accomplishing something," the president told Speakes. It was Donald Regan, in his 1988 *For the Record: From Wall Street to Washington,* who told us how the schedule reminded the president when it was time to give a birthday present ("a funny hat or a tee shirt bearing a jocular message") to one or another staff member. "These gifts were chosen by others, and sometimes Reagan barely knew the person to whom he was giving them, but his pleasure in these contacts was genuine. . . . On one occasion, when he was somehow given the wrong date for one man's birthday and called to offer congratulations, nobody had the heart to tell him about the mistake."

"I cannot remember a single case in which he changed a time or canceled an appointment or even complained about an item on his schedule," Regan noted, betraying a certain queasy wonder at his initial encounter with this apparently cheerful lack of interest: Regan, still at Treasury, found himself slotted into the schedule, along with James Baker and Michael Deaver, to introduce to the president the novel notion that he and Baker, then chief of staff, switch jobs. "Reagan listened without any sign of surprise," Regan recalled. "He seemed equable, relaxed—almost incurious. This seemed odd under the circumstances." Notwithstanding Regan's efforts to offer the possibility of further deliberation on so serious a move ("'I appreciate that, Don,' the President said with the bright courtesy that is typical of him. 'But I don't see why we shouldn't just go ahead with it'"), the meeting lasted, including an exchange of Christmas-vacation pleasantries, fewer than its allotted thirty minutes. "I did not know what to make of his passivity," Regan wrote. "He seemed to be absorbing a *fait accompli* rather than making a decision. One might have thought that the matter had already been settled by some absent party." On reflection, Regan understood:

> As President, Ronald Reagan acted on the work habits of a lifetime: he regarded his daily schedule as being something like a shooting script in which characters came and went, scenes were rehearsed and acted out, and the plot was advanced one day at a time, and not always in sequence. The Chief of Staff was a sort of producer, making certain that the star had what he needed to do his best; the staff was like the crew, invisible behind the lights, watching the performance their behind-the-scenes efforts had made possible. . . . Reagan's performance was almost always flawless. If he was scheduled to receive a visitor at ten o'clock, he would finish whatever else he was doing at 9:58, clear off his desk, clear his mind of whatever had gone before, and prepare himself for the next scene.

Dinesh D'Souza, when he arrived at the Reagan White House as a senior domestic policy analyst in 1987, was twenty-six years old, a resident of the United States only since 1978 but already a name within what had come on the right to be called "the movement." He was a native of India who seemed to have arrived in this country with preternatural pitch for the exact charged chords (affirmative action, multiculturalism, gender studies, the academy in general) that drove its politics of resentment, and he played them, first as a founding editor of *The Dartmouth Review,* then as editor of the equally strident Princeton *Prospect,* managing editor of the Heritage Foundation's *Policy Review,* and biographer of the Moral Majority's Jerry Falwell.

The 1980s were years in Washington when careers were made on undergraduate bliss. One of D'Souza's colleagues on *The Dartmouth Review* became a speechwriter for Reagan, another for George Bush. Another, Keeney Jones, the author of the notorious "Dis Sho' Ain't No Jive, Bro," a puerile but predictably inflammatory *Dartmouth Review* parody of black students ("Dese boys be sayin' that we be comin' here to Dartmut an' not takin' the classics. You know, Homa, Shakesphere; but I hea' dey all be co'd in da ground, six feet unda, and whatchu be askin' us to learn from dem?"), became a speechwriter for Secretary of Education William Bennett. Another, Laura Ingraham, who became famous at *The Dartmouth Review* for publishing the secretly taped transcript of a meeting of the Gay Students' Association and to whom D'Souza dedicated *Illiberal Education,* went on to clerk for Clarence Thomas and then to become one of the most visible blonde pundits on MSNBC. "What could be more exciting?" D'Souza, who had been editor of *The Dartmouth Review* at the time "Dis Sho' Ain't No Jive, Bro" was published, later wrote of those years in Washington when to be young and movement was very heaven. "We were a generation of young conservatives who came to Washington in the 1980s inspired by Reagan and the idea of America that he espoused and embodied. The world was changing, and we wanted to be instruments of that change. Reagan was a septuagenarian with a youthful heart. He hired people like me because he wanted fresh faces and new ideas in the White House. Full of vigor and determination, we rallied to his cause."

"He hired people like me" may seem to suggest excessive executive volition on the part of a president who by all accounts expressed no interest in who his secretary of the treasury or chief of staff was to be, but the choice of the active tense is key here. D'Souza's intention in his 1997 *Ronald Reagan: How an Ordinary Man Became an Extraordinary Leader* (which, like his 1991 *Illiberal Education: The Politics of Race and Sex on Campus* and his 1995 *The End of Racism: Principles for a Multiracial Society,* was written within the nurturing framework of the American Enterprise Institute) was to offer what he presented as a "revisionist" view of the Reagan years, a correction of the record for "a new generation of young people" who, because they have had "no alternative source of information," have been unable to detect the "transparent bias" of their teachers and the media.

It was D'Souza's thesis, honed by his useful and apparently inexhaustible ability to present himself as one of a besieged minority, that Reagan had been systematically misread. The misreading only began, in this view, with Reagan's "liberal critics," who were further identified as "the pundits, political scientists, and historians," "the wise men," "the intellectual elite," and "the cognoscenti." The more grave misreading, as D'Souza sees it, came from within Reagan's own party, not only from his more pragmatic aides (the "prags," or "ingrates and apostates," whose remarkably similar descriptions of the detachment at the center of the administration in which they served suggested to D'Souza "an almost defiant disloyalty") but even from his "hard-core" admirers, or "true believers," those movement conservatives who considered Reagan a "malleable figurehead" too often controlled by the pragmatists on his staff. "I was one of those conservatives," D'Souza allowed:

> Even when Reagan proved us wrong and showed how effective a president he was, many of us in his ideological camp nevertheless failed to understand the secret of his success. We could not fathom how he conceived and realized his grand objectives, effortlessly overcame his powerful adversaries, and won the respect of the American people. Many who worked with him are still bewildered. This study seeks to solve the mystery.

In his casuistical pursuit of the elusive frame in which Reagan can be seen as the "prime mover," the "decisive agent of change," and the "architect of his own success," D'Souza was not actually breaking new ground. Such attempts to "solve the mystery" date back at least to the 1980 transition, during which it became apparent to some that the president-elect, without benefit of constructive interpretation, could appear less than fully engaged. During a transition briefing on secret international agreements and commitments, according to Jimmy Carter, Reagan listened politely but asked no questions and took no notes. Two hours before his 1981 inauguration, according to Michael Deaver, he was still sleeping. Deaver did not actually find this extraordinary, nor would anyone else who had witnessed Reagan's performance as governor of California. "I remember sitting there in the governor's office with him, a couple of days after I had been elected to succeed him," Jerry Brown recalls in *Recollections of Reagan: A Portrait of Ronald Reagan:*

> We didn't have a nuts-and-bolts conversation about the transition that day. I didn't see Ronald Reagan as a nuts-and-bolts kind of guy. . . . He was definitely performing his ceremonial role as governor, and doing it quite well. I think a great deal of the job is ceremonial. The way I look at it now, most politicians holding office think they are doing things but it's all staffed out. . . . Most of the day-to-day stuff is very symbolic. That was one of the frustrations I found in being governor. At first, I took literally the nature of the material being presented at meetings, but I soon found that visiting delegations often were satisfied just being in the same room as the governor. There is some-

> thing illusory about it, like a play. Then again, if that satisfies people, it has some value. Reagan seemed to understand all that.

This was in fact the very understanding that would come to power Reagan's performance as president, and many people knew it, but to have said so at the time would have been out of synch with the somewhat less Zen story line (West Wing lights burn late as dedicated workaholics hit the ground running) preferred in Washington. From the outset, then, the invention of a president who could be seen as active rather than passive, who could be understood to possess mysteriously invisible and therefore miraculously potent leadership skills, became a White House priority. "Reagan's aides have been telling reporters of decisions that the President himself has made, as if they found it necessary to explain that he has made some," Elizabeth Drew reported two months into the administration, when both NBC and *Time* had been enlisted to do "A Day with President Reagan" stories. "A White House aide told me, 'We thought it was important to do those, because of the perception out there that this is a marionette president. It's simply not true.'"

This president who was not a marionette would be shown making decisions, and not only that: the decisions he was shown making (or more often in this instance, where rhetoric was soon understood to be interchangeable with action, the speeches he was shown making) would have demonstrable, preferably Manichean, results. Victory, particularly in the realm of foreign affairs, which offered dramatic "standing tall" roles for the active president to play, would be narrowly defined: the barest suggestion of an election or a reform would serve to signal the enlistment of another fledgling democracy. So defined, all victories could assume equal import: the decision to invade Grenada, D'Souza tells us, reversed the Brezhnev Doctrine. "Reagan had listened intently but said little," D'Souza wrote about the moment of standing tall that preceded the Grenada invasion. "Finally he asked the Joint Chiefs of Staff whether they believed that a military operation was likely to succeed." The Joint Chiefs, according to D'Souza, who credits his account of this meeting to Edwin Meese and Caspar Weinberger, said they believed that the operation, which entailed landing six thousand marines and airborne rangers on an island significantly smaller than Barbados, "could be done."

"Very well," Reagan is said to have said. "In that case, let's go ahead."

The invasion of Grenada is instructive. The operation, which involved one of Reagan's few overt (and his only, on his own terms, "successful") uses of military power, was justified by the administration on the ground that a ten-thousand-foot landing strip was under construction on the island, but secondarily (or primarily, depending on who was talking) because American medical students were "captive" (in fact they could have left on either regularly scheduled or charter flights) at an island medical school. "I don't think it was an invasion," Jeane Kirkpatrick said on *Meet the Press* a few days after the operation. "I think it was a rescue, and I think that we ought to stop calling it an invasion." Norman Podhoretz, on the op-ed page of *The New York Times,* wrote that the invasion, or the rescue, suggested a return to "recovery and health" for "a United States still suffering from the shell-shocked condition that has muddled our minds and paralyzed our national will since Vietnam." D'Souza characterizes it as "Reagan's first opportunity to overthrow a communist regime," an occasion when "Reagan's leadership was exercised in the face of apprehension on the part of his staff and skepticism on the part of the congressional leadership."

Not long after the Grenada invasion, for which the number of medals awarded eventually exceeded the number of actual combatants, the president, in his commander-in-chief role, spoke at a ceremony honoring the nation's Medal of Honor recipients. "Our days of weakness are over," he declared, standing under a huge representation of the medal's pale-blue ribbon and five-pointed star. "Our military forces are back on their feet and standing tall." Grenada, then, virtually as it happened, had materialized into the symbolic centerpiece of the rollback scenario that was the Reagan Doctrine. In the first dozen pages of *Ronald Reagan: How an Ordinary Man Became an Extraordinary Leader,* D'Souza laid out, presumably for that "new generation of young people with no alternative source of information," a kind of Young Adults timeline in which the Reagan administration is seen to begin at modern history's lowest tide ("capitalism and democracy . . . on the retreat in much of the world," America itself facing "the greatest economic crisis since the Great Depression") and to conclude at its highest, the triumphal surge of reborn patriotism and purpose that was to raise all boats and end the cold war.

In this version of what happened between 1980 and 1988, Reagan's role as prime mover is seen to reside, before and after Grenada, less in actual actions than in his speeches, those moments when the president was primed to "go over the heads" of the Congress or the media or whoever was at the moment frustrating the aims of the administration. D'Souza, in *Ronald Reagan: How an Ordinary Man Became an Extraordinary Leader,* devoted four of his 264 pages to a close textual analysis of the 1983 "Evil Empire" speech (further comment appears on four more pages), which was, he assures us, "the single most important speech of the Reagan presidency, a classic illustration of what Vaclev Havel terms 'the power of words to change history.'"

This faith in the laser-like efficacy of Reagan's rhetoric seems undiminished by the fact that it remains largely a priori. "Going after a major policy change, crafting a practical policy initiative, and sticking with it is an accomplishment," Martin Anderson, who was Reagan's chief domestic policy adviser in the early administration, tells us in *Recol-*

lections of Reagan. Yet the accomplishment he cites is the 1983 SDI, or "Star Wars," speech. "Another very important event in 1983 took place two weeks after the SDI speech," he adds, and, again, it develops that he is talking about not an actual "event" but another speech, in this instance the popular "Evil Empire."

William Kristol made recent reference to our need to credit Reagan's "magnificent" 1984 speech at Normandy, as if the speech, which was written by Peggy Noonan, were somehow at one on the "magnificence" scale with the invasion it was delivered to commemorate. ("The State/NSC draft that I'd been given weeks before wanted the president to go off on this little tangent about arms control," Miss Noonan later wrote about her Normandy speech, "and as I read it I thought, in the language of the day, Oh gag me with a spoon, this isn't a speech about arms negotiations, you jackasses, this is a speech about splendor.") As evidence that Reagan had the force of calculation behind his "predictions" and "prophecies," D'Souza offers the "tear down this wall" speech delivered at the Brandenburg Gate in 1987. "Not long after this," he writes, "the wall did come tumbling down, and Reagan's prophecies all came true. The most powerful empire in human history imploded. These were not just results Reagan predicted. He intended the outcome."

The consequences of reinventing Reagan as a leader whose leadership was seen to exist exclusively in his public utterances, the ultimate "charismatic" president, were interestingly studied by the political historian Jeffrey K. Tulis, who, in his 1987 *The Rhetorical Presidency,* outlined in some detail the dilemmas presented by a presidential style that tends to delegitimize both constitutional and bureaucratic authority, to depend for its effect on created crises (to "go over the heads" of the opposition requires the presence of some urgent message to be conveyed), and so to place unusual policy-making power in the hands of speechwriters:

> Many speeches are scheduled long before they are to be delivered. Thus the commitment to speak precedes the knowledge of any issue to speak about, often causing staff to find or create an issue for the speech. . . . The routinization of crisis, endemic to the rhetorical presidency, is accompanied by attempted repetitions of charisma. In Reagan's case this style was further reinforced by an ideology and a rhetoric opposed to the Washington establishment, to bureaucrats and bureaucracies. . . . He serves as a better illustration than any other president of the possibility and danger that presidents might come themselves to think in the terms initially designed to persuade those not capable of fully understanding the policy itself. Having reconfigured the political landscape, the rhetorical presidency comes to reconstitute the president's political understanding.

Since D'Souza's account of the Reagan presidency derived from and differed in no substantive factual detail from those of the "ingrates and apostates" who were already on their book tours when that presidency ended, the superimposition of the "leadership" narrative meant grappling with some fairly intractable material already on the record. The peculiarities noticed by others (the president was "detached," or "not entirely informed," or "vague on details," or "passive") would need to be translated into evidence of a grand design. Biographical details would need to be mined for "character" points, often to less than coherent effect. "Here was the son of the town drunk who grew up poor in the Midwest," D'Souza tells us on page 10. "Without any connections, he made his way to Hollywood and survived its cutthroat culture to become a major star."

This was not literally true: Reagan was never a "major star," but a reliable studio contract player who hit an era of diminished demand and was reduced, before finding a role as a spokesman for General Electric, to introducing a club act, The Continentals, at the Last Frontier in Las Vegas. "Survived its cutthroat culture to become a major star," however, fit the point D'Souza was trying to make on this page, which had to do with "the personal [and] political mystery" that had enabled Reagan to change "both his country and the rest of the world." By page 45, where the point to be made had to do with the president's flexibility and skill at "the art of negotiating and being part of a team," D'Souza had reworked the bio to yield what he needed: "Reagan was never a big enough star to permit himself such consuming narcissism. . . .

When many actors were too fastidious to be seen on television, regarding it as inferior to film, Reagan obligingly switched to the new medium, thus guaranteeing himself more parts."

This constant trimming and tacking leads D'Souza into fairly choppy water, where logical connections tend to get jettisoned. If the famous Reagan "gaffes" were calculated, as D'Souza suggests ("When we recall Reagan's gaffes, we see that he sometimes used them as a kind of code to transmit important political messages that would be incomprehensible to a hostile media"), then could the president not be seen as a demagogue, deliberately manipulating the electorate with "facts" (the welfare queens, the student loans used to buy certificates of deposit, the young man who went into the grocery store and bought an orange with food stamps and a bottle of vodka with the change) he knew would never stand scrutiny? Not at all: the president dealt in "morality tales," in the "illustration of a broader theme," and "just because this or that particular detail might be erroneous did not mean that the moral of the story was invalid." If Reagan failed to recognize his black secretary of housing and urban development, Samuel Pierce, addressing him as "Mr. Mayor," did that not suggest a relationship both with his own administration and with urban America that remained casual at best? No, only an "oversight": "He was wrong not to recognize Sam Pierce, but the reason for his oversight was that he had no interest in the Department of Housing and Urban Development, which he saw as a rat hole of public policy."

If Reagan set out to reduce the size and cost of the government and left it, in 1990 dollars, $1.5 trillion deeper in debt than when he started ("You and I, as individuals, can, by borrowing, live beyond our means, but only for a limited period of time," he had said in his 1981 inaugural address. "Why then should we think that collectively, as a nation, we are not bound by that same limitation?"), could not the president be said to have failed at his own mission? No, because Reagan's unique approach to that mission, which allowed him to cut taxes while increasing domestic entitlements and boosting defense spending to a rough total, for the eight years, of $2 trillion, turned out to have "a silver lining." D'Souza explains: "by a strange turn of fate, the deficit accomplished for Reagan what he was unable to achieve directly: for the first time in this century, Congress began to impose limits on the growth of government." If Reagan lacked, as D'Souza allows, not only "historical learning" and "encyclopedic knowledge" but also "the two characteristics of the liberally educated person: self-consciousness and open-mindedness," did dogmatism not tend to undermine the value of his opinions? Not exactly: Reagan "saw the world through the clear lens of right and wrong," and so possessed a knowledge that "came not from books but from within himself."

The knowledge that "came not from books but from within himself" is where we reenter the real woo-woo of the period, the insistence on the ineffable that began with the perceived need to front the administration with a "leader" and ended by transforming the White House into a kind of cargo cult. "There is no point in pining for 'another Ronald Reagan,'" D'Souza concludes, exactly if unwittingly capturing this aspect of the period. "He isn't returning, and there will never be another quite like him." Since it was the given of the Reagan administration that Reagan was at its helm, and since a good deal of the visible evidence suggested otherwise, the man must be a "mystery," with skills pitched, like a dog whistle, beyond our defective ability to hear them.

D'Souza tells us that Edmund Morris, Reagan's official biographer, in 1990 characterized his subject as the most incomprehensible figure he had ever encountered. He tells us that Lou Cannon, who covered Reagan in Sacramento and in Washington and wrote three books about him, regards Reagan as a puzzle, and is "still trying to understand the man." He tells us that Reagan and Edwin Meese, whose daily lives were inseparable in both Sacramento and Washington, never saw each other socially. Reagan had "countless acquaintances," D'Souza observes, but apparently only one close friend, the actor Robert Taylor. Nancy Reagan spoke regularly to friends on the telephone, but her husband did not: "He would say hello, exchange a few pleasantries, then hand the receiver to her." Frustrated by "the paradoxes of Reagan's personality," D'Souza writes, "some who worked with him for years have given up trying to understand him."

Yet these "paradoxes" existed only within what was essentially a category confusion. Defined as "president," or even as "governor," Reagan did indeed appear to have some flat sides, some missing pieces. Defined as "actor," however, he was from the beginning to the end of his public life entirely consistent, a knowable and in fact quite predictable quantity. D'Souza allows that Reagan's life as an actor was a significant part of his makeup, but sees "actor" as a stepping stone, a role the real Ronald Reagan, or "president," had mastered and shed, although not before absorbing certain lessons that "enabled him to govern more effectively": the importance of appealing to a mass audience, say, or the knowledge that "noble ideals" could be more effectively communicated "if they were not abstract but personalized and visualized." Grappling with the question of how Reagan could be "uniformly fair-minded and pleasant with aides" but "not get close to them personally," D'Souza, laboring from within the definition "president," extracts a "leadership" solution: "He saw them as instruments to achieve his goals."

"People would work for him for a decade, then they would leave, and he would not associate with them—not even a phone call," D'Souza notes, and again draws the "leadership" lesson: "Thus the conventional wisdom must be turned on its head: he wasn't their pawn; they were his." This fails to compute (if they were the pawns and he their leader, would he not instead be inclined to keep them on speed dial, available for further deployment?) and will continue to do so, since the category is wrong: what might be seen as mysterious behavior in one occupation can be standard operating procedure in another, and it is within the unique working rhythms of the entertainment industry that the "mysteries" of the man and the administration evaporate. Reagan could be "uniformly fair-minded and pleasant with aides" without getting close to them personally (or knowing where their offices were or even their names) not because he "saw them as instruments to achieve his goals" but because he saw them as members of the crew ("invisible behind the lights," in Donald Regan's words), as gaffers and best boys and script supervisors and even as day players, actors like himself but not featured performers whose names he need remember.

Similarly, the ability to work with people for a decade and never call them again precisely reflects the intense but temporary camaraderie of the set, the location, where the principals routinely exchange the ritual totems of bonding (unlisted home numbers, cell numbers, car numbers, triple-secret numbers, and hour-by-hour schedules for sojourns in Aspen and Sundance and Martha's Vineyard) in full and mutual confidence that the only calls received after the wrap will be for ADR, or for reshoots. Even that most minor of presidential idiosyncracies, the absolute adherence to the daily schedule remarked upon by virtually all Reagan's aides, the vertical line drawn through the completed task and the arrow pointing to the next task (D'Souza tells us again about the arrows, as evidence of "the brisk thoroughness with which he discharged his responsibilities"), derives from the habits of the set, where the revised shooting schedule is distributed daily. "SC. 183A—EXT. WASHINGTON STREET—MOTORCADE—DAY," such a schedule might read, and, once Scene 183A was completed, a vertical line would be drawn through it on the schedule, with an arrow pointing to "SC. 17—ANDREWS AFB—ESTABLISHING—DAY": not in any sequence the principals need to understand, but the day's next task.

Asked whether he liked being president better than being an actor, Ronald Reagan, according to D'Souza, replied, "Yes, because here I get to write the script too." D'Souza presents this as the president's amusing deprecation of the way in which he achieved objectives "against the odds," and so it may have been intended, but the deeper peculiarities of Reagan's tenure could even at the time be seen to derive from his tendency to see the presidency as a script waiting to be solved. There is in the development of every motion picture a process known as "licking the script," that period during which the "story" is shaped and altered to fit the idealized character who must be at its center. A president who understands the "character clarity" that results from this process would sense immediately that a scene with, say, Prime Minister Yitzhak Shamir of Israel could be improved by a dramatization of how he, the president, or star, personally experienced the Holocaust.

It would be only logical, then, for Reagan to tell Shamir, as he did in 1983, that during World War II he had filmed Nazi death camps for the Signal Corps (in fact he had spent the entire war in Culver City, making training films at the Hal Roach studio), that he had (presciently) kept one reel in case the Holocaust was ever questioned, and that he had (just recently!) found occasion to convert a doubter by running this reel. A president who understands how a single scene can jump a script would naturally offer reporters in Charlotte, North Carolina, as Lou Cannon tells us that Reagan did during his 1975 primary campaign, this improved version of how segregation ended in the military:

> "When the Japanese dropped the bomb on Pearl Harbor there was a Negro sailor whose total duties involved kitchen-type duties. . . . He cradled a machine gun in his arms, which is not an easy thing to do, and stood on the end of a pier blazing away at Japanese airplanes that were coming down and strafing him and that [segregation] was all changed." When a reporter pointed out that segregation in the armed services actually had ended when President Truman signed an executive order in 1948 three years after the war, Reagan stood his ground. "I remember the scene,"

Reagan told me on the campaign plane later. "It was very powerful."

The question most frequently asked in a script meeting is, in one variation or another, always this: *Why do we care, how can we up the stakes, what's going to make America root for this guy?* The "guy," of course is the main character, the star part, and infinite time and attention is devoted to finding his "hook," the secret to his character that gets hinted at in Act One, revealed at the end of Act Two, and turned in Act Three: "son of the town drunk," say, could even be the secret behind "stood on the burning pier and cradled in his arms the machine gun that would end segregation." Ronald Reagan, we later learned from his personal physician, Brigadier General John Hutton, first grasped the import of the AIDS epidemic in July 1985 (until then he had seemed to construe it as a punishment for bad behavior, and "would say words to the effect: 'Is there a message in this?'"), when he learned from a news report that it had happened to someone America could root for, Rock Hudson.

There is in *Ronald Reagan: How an Ordinary Man Became an Extraordinary Leader* one arresting account, which seems to be based not on D'Souza's access to the famous and less known movers of the period (his two-page list of acknowledgments recalls with considerable poignancy the fervor of the moment, including as it does such evocative names as "Elliott Abrams," "George Gilder," "Josh

Gilder," "Michael Ledeen," "Joshua Muravchik," "Grover Norquist," "Robert Reilly," "Joseph Sobran," and "Faith Whittlesey") but on reporting done by Jane Mayer and Doyle McManus for their *Landslide: The Unmaking of the President, 1984—1988.* The place is the White House. The time is October 26, 1983, when the American students "rescued" by the invasion of Grenada were on their way to Charleston Air Force Base in South Carolina. "On the day of their arrival," D'Souza writes, "Oliver North, who had helped plan the Grenada operation, came rushing into the president's office."

> He said that the students had not been briefed on the reasons for the invasion, and no one knew what they would tell the press. "Come with me," Reagan said. He led North into a room with a television monitor. There the two of them watched as the first young man got off the plane, walked over to the runway, dropped to his knees, and kissed the soil of the United States. "You see, Ollie," Reagan said, "you should have more faith in the American people." Reagan knew that with the student's dramatic gesture, the national debate over the legitimacy of the Grenada invasion was effectively over.

Among the several levels on which this passage invites the reader to linger (Why would students in need of rescue need to be briefed on the reasons for the rescue? How exactly would "more faith in the American people" lead to the expectation that the first student off the plane would show the cameras what the administration wanted shown?), the most rewarding has to do with "Ollie," and his apparently easy access, as early as October 1983, to the president's office. It would, in due time, be repeatedly suggested that Lieutenant Colonel North was a rogue fantast who had inflated or even invented his proximity to the president. "He said he sometimes spent time alone with Ronnie in the Oval Office," Nancy Reagan wrote in *My Turn,* her own essay into correcting the record. "But that never happened." Larry Speakes called North's assertion that he had been in the Oval Office when the medical students arrived home from Grenada "an outright lie." "We researched the records," he wrote, "and there was never a time when Ollie was alone with the President in the Oval Office." Yet D'Souza's vignette casts North, whose several code names included "Mr. Goode" and "Mr. White," in what seems to have been his own preferred light: he was on the scene, he was in the picture, he was able in a moment of threatened crunch to regard the president as his confidant.

By October 1983, the sequence of events that became known as "Iran-contra," or, as D'Souza calls it, the "historical footnote that future generations will not even remember," was well underway, and the White House deep in that perilous territory where certain spectral missions were already coinciding, to deleterious effect, with the demands of the script. Iran-contra, D'Souza assures his Young Adult readers, "seems to have been transacted in the White House without Reagan's knowledge or approval," but even if we discount the assertions of Reagan's aides that he was briefed on every detail except possibly (this point remains unclear) the diversion of funds, and even if we discount the president's own statement that "it was my idea to begin with," Iran-contra was not a series of events that professionals of the Washington process would naturally think of transacting.

It was instead a scenario that suggested the addled inspiration of script meetings, the moment when the elusive line materializes: on the one hand we have the "lion in winter," as D'Souza calls Reagan, the aging freedom fighter (*NB, possible: we learn in Act Two he knows he has something terminal but hasn't told anybody???*) whose life has been dedicated to the eradication of tyranny and who is now, apparently alone (*NB, everyone opposes, scene where even trusted aide backs away*), facing his last and toughest battle with the forces of injustice. The inspiration, of course, the solution to the script, the always startlingly obvious idea that comes only when the table is littered with takeout and the producer is inventing pressing business elsewhere, is this: the lonely lion in winter turns out not to be alone after all, for we also have the young colonel, "Mr. Goode," a born performer, a larger-than-life character, a real character, actually, one who (according to Larry Speakes) "loved to operate big in the Situation Room . . . standing in the middle of the floor, a phone at each ear, barking cryptic orders to some faraway operative" and who (according to

Peggy Noonan) could convincingly deliver such lines as "And don't forget this is in accord conversation Casey-North approximately 1500 this date" or "Don't talk to me about Pastora [the contra leader Eden Pastora, aka "Comandante Zero"], I'm not speaking to Pastora."

For the "President," a man whose most practiced instincts had trained him to find the strongest possible narrative line in the scenes he was given, to clean out those extraneous elements that undermine character clarity, a man for whom historical truth had all his life run at twenty-four frames a second, Iran-contra would have been irresistible, a go project from concept, a script with two strong characters, the young marine officer with no aim but to serve his president, the aging president with no aim but to free the tyrannized (whether the tyrants were Nicaraguans or Iranians or some other nationality altogether was just a plot point, a detail to work out later), a story about male bonding, a story about a father who found the son he never (in this "cleaned out" draft of the script) had, a buddy movie, and better still than a buddy movie: a mentor buddy movie, with action.

"Reagan didn't violate the public trust in the pursuit of personal power," we are told by D'Souza, who, possibly because he noticed that he had "Ollie" running into the president's office on page 158, seems by page 247 of *Ronald Reagan: How an Ordinary Man Became an Extraordinary Leader* to have somewhat amended his earlier (page 16) assessment of Iran-contra as a series of events "transacted in the White House without Reagan's knowledge or approval." Here, on page 247, we see a change from passive to active voice: "He did it because he empathized with the suffering of the hostages and their families. . . . He refused to listen to Shultz and Weinberger's prudent recommendations that he avoid the foolish enterprise altogether." D'Souza seems not to entirely appreciate that for this actor, given this script, it would have been precisely the suggestion that he was undertaking a "foolish enterprise" that sealed his determination to go with it. "There are those who say that what we are attempting to do cannot be done," he had said in a hundred variations in as many speeches. This was a president who understood viscerally—as the young colonel also understood—that what makes a successful motion picture is exactly a foolish enterprise, a lonely quest, a lost cause, a fight against the odds: undertaken, against the best advice of those who say it cannot be done, by someone America can root for. *Cut, print.*

Eyes on the Prize

September 24, 1992

1.

In the understandably general yearning for "change" in the governing of our country, we might pause to reflect on just what is being changed, and by whom, and for whom. At Madison Square Garden in New York from July 13, 1992, until the balloons fell on the evening of July 16, four days and nights devoted to heralding the perfected "centrism" of the Democratic Party, no hint of what had once been that party's nominal constituency was allowed to penetrate prime time, nor was any suggestion of what had once been that party's tacit role, that of assimilating immigration and franchising the economically disenfranchised, or what used to be called "co-opting" discontent.

Jesse Jackson and Jimmy Carter got slotted in during the All-Star Game. Jerry Brown spoke of "the people who fight our wars but never come to our receptions" mainly on C-SPAN.

"This convention looks like our country, not like a country club," Representative Tom Foley declared, and a number of speakers echoed him. Yet the preferred images of the convention were those of a sun-belt country club, for example that of Tipper and Al Gore dancing sedately on the podium. The preferred sound was not "Happy Days Are Here Again" but Fleetwood Mac, Christine McVie's request before the New Hampshire primary that the Clinton campaign stop using her song "Don't Stop" notwithstanding. Those who wanted to dance with the Gores, join the club, made it clear that they were prepared to transcend, as their candidate had often put it, "the brain-dead policies in both parties," most noticeably their own. "Democrat" and "Republican," we heard repeatedly, as if a prayer for electoral rain, were old words, words without meaning, as were the words "liberal" and "conservative." "The choice we offer is not conservative or liberal, in many ways it is not even Republican or Democratic," the candidate told us. "It is different. It is new. . . . I call it a New Covenant."

What Governor Clinton had been calling "a New Covenant" (for a while he had called it "a Third Way," which had sounded infelicitously Peruvian) was essentially the Democratic Leadership Council's "New Choice," or more recently its "New Social Contract," a series of policy adjustments meant to "reinvent government" (as in *Reinventing Government* by David Osborne, a Clinton adviser) not at all by diminishing but by repackaging its role. There was in the New Covenant or the Third Way or the New Choice or the New Social Contract much that was current in Republican as well as Democratic thinking, but there was also a shell game: part of the "New Covenant," for example, called for the federal government to "cut 100,000 bureaucrats" by attrition, but it was unclear who, if not a new hundred thousand bureaucrats, would administer the new federal programs ($133.7 billion to "Put America to Work," $22.5 billion to "Reward Work and Families," $63.3 billion to encourage "Lifetime Learning") promised in the ticket's *Putting People First: How We Can All Change America*. The "New Covenant" was nonetheless the candidate's "game plan," and it was also, covering another Republican base, his "new choice based on old values."

In certain ways this convention's true keynote address was delivered not by the keynote speakers of record but by the Democratic National Committee's finance chairman, Senator John D. (Jay) Rockefeller IV of West Virginia. Senator Rockefeller, describing himself as "one of those Democrats who doesn't threaten big donors," reported that this was a year in which it was possible to mount "the best financed Democratic presidential campaign ever," one in which the "donor base is bigger than ever," enabling the party to buy "focus groups, polling, research, whatever it takes to get the message out." The message was this: we're tough, kick ass, get a life. "We Democrats have some changing to do," the candidate said, accepting the nomination on behalf of those who "pay the taxes, raise the kids and play by the rules," by which he meant "the forgotten middle class" that had been the target of his campaign since New Hampshire. He had an ultimatum for "the fathers in this country who have chosen to abandon their children by neglecting their child support: take responsibility for your children or we will force you to do so." He had a promise to "end welfare as we know it," to put "100,000 more police on your streets," to set right a situation in which "the prime minister of Japan . . . actually said . . . he felt sympathy for America."

This world the candidate evoked, one in which the prime minister of Japan conspired with welfare queens and deadbeat dads (referred to in *Putting People First* as "deadbeat parents") to deride those who paid the taxes and raised the kids and played by the rules, began and ended with the woolly resentments of the focus group, and so remained securely distanced from what might be anyone's actual readiness to address actual concerns. The candidate spoke about "taking on the big insurance companies to lower costs and provide health care to all Americans," but *Putting People First* made it clear that this more comprehensive health care was to be paid for not only by decreasing Medicare benefits for those with incomes over $125,000, a proposal with which no one could argue, but also by "cutting medical costs," which, in practice, again means reducing benefits, this time at all income levels. (This is a thorny business. One reason medical costs keep rising is not necessarily because the insured consumer is being "gouged," as *Putting People First* suggests, but precisely because insured consumers now make up certain deficits incurred by the treatment of patients subject to the already restricted payment schedules specified by Medicare and Medicaid.)

The candidate spoke about "less entitlement" and more "empowerment," the preferred word among the Bush administration's own "New Paradigm" theorists for such doubtfully practicable ideas as selling housing projects to their tenants, but it remained unclear just what entitlement this particular candidate could have the political will to cut. The single "entitlement reform" detailed as an actual monetary saving in *Putting People First* was the Medicare cutback for those with incomes over $125,000, and it was hard not to remember that Governor Clinton, just four months before, had saturated Florida retirement condos with the news that Paul Tsongas, who had proposed to limit cost-of-living increases on Social Security benefits to recipients with incomes over $125,000, was against old people.

He spoke about reducing defense spending, but also about maintaining "the world's strongest defense"; the projected figure for "1993 defense cuts (beyond Bush)" offered by *Putting People First,* however, was only two billion dollars, and Governor Clinton, during the press of his losing primary campaign in Connecticut, had promised to save the Groton-based Seawolf submarine program, one multibillion-dollar defense expenditure marked for a cut by the Bush administration. He spoke about the need to "clean out the bureaucracy," as he had during all his primary campaigns except one, that in New York, where his key union endorsements included the Civil Service Employees Association (some 200,000 members in New York State) and District Council 37 (135,000 members in New York City) of the American Federation of State, County, and Municipal Employees. "There is a real opportunity in the citadel of the failures of the old bureaucratic approaches to talk about new ideas," Will Marshall, the president of the Democratic Leadership Council's Progressive Policy Institute and a Clinton adviser, had acknowledged to Ronald Brownstein of the *Los Angeles Times* on this point. "On the other hand, he's got a lot of support from public employee unions, he's fighting for his life and he needs support wherever he can get it."

These were Democrats, in other words, who accepted the responsibility with which Ron Brown had charged them: to "keep our eye on the prize, so to speak." These were Democrats who congratulated themselves for staying, as they put it, on message. Not much at their convention got left to improvisation. They spoke about "unity." They spoke about a "new generation," about "change," about "putting people first." As evidence of putting people first, they offered "real people" videos, soft-focus videos featuring such actual citizens as "Kyle Harrison," a student at the University of Arkansas in Fayetteville who cooperatively described himself as a member of "the forgotten middle class." Convention delegates were given what a Clinton aide called the "prayerbook," a set of six blue pocket cards covering questions they might be asked, for example about "The Real Bill Clinton." ("His father died before he was born and his mother had to leave home to study nursing. . . . Bill grew up in a home without indoor plumbing.") The volunteers who worked the DNC's "VVIP" skyboxes at the Garden were equipped with approved conversation, or "Quotable Lines" ("Al Gore complements Bill Clinton, they are a strong team," or "The Republicans have run out of ideas, they're stuck in a rut . . . all Americans are losing out"), as well as with answers to more special, more VVIP-oriented questions, as in "Celebrity Talking Points" #3 and #4:

> 3. "Tipper Gore previously worked on a drive to put warning labels on albums classified violent or obscene. Isn't this a restriction of our 1st Amendment right to freedom of speech?"
>
> First, let's be clear—Al Gore is the Vice-Presidential candidate and this convention will determine the platform for this party and for this campaign. Second, Tipper Gore is entitled to her own opinions as is any other American. She is a good campaigner and will work hard on behalf of

the platform of this party and the Clinton-Gore ticket.

4. "Why are some entertainment personalities who normally endorse Democratic candidates sitting this election year out or going to Ross Perot?"

There are many other issues such as Human Rights, the Environment, Women Rights, AIDS and other such important issues which have become a priority for certain individuals. Also, those who have chosen other campaigns must have their reasons and I respect their right to do that.

"When in doubt," skybox volunteers were advised, "the best answer is, 'Thank you, I'll get a staff person to get you the campaign's position on that issue.'" It was frequently said to be the Year of the Woman, and the convention had clearly been shaped to make the ticket attractive to women, but its notion of what might attract women was clumsy, off, devised as it was by men who wanted simultaneously to signal the electorate that they were in firm control of any woman who might have her own agenda. There was the production number from *The Will Rogers Follies* with the poufs on the breasts. There was the transformation of two mature and reportedly capable women, Mrs. Clinton and Mrs. Gore, into double-the-fun blondes who jumped up and down, clapped on cue, and traveled, as Mrs. Reagan had, with a hairdresser on the manifest for comb-outs.

The party did introduce its five women candidates for the Senate (Carol Mosley Braun, Jean Lloyd-Jones, Lynn Yeakel, Barbara Boxer, and Dianne Feinstein) as well as four of its most visible ingenues (Kathleen Brown, Barbara Roberts, Sharon Pratt Kelly, and Pat Schroeder), but had originally hedged the possibility that the presence of too many women might threaten any viewer by ghettoizing them, scheduling them, with Jimmy Carter and Jesse Jackson and the AIDS presentations, on Tuesday night, which on the Monday-through-Thursday convention schedule had traditionally been known as "losers' night." (After some complaints, the Senate candidates, although not the ingenues, got moved to the Monday schedule.) "What used to be losers' night we're making women's night," Ron Brown had said about this to one woman I know, a prominent Democrat in the entertainment industry.

The proceedings ran so relentlessly on schedule that it was sometimes necessary to pad out the pre-primetime events with unmotivated musical interludes, and on one occasion with an actual ten-minute recess. "The people running this convention are just impossible," an aide to Governor Ann Richards of Texas, who as convention chair might in past years have been thought to be one of the people running the convention, said on its second night. "Wouldn't give us a minute of time when the networks were on. Finally she [Governor Richards] said to us, girls, my ego doesn't need this, so don't let yourselves get dragged down." Jodie Evans, who managed Jerry Brown's campaign, was told that to enter his name in nomination would "clutter up the schedule."

Governor Brown, who did not get to be governor of California for eight years by misunderstanding either politics or the meaning of political gestures, remained a flaw in the convention's otherwise seamless projection of its talking points. It was not by accident that he had been the only one of the Democratic primary candidates who, on the evening of the primary campaign's first Washington debate, did not go to dinner at Pamela Harriman's. He maintained so apparently quixotic a guerrilla presence in New York that Maureen Dowd began referring to him in the *Times* as The Penguin. He worked out of the *Rolling Stone* office. He got messages at Dennis Rivera's Hospital Workers Union Local 1199. He camped one night at a homeless shelter and other nights at my husband's and my apartment. He passed up the balloon drop and the podium handshake to end the convention with his volunteers, finishing the night not at the DNC's four-million-dollar fundraising gala but at Elaine's.

He told Governor Clinton that the ticket would have his "full endorsement" in the unlikely eventuality that the platform was amended to include four provisions: "a $100 ceiling on all political contributions, a ban on political action committees (PACs), universal registration undertaken by government itself (together with same-day registration), and finally election day as a holiday." That these were not provisions the Clinton campaign was prepared to discuss ("I want to work with you on these critical issues throughout my campaign," the response went) freed Brown on what was for him, since he had shaped his campaign as a "fight for the soul of the Democratic Party," a quite sticky and isolating point, that of endorsing a ticket that could be seen as the very model of who his adversary might be in any "fight for the soul of the Democratic Party."

"I'd like to thank someone who's not here tonight," he said on the evening he declined to endorse but nonetheless did opt to clutter up the schedule. "Someone who's missing his first Democratic convention since the Depression. Someone I think of as the greatest Democrat of all. My father, Pat Brown." Referring as it did to a Democratic past, a continuum, a collective memory, this was jarring, off the beat of a party determined to present itself as devoid of all history save that one sunny day in the Rose Garden, preserved on film and repeatedly shown, when President John F. Kennedy shook the hand of the Boy's Nation delegate Bill Clinton, who could be seen on the film elbowing aside less motivated peers to receive the grail: the candidate's first useful photo opportunity.

2.

More recent opportunities had given us, early on, the outline of the campaign the Democrats planned to run. There was, first of all, the creation, or re-creation, of Governor Clinton. By all accounts, and particularly by certain contradictory threads within those accounts, this was a dramatically more interesting character than candidate, a personality so tightly organized around its own fractures that its most profound mode often appeared to be self-pity. "I was so young and inexperienced," Governor Clinton told *The Washington Post* about his 1980 Arkansas defeat, "I didn't understand how to break through my crisis and turn the situation around." In his famous and extremely curious letter to the director of the ROTC program at the University of Arkansas, Colonel Eugene Holmes, who could not reasonably have been thought to care, he had spoken of his "anguish," of his loss of "self-regard and self-confidence"; of a period during which, he said, he "hardly slept for weeks and kept going by eating compulsively and reading until exhaustion set in." He spoke of the continuing inclination of the press to dwell on this and other issues as "the trials which I endured."

"When people are criticizing me, they get to the old 'Slick Willie' business," he had explained before the New York primary to Jonathan Alter and Eleanor Clift of *Newsweek*. "Part of it is that I'm always smiling and try to make it look easy and all that. And part of it is the way I was raised. I had such difficulties in my childhood." Governor Clinton spoke often about these difficulties in his childhood, usually, and rather distressingly, in connection with questions raised about his adulthood.

Such questions had caused him to wonder, he confided to *The Wall Street Journal,* "whether I'd ever be able to return to fighting for other people rather than for myself. I had to ask myself: what is it about the way I communicate or relate? Was it something in my childhood? I didn't wonder if I was a rotten person. I knew I was involved in a lifelong effort to be a better person."

He was sometimes demonstrably less than forthcoming when confronted with contradictions in this lifelong effort. By mid-May of the 1992 campaign he was still undertaking what he called an "enormous effort" to reconstruct his draft history, which had first come into question in Arkansas in October 1978, but was clear on one point: "Did I violate the laws of my state or nation? Absolutely not." Still, from the angle of "something in my childhood," this personal evasiveness could be translated into evidence of what came to be called his "reaching to please," his "need to bring people together": the heroic story required by the campaign coverage. "I'm always trying to work things out because that's the role I played for a long time," the candidate told David Maraniss of *The Washington Post* at one point, and, at another: "The personal pain of my childhood and my reluctance to be revealing in that sense may account for some of what may seem misleading."

He frequently referred to "my pain," and also to "my passion," or "my obsession," as in "it would be part of my obsession as president." He spoke of those who remained less than enthusiastic about allowing him to realize his passion or obsession as "folks who don't know me," and of his need to "get the people outside Arkansas to know me like people here do"; most of us do not believe that our best side is hidden. "I can feel other people's pain a lot more than some people can," he told Peter Applebome of *The New York Times.* What might have seemed self-delusion was transformed, in the necessary reinvention of the coverage, into "resilience," the frequently noted ability to "take the hits." "The comeback kid" was said at the convention to be Governor Mario Cuomo's tribute to the candidate, but of course it had initially been the candidate's own tribute, a way of positioning his second-place finish in New Hampshire as a triumph, and there was in Governor Cuomo's echo of it a grudging irony, a New York edge.

What else did we know about this candidate? We knew that he, or his campaign, was adept at what is generally called negative campaigning. There was the knockout punch in Florida, on the eve of Super Tuesday, when Clinton supporters distributed leaflets suggesting that his principal rival there, Senator Tsongas, besides being against old people, was against Israel. (Governor Clinton, who had himself campaigned in Delray Beach wearing a white yarmulke, allowed after the primary that the leaflets had been misleading.) There was, on the weekend before the New York primary, the Clinton radio commercial, run for a few hours before it was pulled off the air, accusing Jerry Brown, the only Clinton challenger then extant, of being against "choice," or the right to abortion. In fact Governor Brown's position on choice in California had been exactly that of Governor Cuomo in New York: each had said that he personally accepted the position of the Catholic Church on abortion but as governor supported both the right to choose and full public funding for abortion. This was a notably less equivocal position than that previously taken by Governor Clinton, who had signed into Arkansas law a measure requiring minors to notify both parents before abortion and had apparently taken no position on the state's 1988 constitutional amendment banning public financing for abortion.

There remained some cloudiness about this amendment. "I opposed the vote of the people to ban public funding on that," Governor Clinton had said, fairly unequivocally, when he was asked about it on WNBC the Sunday before the New York primary. That was April 1992. By July 1992, a letter dated 1986 (the year an earlier version of the Arkansas amendment was proposed) had turned up, and seemed equally unequivocal. This letter, which, according to *The New York Post,* was "made available" to news organizations by "Republican operatives," was from Governor Clinton to Arkansas Right to Life. "I do support the concept of the proposed Arkansas Constitutional Amendment 65 and agree with its stated purpose," the letter read. "I am opposed to abortion and to government funding of abortions. We should not spend state funds on abortions because so many people believe abortion is wrong."

Apparent accidents, and even some apparent mistakes in judgment, had emerged over time as less accidental than strategic. There was Hillary Clinton's "gaffe" in complaining to Gail Sheehy, interviewing her for *Vanity Fair,* that the press was following a "double standard" in dwelling on her husband's alleged friendship with Gennifer Flowers, since Anne Cox Chambers ("sittin' there in her sunroom") had told her about "Bush and his carrying on, all of which is apparently well known in Washington." This was an "embarrassment," a "mistake," and yet the appearance of the *Vanity Fair* piece coincided with Clinton strategists issuing the same preemptive warning to the Bush campaign; with Ron Brown suggesting that if questions about adultery were to persist, he thought similar questions should be put to Bush; and with Democratic consultant Robert Squier suggesting on the NBC *Today* show that Bush be asked what he called "the Jennifer question." Nor was just the single point scored: there was also considerable secondary gain in showing Mrs. Clinton as "feminine," a weaker vessel, gossiping with a friend over tea in the sunroom and then retailing the gossip to a new friend—who, in the "unfeminine" role of reporter, could be seen to have taken unfair advantage of the shared confidence, the wife's moment of indiscretion in her husband's defense. The erring but contrite wife could then be firmly but gently "reprimanded" by the presumptive CINC, her husband ("The main point is, she apologized . . . she made a mistake and she's acknowledged it"), an improved role for them both.

What else did we know? We knew that this was a candidate who arrived on the national scene with a quite identifiable set of regional mannerisms and attitudes, the residue of a culture that still placed considerable value on playing sports and taking charge and catting around with one kind of woman and idealizing the other kind. It was true that this "southernness" sometimes seemed in Governor Clinton's case less inherited than achieved; it was also true that the achievement seemed to have cost the candidate a certain reliability of pitch. "You're not worth being on the same platform as my wife," which is what he said to Governor Brown when the latter suggested a possible conflict of interest between Mrs. Clinton's law firm and the state of Arkansas, seemed so broad as to raise doubts that he really had the manner down. Yet the rudiments of the style were in place, and they worked to convey the image of a candidate uniquely free of entangling alliances with the exact "special interests" that many voters believed to be receiving undue attention.

Women were one such "special interest." Blacks were another. Appearing to take a firm line on women presented a delicate problem, since the party was increasingly dependent on the support of women who were declaring their intention to vote a single issue, that of choice; the candidate covered this by repeating that he wanted to see abortion made "safe, legal, and rare," an unarguable but safely paternalistic construction. When it came to blacks, the candidate claimed an ambiguous regional expertise. "Where I come from we know about race-baiting," Governor Clinton had said when he announced for the presidency at the Old State House in Little Rock, and in many variations, most of which made reference to "the politics of division," thereafter. "They've used it to divide us for years. I know this tactic well and I'm not going to let them get away with it." This was generally seen, for example in a *New York Newsday* editorial, as the candidate "at his most believable," evidence of his "fidelity to the cause of ending racial divisiveness in America." In *The Washington Post,* Richard Cohen even managed to cite, as "an early indication of why Bill Clinton enjoys such wide support in the black community," the draft letter, in which the twenty-three-year-old Clinton had told Colonel Holmes that his opposition to the Vietnam War had plumbed "a depth of feeling I had preserved solely for racism in America."

Yet there remained an odd undertone in what Governor Clinton actually said on this subject. The "race-baiting" about which he claimed the special southern knowledge, for example, worked more than one way: "race-baiting" was what Governor Clinton accused Senator Tsongas of doing, after Tsongas ran commercials in the South showing film on which Governor Clinton, unaware that a camera was running and enraged by a misunderstanding (he had just been told mistakenly that Jesse Jackson was endorsing Senator Harkin), spoke of Jackson's "backstabbing" and "dirty double-crossing." Similarly, letting "New York be split apart by race" was what Governor Clinton accused Governor Brown of doing, when the Clinton campaign wanted to remind New York primary voters that Brown had named Jesse Jackson as his choice for vice president. There was often this chance, when Governor Clinton spoke about race, to hear what he very clearly said and yet to understand it quite another way. The "them" who would not be allowed to "get away with it," for example, were clearly those who practiced "the politics of division," yet "the politics of division" remained, like "race-baiting," open to conflicting interpretation: it has been within memory the contention of large numbers of white Americans that civil rights legislation itself represented the politics of division.

This has not been a sphere in which very many American politicians have known how to talk straight. Susan Estrich, who managed Michael Dukakis's 1988 campaign, later pointed out to Peter Brown, the chief political writer for Scripps Howard and the author of *Minority Party: Why Democrats Face Defeat in 1992 and Beyond,* that she did not hear voters in the party's 1988 focus groups say they were "against" blacks. What she did hear, she said, was, "I want to get a decent job, send my kid to a good school." What was being said, as she saw it, was, "Are you the party that is going to bend over backwards for blacks when the rest of us just want to walk straight?" Although the Democratic Party's 1992 candidate told us in Madison Square Garden where he got what he called "my passionate commitment to bringing people together without regard to race" (from his grandfather, who ran a grocery in a black neighborhood and "just made a note of it" when customers couldn't pay), this was a campaign that took extraordinary care not to leave the impression that it was bending over backwards for blacks.

There was the picture, taken the day before the Georgia, Maryland, and Colorado primaries, showing Governor Clinton standing with Senator Sam Nunn of Georgia in front of a formation of mostly black prisoners at the Stone Mountain Correctional Facility, a less than conventional setting in which to make time for photos on the eve of three contested primaries. Senator Tom Harkin had promptly blanketed rural South Carolina with some eighty thousand copies of this Stone Mountain shot (juxtaposed with one of himself with Jesse Jackson), and its explication had for a while been a staple of Jerry Brown's stump speech: "Two white men and forty black prisoners, what's he saying? He's saying, We got 'em under control, folks, don't worry." There was, when Governor Clinton was campaigning in a white Detroit suburb before the Michigan primary, his rather unsettling take on the Bush campaign's

1988 use of Willie Horton: "This guy runs Willie Horton, scares the living daylights out of people, then cuts back on aid to local prosecutors, cuts back on aid to local law enforcement, cuts back Coast Guard, Customs, and Border Patrol funding to intercept drugs."

There was the apparently unmonitored decision, the day after the Illinois and Michigan primaries, to play nine holes of golf, accompanied by at least one television camera crew, at an unintegrated Little Rock country club, a recreational choice so outside the range of normal political behavior that it seemed aberrational, particularly since the issue was not unfamiliar in Little Rock; a group of twelve Arkansas legislators had a year or so before boycotted an event at another unintegrated local club, and both *The Boston Herald* and *The New York Post* had already run stories about Governor Clinton's honorary memberships in unintegrated Little Rock clubs. There was the equivocal response to the May 1992 Los Angeles riots (the desirability of "personal responsibility" and "an end to division" remained the unexceptionable but elusive Clinton position on discontent of all kinds), followed six weeks later by the campaign's cleanest surgical strike: the Sister Souljah moment.

Sister Souljah, born Lisa Williamson, was in 1992 a twenty-eight-year-old rap artist, writer, and community activist. She was a graduate of Rutgers. In high school she had won a prize in a constitutional oratory competition sponsored by the American Legion. Not long after the Los Angeles riots, in the course of an interview in *The Washington Post,* she had said this: "I mean, if black people kill black people every day, why not have a week and kill white people? You understand what I'm saying? In other words, white people, this government and that mayor were well aware of the fact that black people were dying every day in Los Angeles under gang violence. So if you're a gang member and you would normally be killing somebody, why not a white person?" What happened next was fortuitous, one of those random opportunities by which campaigns live or die: just a few weeks later, during a meeting of Jesse Jackson's Rainbow Coalition at which Governor Clinton was scheduled to speak, it came to the attention of the Clinton campaign that this same Sister Souljah had spoken the day before. A number of reporters had apparently been told in advance by Clinton aides that Governor Clinton would use his Rainbow Coalition speech to demonstrate his "independence" from Jesse Jackson, and the opportunity to signal white voters by denouncing Sister Souljah's "message of hate" was seamless, a gift from heaven, the most unassailable possible focus for such a signal. That this opportunity had been seized was precisely what constituted, for the campaign and for its observers, the incident's "success," and the candidate's "strength."

The extent to which many prominent Democrats perceived their party as hostage to Jesse

Jackson was hard to overestimate. I recall being told by one of the party's 772 "superdelegates," a category devised to move control of the nominating process back from the primary electorate to the party leadership, that Jackson's speech at the 1988 Atlanta convention had been "a disaster" for the party, and had "lost the election for Dukakis." Duane Garrett, a San Francisco attorney and fundraiser, told the Scripps Howard political writer Peter Brown that "the key thing that would have helped Dukakis enormously would have been to go to war with Jesse at the convention. Not to be mean-spirited or petty, but to make it clear that Dukakis was the guy in charge." A good deal of Governor Clinton's 1992 campaign was about creating situations in which he could be seen to do what Dukakis had not done. Eleanor Clift, for example, on one of the Sunday-morning shows, interpreted "You're not worth being on the same platform with my wife" as a success on the not-Dukakis scale. The candidate, she said, had "needed to pass the Dukakis test, needed to show true strong emotion toward his wife." The Sister Souljah moment, in this view, represented a Clinton call for "an end to division" that had at once served to distance him from Jackson and to demonstrate that he was "the guy in charge," capable of dominating, or "standing up to," a kind of black anger that many white voters prefer to see as the basis for this country's racial division.

"It was a brilliant coup," Mary McGrory concluded in *The Washington Post.* "Clinton didn't take on Jackson directly. He didn't pick the fight on a central black concern." That Sister Souljah herself was a straw target was, then, beside the point, and what Clinton actually said at the Rainbow Coalition meeting (he said that Sister Souljah's comments in the *Post* had been "filled with the kind of hatred that you do not honor," that they were an example of "pointing the finger at one another across racial lines," and that "we have an obligation, all of us, to call attention to prejudice wherever we see it") was less important than the coverage of it, and the way in which the candidate capitalized on the coverage: the message had been sent and he reinforced it, just as he had reinforced his willingness to make "tough choices" by allowing the Arkansas execution of Rickey Ray Rector to proceed by lethal injection forty-eight hours before the Super Bowl Sunday on which Governor and Mrs. Clinton would address the Gennifer Flowers question on *60 Minutes.* The measures Governor Clinton had apparently taken to avoid the draft were adroitly reframed as another "tough choice," a decision to do what he saw as "right" ("I supported the Persian Gulf War because I thought it was right and in our national interest, just as I opposed the Vietnam War because I thought it was wrong and not in our national interest"); this was his commander-in-chief transformation, a mode in which he was moved to mention, as evidence of his ability to handle crises abroad, the several venues, including Honduras, to which he had deployed the Arkansas National Guard.

"If you want to be president you've got to stand up for what you think is right," Governor Clinton said about his Sister Souljah moment. "They have chosen to react against me, essentially taking the position, I guess, that because I'm white I shouldn't have said it, and I just disagree with that," he told *Larry King Live.* One of his principal advisers, Stuart Eizenstat, a former Carter adviser and then a lobbyist, for example representing the National Association of Manufacturers against a workers' right-to-know law on toxic chemicals, was more forthcoming: "Clinton's strategy is not without risk," he told *The New York Times* about the calculation that reaching out to unhappy white voters should be the campaign's first priority. "But we have no real choice. Our base is too small to win, even in a three-way race, so the old-time religion just won't work any more."

3.

This wisdom, that the failure of Democratic candidates in five of the six national elections preceding 1992 derived from an undesirable identification with the party's traditional base, was of course not new. It had its roots during the Vietnam War, with the 1968 and 1972 Nixon victories over the "liberals" Hubert Humphrey and George McGovern; was crystallized by Kevin Phillips's 1970 *The Emerging Republican Majority;* and became a fixed idea among the party's revisionist mainstream after the 1980 and 1984 defections of the so-called Reagan Democrats. These "Reagan Democrats," statistically quite a small group of people, thereafter became the voters to whom all election appeals would be directed, a narrowing of focus with predictable results, not the least significant of which was that presidential elections would come to be conducted almost exclusively in code.

Governor Clinton, for example, did not speak of Reagan Democrats. He spoke instead of being stopped in an airport by a police officer who wanted to tell him that he was "dying to vote for a Democrat again." He spoke of "the forgotten middle class," or, in a 1991 speech to the Democratic Leadership Council, of "the very burdened middle class," also known as "the people who used to vote for us." The late Paul Tully, at that time the political director of the Democratic National Committee, described one of those hypothetical "people who used to vote for us" to *The New York Times* as "a suburbanite, in a household with about $35,000 income, younger than forty-five, with a child or two, and in a marriage in which both partners work." James Carville spoke of "a thirty-two-year-old with two kids in day care who works in some suburban office building."

The point on which everyone seemed to agree was that this suburban working parent of two was "middle class," which was, according to Ted

Van Dyk, the Democratic strategist who advised Paul Tsongas, the phrase that signaled Reagan Democrats "that it is safe to come home to their party because poor, black, Hispanic, urban, homeless, hungry, and other people and problems out of favor in Middle America will no longer get the favored treatment they got from mushy 1960s and 1970s Democratic liberals." That "middle class" had been drained of any but this encoded meaning was clear when, at a Clinton rally in Atlanta, Governor Zell Miller of Georgia derided Senator Tsongas as "an anti-death-penalty, anti-middle-class politician." Middle class, Governor Clinton told the Rainbow Coalition, by way of answering a direct question, was not "a code word" for racism. In fact this was accurate, since the use of the code was never an appeal exclusively to racism; the appeal was broader, to an entire complex of attitudes held in common by those Americans who sensed themselves isolated and set adrift by the demographic and economic and cultural changes of the last half century. "Middle class," Governor Clinton explained, referred "to values nearly every American holds dear: support for family, reward for work, the willingness to change what isn't working."

This again was accurate, but since the phrase "nearly every American" raised the specter of unspecified other Americans who did not hold these values dear, it appealed to those who would prefer to see the changes of the last half century as reversible error, the detritus of too "liberal" a social policy. "I have spent most of my public life worrying about what it would take to give our children a safe place to live again," Governor Clinton also said, striking the same note of seductive nostalgia. Such reduction of political language to coded messages, to "middle class" and "reward for work," to safe children and Sister Souljah, has much to do with why large numbers of Americans report finding politics deeply silly, yet the necessity for this reduction is now accepted as a given: in his *Minority Party,* Peter Brown quoted suggestions made to Alabama party officials by the Democratic pollster Natalie Davis:

- Instead of talking about Democrats lifting someone out of poverty, describe the party's goal as helping average Americans live the good life.
- Instead of saying Democrats want to eliminate homelessness and educate the underclass, talk about finding a way for young couples to buy their first home and offer financial help to middle-class families to send their kids to college.
- Instead of saying the Democrats want to provide health care for the poor, focus on making sure all working Americans have coverage.

The way of talking here was familiar, that of salesmanship, or packaging. If this seemed a way of talking that the average "young couple" or "middle-class family" or "working American" could instinctively tune out, flick the channel, press the mute button, it was also a way of talking that the Democratic candidate nominated by the 1992 convention instinctively understood: Bill Clinton was the son of a traveling salesman, the stepson of a Buick dealer, he knew in his fingernails how the deal gets closed. "If we lead with class warfare, we lose," he had told Peter Brown after the 1988 campaign. With Governor James Blanchard of Michigan and Senators Nunn of Georgia and Charles Robb of Virginia, he had been a founder in 1985 of the Democratic Leadership Council, which was instrumental in reshaping the "image" of the Democratic Party to attract the money of major lobbyists. The chairman of this repackaged Democratic Party, Ron Brown, was himself a lobbyist, a partner at one of Washington's most influential law firms, Patton, Boggs, and Blow. Ron Brown was in 1988 lobbying for the Japanese electronics industry, including Hitachi, Mitsubishi, and Toshiba, but he was on the podium in Madison Square Garden on the evening when Governor Clinton got the delegates hissing and booing over how "the prime minister of Japan actually said he felt sympathy for America"; this was of course just more code, and accepted as such.

The role played by the Democratic Leadership Council was central to the eventual narrowing of American politics. It was the DLC that invented Super Tuesday, the strategy of concentrating primaries in southern states to "front-load" the process against visibly liberal candidates. After this backfired in 1988, enabling Jesse Jackson to gain enough momentum from newly registered voters on Super Tuesday to go on to Atlanta with a real hand to play, Jackson opened his remarks at a DLC-sponsored debate by thanking Senator Robb for Super Tuesday. This had, according to Peter Brown, so amused Governor Clinton, "sitting in the front row next to Robb," that he nearly fell off his chair, but it altered the thinking of the new Democratic leadership only to the extent that Ron Brown took care to deal Jackson out before play began for 1992.

The wisdom of the DLC analysis, which tacitly called for the party to jettison those voters who no longer turned out and target those who did, or "hunt where the ducks are," has not been universally shared. Jesse Jackson had tried to prove it was possible to just register more ducks, and appeared in Madison Square Garden to endorse the 1992 ticket as that classic tragic figure, a man who had tried and failed to incorporate his constituency into the system and who subsequently risked being overtaken by that constituency. Jerry Brown had tried to prove that what the political scientist Walter Dean Burnham had called "the largest political party in America," the party of those who see no reason to vote, could be given that reason within the Democratic Party, but had been led by his quite fundamental party allegiance into a campaign that remained for most Americans inexplicably internecine and finally recondite, a fight for the "soul" of a party about which they no longer or had never cared. "The last thing the Democratic Party has wanted to do is declare that there is a possibility for class struggle," Burnham noted in a discussion in *New Perspectives Quarterly.* "The Republicans, however, are perfectly happy to declare class struggle all the time. They are always waging a one-sided class war against the constituency the Democrats nominally represent. In this sense, the Republicans are the only real political party in the United States. They stand for ideology and interest, not compromise."

4.

The 1988 loss of Michael Dukakis was widely seen, both within the Democratic Party and outside it, as another example of the same malaise that had afflicted the party in 1968 and 1972 and in 1980 and 1984. Governor Dukakis, it was said after the fact, was not only "too liberal" but too northeastern, too closely identified with a section of the country that had once been a Democratic stronghold and no longer had the votes to elect a president. (Mario Cuomo, in this view, presented the same problem, one magnified by his very visibility and attractiveness as a candidate.) But in fact Governor Dukakis had not been nominated as a "liberal"; the party had closed ranks around him precisely because he had seemed at the time to offer the possibility of a "centrist" campaign, a campaign "not about ideology but about competence," which was what Governor Dukakis had promised in Atlanta in 1988 and which sounded not unlike what Governor Clinton promised (the choice that was "not conservative or liberal, Democratic or Republican" but "will work") in Madison Square Garden in 1992.

There were in fact a number of such dispiriting similarities between what was said at the Democratic convention in Atlanta in 1988 and what was said at the Democratic convention in New York in 1992. There was the same insistent stress on "unity," on "running on schedule." "This party's trains are running on time," I recall someone saying in Atlanta to dutiful applause. There was the same programmatic emphasis, tricked out in the same sentimental homilies. There were the same successful arguments to keep the platform free of any minority planks that could suggest less than total agreement with the platform, or lack of "unity." There was even the same emphasis on social control, on "enforcement," although nothing said in 1988 went quite so far in this direction, or suggested quite such a worrisome indifference to what such agencies of enforcement have meant in other countries, as the Clinton-Gore proposal to gather up "unemployed veterans and active military personnel" into what they called a "National Police Corps."

"Until now," Mary McGrory wrote in *The Washington Post* on the last day of the 1992 convention, the 1988 Democratic convention in Atlanta had been "considered the best." Clinton, she said, "hopes to top it, and of course, go on to a far different outcome in November." Not long after the 1988 defeat I was told by Stanley Sheinbaum, a major California Democratic fundraiser who had become distressed in the mid-1980s by the direction the party was taking, about having been excluded from a meeting at which leading Democrats had discussed the disaster and what to do next. "Don't ask Sheinbaum, I kept hearing from someone who was there, he'll only want to discuss issues," he said. It seemed that these Democrats had already convinced themselves that they had once again lost on "issues," specifically on what they saw as too close an association with Jesse Jackson, and they wanted now only to discuss mechanics, know-how, money: what Senator Rockefeller would describe, four years later at Madison Square Garden, as "focus groups, polling, research, whatever it takes to get the message out." The problem, as Sheinbaum saw it, was that there was no longer any message to get out:

> When you're caught up in this dance of how to run campaigns better, rather than what you can do for that constituency that used to be yours, you're not going to turn anybody on. The whole focus is on big money. The Democrats under Dukakis and this guy Bob Farmer mastered how to get around the campaign finance limitations, both with PACs and soft money. They were magnificent in what they raised and it didn't do them a fucking bit of good. I mean it's no longer a thousand dollars. To

> get into the act now you've got to give a hundred thousand. So who are the players? The players are the hundred-thousand people. Who are the hundred-thousand people? They're the people who don't go into Harlem, don't go into South Central. They don't even fly MGM [MGM Grand Air, at the time the transcontinental airline of choice for the entertainment industry] any more, they have their own planes. You get this whole DLC crowd, their rationale is that to talk about the issues will alienate too many people.

What was important, in 1992 as in 1988, was "winning this election," which was why each major DNC fundraiser, or "Managing Trustee," had been asked to raise for 1992 not $100,000 but $200,000. What was important, in 1992 as in 1988, was "not saddling the candidate with a position he'll have to defend." What was important, in 1992 as in 1988, was almost exclusively semantic, a way of presenting the party as free of unprofitable issues for which it might conceivably need to fight. "I don't only think George Bush is popular on many of these issues, I think he's absolutely right," the 1992 Democratic candidate had said in 1991 on one subject that might traditionally have been considered an issue, the incumbent Republican administration's foreign policy. By the time the candidate reached Madison Square Garden he had incorporated into his acceptance speech the very line with which the incumbent Republican president, in

February 1992 at Concord, New Hampshire, had formally opened his campaign for reelection: "If we can change the world we can change America."

In this determined consensus on all but a few carefully chosen and often symbolic issues, American elections are necessarily debated on "character," or "values," a debate deliberately trivialized to obscure the disinclination of either party to mention the difficulties inherent in trying to resolve even those few problems that might lend themselves to a programmatic approach. A two-party system in which both parties are committed to calibrating the precise level of incremental tinkering required to get elected is not likely to be a meaningful system, nor is an election likely to be meaningful when it is specifically crafted as an exercise in *personalismo,* in "appearing presidential" to that diminishing percentage of the population that still pays attention. Governor Clinton, interestingly, began to "appear presidential" on the very morning he left New Hampshire, despite both his much-discussed "character problem" and the previous day's vote, which had shown him running eight points behind Senator Tsongas and incapable of raising more than twenty-five percent of the Democratic vote.

He appeared presidential largely because he was sufficiently well financed and sufficiently adroit to exit this disappointing performance via motorcade and private plane, in the authenticating presence of his own press entourage and ten-man Secret Service detail. By the day before the California primary he had begun to assume even the imperial untouchability of the presidency: plunging into a crowd on the UCLA campus, live on C-SPAN, the candidate and his Secret Service cordon became suddenly invisible in the sea of signs and faces. Only voices could be heard: "Bill, Bill, here, Bill," someone had kept saying. "You got a joint? Just one? I promise not to inhale?" And then, the same voice said, apparently to someone in the cordon of aides and agents: "I'm not touching him, hey, I said I'm not touching him, get your fucking hands off me."

Some weeks later, on the hot July morning when he stood outside the governor's mansion in Little Rock to introduce his choice for the vice-presidential nomination, Governor Clinton, in one simple but novel stroke, eliminated what some found the single remaining false note in this performance of presidentiality: he resolved the "character problem" by offering the electorate, as his running mate, an improvement on himself, a putatively more respectable Bill Clinton. In Senator Gore, he could present a version of himself already familiar to large numbers of Americans, a version of himself who had already produced the requisite book on a curve issue (Gore's *Earth in the Balance: Ecology and the Human Spirit*) and need not turn defensive about Arkansas whenever the subject of the environment was raised; a version of himself who, most importantly, had spent fifteen years in Congress free not only of identified character flaws but also of too many positions that might identify him as a Democrat.

Senator Gore, it was generally agreed, grounded the ticket, raised what had been its rather uneasy social comfort level: the Gore family had been with us for two generations now, and did not suggest, as the Clintons sometimes did, the sense of being about to spin free, back to the hollow. (This ungrounded quality reflects the oldest and deepest strain in actual American life, but we do not often see it in our candidates. We saw it in Gary Hart, where it was called "the weird factor," and engendered the distrust that ended his political career.) Senator Gore, moreover, lent Governor Clinton the gravitas of the Senate, and a presumed senatorial depth in foreign policy that the ticket might otherwise have been seen to lack. He supported the Bush administration on the use of force in the Persian Gulf. He had supported nonlethal aid to the Nicaraguan contras. He had supported the Reagan administration on the bombing of Libya. He had supported the Reagan administration on the invasion of Grenada.

Closer to home and to what his party had recently come to view as its terminal incubus, Senator Gore had been seen, during his aborted 1988 campaign for the presidency, as the only Democratic candidate willing to criticize, or "take on," Jesse Jackson. This was a Democratic candidate for vice president who could stand there in the hot midday sun in Little Rock and describe his birthplace—Carthage, Tennessee—as "a place where people know about it when you're born and care about it when you die." He could repeat this at Madison Square Garden, where he could also offer this capsule bio of his father, Senator Albert Gore Sr., who served seven terms in the House and three in the Senate before losing his seat in 1970 after opposing the war in Vietnam (a lesson learned for the son here): "a teacher in a one-room school who worked his way to the United States Senate." As presented by the younger Senator Gore, Carthage had its political coordinates somewhere in Reagan Country, as did the father's one-room school, as for that matter did the entire tableau on the lawn behind the governor's mansion in Little Rock, the candidate and the running mate and the wives and the children with the summer tans and the long straight sun-bleached hair that said *our kind, your kind, good parents, country club, chlorine in the swimming pool.* "This is what America looks like," Governor Clinton said on the eve of the nominating convention when he led the same successful cast off the plane at LaGuardia, "and we're going to give it to you."

5.

He said this in a summer during which one American city, Los Angeles, had already burned. He said this in another American city, New York, that had a week before in Washington Heights come close to the flashpoint at which cities burn. This was a year in which 944,000 American citizens and businesses filed for bankruptcy, a figure up twenty-one percent from the year before. This was a year in which 213,000 jobs vanished in the city of New York alone, or 113,000 more than the "100,000 bureaucrats" Governor Clinton proposed to lose by attrition from the federal government. This was a year in which the value of real property had sunk to a point at which Citicorp could agree to sell a vacant forty-four-story office tower at 45th Street and Broadway to Bertelsmann A.G. for $119 million, $134 million less than the $253 million mortgage Citicorp held on the property. Four years before, in the same 1988 interview in *New Perspectives Quarterly,* Walter Dean Burnham had argued that neither of the two existing parties would have sufficient political resources to impose the austerity required to resolve America's financial crisis, the Republicans because their base was narrow to begin with and the Democrats "because a substantial number of people who would be followers of the Democrats if they had credibility, have dropped out of the political system and don't vote":

> It is already clear that when the fiscal crunch gets serious enough, we are going to find ourselves further away from anything that can be called democracy . . . and the more turned off the public becomes, the more they drop out. There is probably no recourse for this situation. The system is becoming more conspicuously oligarchic all the

time. Both the politics of deadlock and, increasingly the bipartisan politics of resolving the fiscal crisis, are accelerating this dynamic.

Half those eligible to vote did not do so in the 1988 presidential election. The percentage of those eligible to vote who actually did vote in the 1992 California primary was forty-four percent. Only twenty-six percent of those registered to vote, or seven percent of the actual voting-age population, voted in the 1992 New York primary. The question of what happens when fifty percent of the electorate (or fifty-six percent, or seventy-four percent, or, in the case of New York, ninety-three percent) believes itself insufficiently connected to either the common weal or the interests of the candidates to render a vote significant could mean, in hard times, something other than it might have meant in good times, and a working instinct for self-preservation might suggest that one's own well-being could well depend on increasing the numbers of those who feel they have a stake in the society.

Yet this was not a year in which the Democratic Party was inclined to address the question of bringing these nonvoting citizens into the process. The party leadership was focused instead on its phantom Reagan Democrats, on what Robert J. Shapiro, a Clinton adviser and vice president of the DLC's Progressive Policy Institute, described to Ronald Brownstein of *The Los Angeles Times* as "an attempt to take the traditional goals of the Democratic Party . . . and find means to achieve them that embody the values of the country." The "values of the country," which is to say the values of that fraction of the country that had come to matter, also known as "the swing vote," began to be defined in 1985, when the Michigan House Democratic Caucus commissioned Stanley Greenberg to do what became a seminal study of voters in Macomb County, Michigan. At a motel in Sterling Heights, Michigan, Greenberg assembled a focus group made up of three dozen registered Democrats who had voted for Ronald Reagan. According to Peter Brown,

> The voters were broken into four groups. Each participant was paid $35 for two hours and fed cold cuts. The tone was set when Greenberg read a quote from Robert Kennedy, a man held in reverence by these heavily Roman Catholic voters. The quote was RFK's eloquent call for Americans to honor their special obligation to black citizens whose forefathers had lived through the slave experience and who themselves were the victims of racial discrimination. . . .
>
> "That's bullshit," shouted one participant.
>
> "No wonder they killed him," said another.
>
> "I'm fed up with it," chimed a third. . . .
>
> The resulting report sent a shudder through state and national Democrats. It was the first of a continuing series of research projects during the latter half of the decade that explained the problem, quite literally, in black and white.

> The votes for Reagan among these traditional Democrats, Greenberg reported, stemmed from . . . a sense that "the Democratic Party no longer responded with genuine feeling to the vulnerabilities and burdens of the average middle-class person. Instead the party and government were preoccupied with the needs of minorities. . . . They advanced spending programs that offered no appreciable or visible benefit" for middle-class people.

"Traditional" has many meanings here. These were "traditional" Democrats, and yet black voters were those who tended to share what Shapiro had called "the traditional goals of the Democratic Party." A candidate bent on at once luring the former and holding the latter will predictably be less than entirely forthcoming on certain points, which is part of what lent the Clinton "program," as outlined in *Putting People First,* its peculiar evasiveness. In the first place its details were hard to extract, since *Putting People First* was essentially a paste job of speeches and position papers, with only the occasional and odd specific, for example a call to "end taxpayer subsidies for honey producers." Read one way, the program could seem largely based on transferring entitlements from what were called "special interests" to those who "work hard and play by the rules," in other words distributing what wealth there was among the voting percentage of the population. *Putting People First* spoke often and eloquently, and in many variations, of "rewarding work," of "providing tax fairness to working families," of "ending welfare as we know it," of "cracking down on deadbeat parents." Read another way, however, *Putting People First* could be seen to stress benefits to accrue to the formerly needy and about to be "empowered":

> *Empower people* with the education, training, and child care they need for up to two years, so they can break the cycle of dependency; expand programs to help people learn to read, get their high school diplomas or equivalency degrees, and acquire specific job skills; and ensure that their children are cared for while they learn.
>
> After two years, *require those who can work to go to work,* either in the private sector or in community service; provide placement assistance to help everyone find a job, and give the people who can't find one a dignified and meaningful community service job.
>
> *Expand the Earned Income Tax Credit* to guarantee a "working wage," so that no American with a family who works full-time is forced to raise children in poverty.

Clues as to how all this might be reconciled seemed absent in the text itself. Much of *Putting People First,* however, appeared to derive from the thinking of the Democratic Leadership Council, particularly as expressed in a document distributed as a "discussion guide" at a May 1992 meeting to which

Governor Clinton, the former chairman made candidate, had returned in triumph. The thrust of this document was later refined as the DLC's "New Social Contract," outlined in the July 1992 issue of its bi-monthly publication, *The New Democrat.* It was this "New Social Contract" that provided an instructive subtext for the Clinton program. "Data suggest that the public is ready to shift the moral foundations of entitlements from a one-way street—if you need it, you are entitled to it—to a more balanced social contract," Daniel Yankelovich suggested in *The New Democrat.* "If the society gives you a benefit, you must, if you are able, pay it back in some appropriate form. This means no more 'freebies,' no more rip-offs, and no more unfairness to the middle class."

A few pages earlier, Will Marshall, president of the DLC's Progressive Policy Institute, quoted Yankelovich by way of explaining how to remedy the fact that an "explosion of new rights and entitlements," among which he counted the rights "to remedial and college education, to abortion, to equal pay for women, to child and health care, to free legal counsel, to public facilities for the disabled, and many, many more," had meant "higher taxes to pay for public transfers to 'special interests'": "What the public is saying is that government programs should require some form of reciprocity: people should no longer expect something for nothing."

"Freebies" and "rip-offs" and "something for nothing" are extremely loaded words to use in reference to entitlement programs already weighted, via Social Security and Medicare and tax exemptions for mortgage interest and for contributions to pension funds, to favor the voting class, but they are the words heard in focus groups. Similarly, the "new right" to abortion does not mean "higher taxes to pay for public transfers to 'special interests'"; women who need funded abortions would tend alternately to need funded births and Aid to Families with Dependent Children, clearly the more expensive choice, but the politics are different: abortion remains, among "swing voters," a deeply freighted issue.

The most discussed and ambitious parts of the Clinton program were his proposals to involve the federal government (in ways and at a cost not satisfactorily detailed in *Putting People First*) not only in medical care but in rebuilding infrastructure and retraining and educating the work force. Yet what was said in *The New Democrat* suggested that even these proposals may have been crafted to reflect "what the public is saying." Daniel Yankelovich, describing the results of a focus-group study conducted for the DLC to gauge the mood of the electorate, noted that since "the American people believe activist government is important in solving the great challenges facing our country,"

> they are rejecting calls to eliminate government and leave problems like helping their kids go to college to the whims of the marketplace.... While any proposal to help families send their chil-

dren to college would appeal both to the growing emphasis on education and to the public's economic worries, national service is especially attractive because it emphasizes the value of reciprocity. [Clinton had proposed national service as a way to pay back universal college loans.] There is a strong belief among the public that "there is no free lunch." In nearly every focus group, people echoed the comments of the man in Detroit who said, "I believe in giving something in return, I don't think anyone should get a free ride." . . . .

Welfare reform proposals that emphasize reciprocal obligation resonate well with the public, because they reinforce core American values. . . .

There is virtual unanimity (76 percent) on the idea that the country's elected leaders are not paying attention to the long-range needs of the country. . . . They are convinced that education, training, and the dedication of the workforce are the keys to economic vitality. . . .

All of this points to a possible solution involving a massive commitment to training, education, and outreach; a practical and realistic examination of what is meant by "most-qualified" so that minorities were not disqualified; and a serious good-faith effort to take black mistrust seriously and work at building a new structure of trust.

This is not an easy or simple strategy to implement. But it offers a basis for compromise, rather than a sure formula for confrontation and defeat—moral as well as electoral.

What was striking about this "new social contract," then, was that its notion of what might resolve our social and economic woes, the "program," had been specifically shaped, like Governor Clinton's Madison Square Garden speech, to reflect what was said in focus groups. The "New Social Contract" talked not about what the Democratic Party should advocate but about what it "must be seen advocating," not about what might work but about what might have "resonance," about what "resonates most clearly with the focus-group participants." The "need for profound changes in the way progressives view economic policy" was confirmed, for Will Marshall and presumably for the new Democratic leadership, not by an economic reality but by an "evolution in the public's thinking."

The reliance on focus groups is not new, nor is it unique to the Democratic Party (the Willie Horton issue, most famously, was born in a 1988 focus group the Bush campaign ran in Paramus, New Jersey) or even to politics. Motion pictures are tested in focus groups at every stage of their production, sometimes even before production, in the "concept" stage. New products have been for at least the past several decades exhaustively exposed to focus research. The use of such groups in marketing, however, has as its general intention the sampling of public opinion at large, the extrapolation of the opinion of the majority from the opinion of a few. What seemed novel about the use of focus groups in the 1992 campaign was the increasingly narrow part of the population to which either party was interested in listening, and the extent to which this extreme selectivity had transformed the governing of the country, for most of its citizens, into a series of signals meant for someone else. "When people are asked to prioritize U.S. foreign policy," Daniel Yankelovich noted, "they favor furthering our economic interests over support for democracy by a two to one margin."

This was what was meant by the DLC's "revolution in government," the revolution, according to *The New Democrat,* that the Democratic Party must lead if it "expects to win back the confidence of the American people." Out where confidence was harder to come by and the largest political party in America—those who did not vote—got larger as we watched, the questions raised in the focus groups of the two leading minority parties about "freebies" and "rip-offs" and "something for nothing," about Willie Horton and about Sister Souljah, remained less clear. At a time when the country's tolerance of participatory democracy had already shallowed, what remained less clear still, and a good deal more troubling, was what kind of revolution might be made after the focus session in Sterling Heights or Paramus or Costa Mesa when "the American people," which is the preferred way of describing the selected dozens of narrowly targeted registered voters who turn out for the cold cuts and the $35, decide to say something else.

Newt Gingrich, Superstar

August 10, 1995

1.

Among the personalities and books and events that have "influenced" or "changed" or "left an indelible impression on" the thinking of the Honorable Newton Leroy Gingrich, (R-Ga.), the Speaker of the House of Representatives and one of the leading beneficiaries of the nation's cultural and historical amnesia, are, by his own accounts, Abraham Lincoln, Thomas Jefferson, Franklin Roosevelt, Isaac Asimov, Alexis de Tocqueville, Tom Clancy, Allen Drury's *Advise and Consent,* Robert Walpole, William Gladstone, Gordon Wood, Peter Drucker, Arnold Toynbee's *A Study of History,* Napoleon Hill's *Think and Grow Rich,* the "Two Cultures" lectures of C. P. Snow (the lesson here for the Speaker was that "if you're capable of being glib and verbal, the odds are that you have no idea what you're talking about but it sounds good, whereas if you know a great deal of what you're saying the odds are you can't get on a talk show because nobody can understand you"), Adam Smith, *Zen and the Art of Archery,* "the great leader of Coca-Cola for many years, Woodruff," an Omaha entrepreneur named Herman Cain ("who's the head of Godfather Pizza, he's an African-American who was born in Atlanta and his father was Woodruff's chauffeur"), Ray Kroc's *Grinding It Out,* and Johan Huizinga's *The Waning of the Middle Ages.*

There were also: Daryl Conner's *Managing at the Speed of Change,* Sam Walton's *Made in America,* Stephen R. Covey's *The Seven Habits of Highly Effective People,* the 1913 *Girl Scout Handbook,* Alcoholics Anonymous's *One Day At A Time,* Gore Vidal's *Lincoln* ("even though I'm not a great fan of Vidal"), the Sydney Pollack/Robert Redford motion picture *Jeremiah Johnson* ("a great film and a useful introduction to a real authentic American"), commercial overbuilding in the sun belt ("I was first struck by this American passion for avoiding the lessons of history when I watched the Atlanta real-estate boom of the early 1970s"), the science fiction writer Jerry Pournelle, the business consultant W. Edwards Deming ("Quality as Defined by Deming" is Pillar Five of Gingrich's Five Pillars of American Civilization), and, famously, the Tofflers, Alvin and Heidi, "important commentators on the human condition" and "dear friends" as well.

It was these and other influences that gave Mr. Gingrich what Dick Williams, an Atlanta newspaperman and the author of *Newt!,* called "an intellectual base that he has been developing since he was in high school, collecting quotes and ideas on scraps of paper stored in shoeboxes." It was in turn this collection of quotes and ideas on scraps of paper stored in shoeboxes (a classmate estimated that Mr. Gingrich had fifty such boxes, for use "in class and in politics") that led in 1984 to Mr. Gingrich's *Window of Opportunity* (described in its preface by Jerry Pournelle as "a detailed blueprint, a practical program that not only proves that we can all get rich, but shows how"); in 1993 to the televised "Renewing American Civilization" lectures that Mr. Gingrich delivered from Reinhardt College in Waleska, Georgia; and in 1995 to two books, the novel *1945* and the polemic *To Renew America.*

1945 is a fairly primitive example of the kind of speculative fiction known as "alternate history," the premise here being that Hitler "spent several weeks in a coma" after a plane crash on December 6, 1941, and so did not declare war on the United States. Now, in 1945, fully recovered, Hitler is poised to launch Operation Arminius, a manifold effort to seize England (which in 1943 had "agreed to a remarkably lenient armistice" after the collapse of the Churchill government) and cripple the ability of the United States to respond by sinking its fleet and knocking out Oak Ridge, where the development of the atomic bomb is still underway. "Kill every scientist at Oak Ridge and we kill their atomic program," the German officer charged with the facility's infiltration and destruction declares. "That is why the Führer is willing to go to war to stop the Americans before they beat us to this truly ultimate weapon." In *To Renew America,* for which HarperCollins originally offered $4.5 million, Mr. Gingrich recycles familiar themes from both *Window of Opportunity* and the "Renewing American Civilization" lectures as he endeavors to "restore our historic principles," most recently evidenced, as he sees it, in "the certainty and convictions of World War II and the Cold War."

To complain that Mr. Gingrich's thinking is "schematic," as some have, seems not exactly to describe the problem, which is that the "scheme," as revealed in his writing and lectures, remains so largely occult. The videotaped "Renewing American Civilization" lecture in which he discusses "The Historic Lessons of American Civilization" (Pillar One of the Five Pillars of American Civilization) offers, for example, clips from several television movies and documentaries about the Civil War, but not much clue about why the lessons of American civilization might be "historic," and no clue at all why the remaining four Pillars of American Civilization ("Personal Strength," "Entrepreneurial Free Enterprise," "The Spirit of Invention and Discovery," and "Quality as Defined by Deming") might not be more clearly seen as subsections of Pillar One, or lessons of civilization. Similarly, the attempt to track from one to five in Mr. Gingrich's "Five Reasons for Studying American History" ("One: History is a collective memory," "Two: American history is the history of our civilization," "Three: There is an American exceptionalism that can best be understood through history," "Four: History is a resource to be learned from and used," and "Five: There are techniques that can help you learn problem-solving from historic experience") leaves the tracker fretful, uneasy, uncertain just whose synapses are misfiring.

What has lent Mr. Gingrich's written and spoken work (or, as he calls it, his "teaching") the casual semblance of being based on some plain-spoken substance, some rough-hewn horse sense, is that most of what he says reaches us in outline form, with topic points capitalized (the capitalization has been restrained in the more conventionally edited *To Renew America*) and systematically if inappositely numbered. There were "Seven key aspects" and "Nine vision-level principles" of "Personal Strength," Pillar Two of American Civilization. There were "Five core principles" of "Quality as Defined by Deming" (Pillar Five); there were "Three Big Concepts" of "Entrepreneurial Free Enterprise," Pillar Three. There were also, still under Pillar Three, "Five Enemies of Entrepreneurial Free Enterprise" ("Bureaucracy," "Credentialing," "Taxation," "Litigation," and "Regulation"), which might have seemed to replicate one another and would in any case have been pretty much identical to Pillar Four's "Seven welfare state cripplers of progress" had the latter not folded in "Centralization," "Anti-progress Cultural Attitude," and "Ignorance."

In *Window of Opportunity,* Mr. Gingrich advised us that "the great force changing our world is a synergism of essentially six parts," and offered "five simple steps to a bold future." On the health care issue, Mr. Gingrich posited "eight areas of necessary change." On the question of arms control, he saw "seven imperatives that will help the free world survive in the age of nuclear weapons." Down a few paragraphs the seven imperatives gave way to "two initiatives," then to "three broad strategic options for the next generation," and finally, within the scan of the eye, to "six realistic goals which would increase our children's chances of living in a world without nuclear war."

"Outlining" or "listing" remains a favored analytical technique among the management and motivational professionals whose approach Mr. Gingrich has so messianically adopted. (Balancing the budget and "finding a way to truly replace the current welfare state with an opportunity society" could both be done by the year 2002, he advised the Congress on the occasion of his swearing-in as Speaker, "if we apply the principles of Edwards Deming and Peter Drucker.") Yet, on examination, few of his own "areas" and "imperatives" and "initiatives," his "steps" and "options" and "goals," actually advance the discourse. The seventh of the seven steps necessary to solve the drug problem, as outlined in *To Renew America,* calls for the government to "intensify our intelligence efforts against drug lords across the planet and help foreign governments to trap them," in other words exactly what both the Drug Enforcement Administration and the United States Southern Command have been doing for some years now. No piety can long escape inclusion in one or another of Mr. Gingrich's five or four or eleven steps; another of the seven steps necessary to solve the drug problem is the reinvigoration of Mrs. Reagan's "Just Say No" campaign.

The first of the "eight areas of necessary change" in our health care system calls for "focusing on preventive medicine and good health," which meant, in *Window of Opportunity,* offering Medicare recipients $500 for not going to the doctor. *To Renew America* expands this notion to "employee insurance plans" that provide each employee with a $3,000 "Medisave" account to either spend on medical care or receive as a year-end bonus, i.e., a way of phasing out the concept of medical insurance by calling the phase-out "Medisave." Mr. Gingrich cites the "very large savings in medical expenses" achieved through Medisave accounts by the Golden Rule Insurance Company, the executives and employees of which happen to have put their savings to work, during the several years since Mr. Gingrich's ascendance into the national eye, by donating $42,510 to his campaign committee, $117,076 to his GOPAC, an undisclosed amount to the foundation that sponsors his lectures, and $523,775 to the Republican Party. The Golden Rule Insurance Company also sponsors *The Progress Report,* the call-in show Mr. Gingrich co-hosts on National Empowerment Television. "Linking their contributions to performance," Mr. Gingrich told us in *Window of Opportunity,* was "the first step for average Americans in learning to organize and systematize their new relationship with elected politicians."

Those arguments in *To Renew America* not immediately suggestive of ethical conflict tend to speed headlong into another kind of collision. We have, according to Mr. Gingrich, "an absolute obligation to minimize damage to the natural world," a "moral obligation to take care of the ecosystem." Since this collides with his wish to lift the "ridiculous burden" of "environmental regulations hatched in Washington," the fulfillment of our moral obligation to take care of the ecosystem is left to a constituent in Mr. Gingrich's district, Linda Bavaro, who turns two-liter Coca-Cola bottles into T-shirts, which she sells at Disney World. "Linda," Mr. Gingrich notes, "has a good chance of doing well financially by doing good environmentally. That is how a healthy free market in a free country ought to work."

Even Mr. Gingrich's most unexceptionable arguments can take these unpredictable detours. The "Third Wave Information Age" offers "potential for enormous improvement in the lifestyle choices of most Americans," opportunities for "continuous, lifelong learning" that can enable the outplaced or downsized to operate "*outside* corporate structures and hierarchies in the nooks and crannies that the Information Age creates" (so far, so good), but here is the particular cranny of the Information Revolution into which Mr. Gingrich skids:

> Say you want to learn batik because a new craft shop has opened at the mall and the owner has told you she will sell some of your work. First, you check in at the "batik station" on the Internet, which gives you a list of recommendations. . . . You may get a list of recommended video or audio tapes that can be delivered to your door the next day by Federal Express. You may prefer a more personal learning system and seek an apprenticeship with the nearest batik master. . . . In less than twenty-four hours, you have launched yourself on a new profession.

Similarly, what begins in *To Renew America* as a rational if predictable discussion of "New Frontiers in Science, Space, and the Oceans" takes this sudden turn: "Why not aspire to build a real Jurassic Park? . . . Wouldn't that be one of the most spectacular accomplishments of human history? What if we could bring back extinct species?" A few pages further into "New Frontiers in Science, Space, and the Oceans," we are careering into "honeymoons in space" ("Imagine weightlessness and its effects and you will understand some of the attractions"), a notion first floated in *Window of Opportunity,* in that instance as an illustration of how entrepreneurial enterprise could lead to job creation in one's own district: "One reason I am convinced space travel will be a growth industry is because I represent the Atlanta airport, which provides 35,000 aviation-related jobs in the Atlanta area."

The packaging of space honeymoons and recycled two-liter Coca-Cola bottles is the kind of specific that actually engages Mr. Gingrich: absent an idea that can be sold at Disney World, he has tended to lose interest. Asked, during a 1995 appearance at the 92nd Street YMHA in New York, what he would have done early on about Bosnia, he essayed "creating a Balkan-wide development zone." The somewhat anticlimactic ninth of his Nine Principles of Self-Government for an Opportunity Society was this: "Finally, try, try again. Self-government is an arduous, demanding task on which the survival of freedom depends." Many of the proposals in *Window of Opportunity* and *To Renew America* fritter out this way, dwindle into the perfunctory, as if the proposer's attention had already hopped on. Mr. Gingrich, we are told by Dick Williams, manages his day in fifteen-minute increments, a lesson learned from Peter Drucker's *The Effective Executive.* Mr. Gingrich, he himself tells us, believes in dedicating as many as possible of those fifteen-minute increments to reading, particularly to the reading of biography, which is seen to offer direct personal benefit: "I don't care what you want to be. If you want to get rich, read the biographies of people who got rich. If you want to be a famous entertainer, read the biographies of people who got to be famous entertainers."

Reading can provide not only this kind of intravenous inspiration but also "quotes," what *Forbes* used to call "Thoughts on the Business of Life," rhetorical backup to be plucked from the shoebox and deployed, or "used." "I was very struck this morning by something Bill Emerson used," Mr. Gingrich said at his swearing-in as Speaker. "It's a fairly famous quote of Benjamin Franklin." Mr. Gingrich tends to weigh whatever he does on this scale of strategic applicability and immediate usefulness; the fourth and fifth, or clinching, of the "Five Reasons for Studying American History" are "History is a resource to be learned from and used" and "There are techniques that can help you learn problem-solving from historical experience."

A considerable amount of what Mr. Gingrich says has never borne extended study. There was the dispiriting view of the future as a kind of extended Delta hub, where "each news magazine would have a section devoted to the week's news from space," and from which we would "flow out to the Hiltons and Marriotts of the solar system, and mankind will have permanently broken free of the planet." There were the doubtful tales offered in evidence of the point at hand, the "personalization" (a key Gingrich concept) that did not quite add up. Mr. Gingrich learned that America was "in transition from one type of economy and lifestyle to another" from reading Peter Drucker's *The Age of Discontinuity* and John Naisbett's *Megatrends,* but the truth of this came home only when he was "shocked to discover" that he could telephone his oldest daughter on her junior year abroad "by first dialing the 001 code for the international telephone computer, then the code for France, then the area code for the region near Paris, and finally the code for my daughter's telephone."

That this discovery would seem to have taken place in 1982 or 1983 (his oldest daughter was born in 1963) was just one suggestion that this was not a mind that could be productively engaged on its own terms. There was also the casual relationship to accuracy, the spellings and names and ideas seized, in the irresistible momentum of outlining, in mid-flight. In *Window of Opportunity* and in the lectures, Peter Drucker's *The Age of Discontinuity* becomes *The Age of Discontinuities.* Garry Wills's *Inventing America* becomes "Garry Will's *Discovering America.*" Gordon Wood becomes Gordon Woods. *To Renew America* shows evidence of professional copy-editing, but it also defines what it calls "situational ethics" and "deconstructionism" as interchangeable terms for "the belief that there are no general rules of behavior." Alexis de Tocqueville is seen as a kind of visiting booster, whose privilege it was to "inform the world that 'Democracy in America' worked." De Tocqueville is also seen, even more peculiarly, as an exemplar of American culture: "From the Jamestown colony and the Pilgrims, through de Tocqueville's *Democracy in America,* up to the Norman Rockwell paintings of the 1940s and 1950s, there was a clear sense of what it meant to be an American."

There was the flirtation with the millennial, the almost astral insistence on the significance of specific but intrinsically meaningless dates and numbers. The "discontinuity" (Peter Drucker again) in American history lasted, according to Mr. Gingrich, from exactly 1965 until exactly 1994: "And what's been happening is that from 1965 to 1994, that America went off on the wrong track. Now that's an important distinction." "A year which ends in three zeroes is a rare thing indeed," he declared in *Window of Opportunity.* "We're starting the 104th Congress," he said at his swearing-in. "I don't know if you've ever thought about the concept: 208 years." This inclination toward the pointlessly specific (we have here a man who once estimated the odds on the survival of his second marriage at "53 to 47") is coupled with a tic to inflate what is actually specific into a general principle, a big concept. The cherry blossoms in Washington, he advised his constituents in 1984, remind us that "there's a rhythm and cycle to life. Winter goes and spring comes." *Forrest Gump* became for Mr. Gingrich "a reaffirmation that the counterculture destroys human beings and basic values." That *Star Wars* made more money than *The Right Stuff* instructs us that "we have allowed bureaucracies to dominate too many of our scientific adventures." In the absence of anything specific to either seize or inflate, he tends to spin perilously out of syntactical orbit:

> I think if you will consider for a moment—and this is part of why I wanted to pick up on the concept of "virtualness"—if you think about the notion that the great challenge of our lifetime is first to imagine a future that is worth spending our lives getting to, then because of the technologies and the capabilities we have today to get it up to sort of a virtual state, whether that's done in terms of actual levels of sophistication or whether it's just done in your mind, most studies of leadership argue that leaders actually are putting out past decisions, that part of the reason you get certainty in great leaders is that they have already thoroughly envisioned the achievement and now it's just a matter of implementation. And so it's very different. So in a sense, virtuality at the mental level is something I think you'd find in most leadership over historical periods.

2.

The real substance of Mr. Gingrich's political presence derives from his skill at massaging exhaustively researched voter preferences and prejudices into matters of lonely principle. The positions he takes are acutely tuned to the expressed fears and resentments of a significant number of Americans, yet he stands, in his rhetoric, alone, opposed by "the system," by "Washington," by "the liberal elite," by "the East Coast elite" (not by accident does a mention of Harvard in *1945* provoke the antipathy of the sympathetic president to "East Coast snobbery and intellectual hauteur"), or simply by an unspecified "they." "I kind of live on the edge," Mr. Gingrich told Dick Williams. "I push the system." When, in a famous GOPAC memo, Mr. Gingrich advised Republican candidates to characterize Democrats with the words "decay," "sick," "pathetic," "stagnation," "corrupt," "waste," and "traitors," and Republicans with the words "share," "change," "truth," "moral," "courage," "family," "peace," and "duty," each word had been tested and oiled in focus groups to function in what the memo called "Language, A Key Mechanism of Control."

The 1994 Contract with America was packaged as, and to a peculiar extent accepted even by its opponents as, a "bold agenda" (opponents said too bold, and were left arguing only to split the difference), a "vision for America's future" (opponents rushed to share the vision, and argued only the means), yet each of its ten items derived from and was later refined in focus groups run by Frank Luntz, who did the 1992 campaign polling first for Pat Buchanan and then for Ross Perot. "The Contract with America was specifically designed to appeal to the swing Perot voter who hates partisan politics," Mr. Gingrich said during his 1995 YMHA appearance. "The ten points basically selected themselves as deeply felt desires of the American people," is his somewhat cryptic version of this process in *To Renew America*. "It can literally be said that the Contract with America grew out of our conversations with the American people and out of our basic conservative values."

The preferences and attitudes discovered through opinion research tend to be, no matter who is paying for the research, fairly consistent. A majority of American voters who end up in political focus groups are displeased with the current welfare system, believe that affirmative action has been carried too far, are opposed to crime and in favor of "opportunity." They say this to researchers working for Republican candidates and they also say it to researchers working for Democratic candidates. Which was why, of course, anyone whose own researcher happened to be having identical conversations with the American people was left, up against the Contract with America, with nowhere to stand. "Now what you've got in this city is a simple principle," Mr. Gingrich told the Republican National Committee in January 1995. "I am a genuine revolutionary; they are the genuine reactionaries. We are going to change their world; they will do anything to stop us. They will use any tool—there is no grotesquerie, no distortion, no dishonesty too great for them to come after us." He described himself to Fred Barnes as "the leading revolutionary in the country. I'm trying to replace the welfare state and the counterculture and the old establishment with a system of opportunity and entrepreneurship and classic American civilization."

What seems grandiose melts down, on the floor, to business as usual. "Replacing the welfare state" turned out to mean, with the passage in the House of the Personal Responsibility and Senior Citizens Fairness Acts, phasing out a $16 billion welfare program for the poor (Aid to Families with Dependent Children) in order to expand, by lifting the level of its earnings test, what was already a $335 billion welfare program for the middle class, Social Security. The unfairness (Frank Luntz has isolated "fairness" and "unfairness" as hot words) of applying any earnings test at all to Social Security benefits was an issue seized early by Mr. Gingrich, who illustrated or "personalized" it in *Window of Opportunity* with another doubtful tale, this one featuring "Warren," a retiree who "wanted to do something to keep his mind and body busy and to contribute to the community and world he loves" but was forced to give up selling his contribution of choice, which happened to be scrimshaw, when the Social Security Administration threatened to reduce, or in Mr. Gingrich's telling "cut off," his benefits. When Dan Balz and Charles R. Babcock of *The Washington Post* suggested that this preference for what the Speaker calls "65 percent issues" could be construed as pandering to public opinion, Mr. Gingrich corrected them: "Politics," he said, "is about public opinion and gathering public support. It's like saying, isn't it pandering for Wal-Mart to stock everything people want to buy."

3.

"I teach a course which is an outline of my thoughts at 51 years of age, based on everything I've experienced, which is, frankly, rather more than most tenured faculty," Mr. Gingrich told *The New York Times* in January 1995. "I'm not credentialed as a bureaucratic academic. I haven't written 22 books that are meaningless." What details we have about the formative experience of the Speaker, who was born Newton Leroy McPherson and took the surname of his mother's second husband, describe a familiar postwar history, one not dissimilar from that of William Jefferson Clinton, who was born William Jefferson Blythe and took the surname of his mother's second husband. Each was the adored first-born son of a mother left largely, in the economic and social dislocations that transformed America during and immediately after World War II, to her own devices. Each was farmed out to relatives while the mother earned a living. Each appears to have reached adolescence firm in the conviction that these would be the make-or-break years, that the point of the exercise was to assert, win over, overcome.

The two relied on different means to this end, but the instinctive technique of each derived from the literature of personal improvement, effective self-presentation, salesmanship, five simple steps. Mr. Clinton, with his considerable personal magnetism, kept extensive lists of people he had met and on whom, when the time arrived, he could call. In the case of Mr. Gingrich, who after his mother remarried was repeatedly uprooted and moved from one army post to another, Kansas to France to Germany to Georgia, such social skills remained undeveloped, forcing him back on his reading, his self-education, his shoeboxes. He recalled being given an article when he was young. "It was about Lincoln's five defeats, I carried it in my wallet for years." At sixteen, en route from Stuttgart to Fort Benning, he concluded "that there was no moral choice except to immerse myself in the process of learning how to lead and how to be effective." His stepfather gave him a set of the *Encyclopedia Americana,* and he read it every night. At Baker High School near Fort Benning he yielded to the southern pressure to play sports, but was sidelined by headaches. His Democratic opponent in 1994 referred to him as a "wuss," and as "the guy who won the science project."

"I think I was very lonely and very driven," Mr. Gingrich told Dick Williams. "If you decide in your freshman year of high school that your job is to spend your lifetime trying to change the future of your people, you're probably fairly weird." The defense he adopted was the persona of "class brain" (his classmates voted him "Most Intellectual"), the one with the pens and slide rule in his shirt pocket, the one who could spark the debating society, tie for highest score in the county on the National Merit Scholarship test, make a strategic detour around his lack of aptitude for high school cool by tutoring the school beauty queen and not-quite-secretly dating the geometry teacher. As a freshman at Emory University he married the geometry teacher and co-founded the Emory Young Republican Club. As a graduate student at Tulane he organized a week-long protest against administration censorship of the college paper, discovered Alvin Toffler, and taught a noncredit class on the Year 2000.

He took for himself, in other words, the ritualized role of breaker of new ground, marcher to a different drummer, which happens to be the cast of mind in which speculative fiction finds its most tenacious hold. *What if* one or another event had not occurred, *what if* one or another historical figure had remained unborn, dropped into a coma, taken another turn: the contemplation of such questions has reliably occupied the different drummers of American secondary education. The impulse is anti-theological, which translates, for these readers, into thrilling iconoclasm. In Isaac

Asimov's *Foundation* trilogy, according to Mr. Gingrich, "the Catholic Church's role in maintaining civilized knowledge through the Dark and Middle Ages is played by a secular group of intellectuals called 'The Foundation.'" The tendency is to see history as random but reversible, the sum of its own events and personalities. Isaac Asimov, Mr. Gingrich notes, "did not believe in a mechanistic world. Instead, to Asimov, human beings always hold their fate in their own hands."

It was this high school reading of Isaac Asimov, Mr. Gingrich tells us in *To Renew America,* that first "focused my attention on the fate of civilization. I came to realize that, while most people were immersed in day-to-day activities, daily behavior actually takes place within a much larger context of constantly changing global forces." Mr. Gingrich is frequently and often deprecatingly described as a "futurist," but even as he talks about those "constantly changing global forces," about a transformation "so large and historic that it can be compared with only two other great areas of human history—the Agricultural Revolution and the Industrial Revolution," his view of the future is a view of 1955, factory-loaded with Year 2000 extras. *To Renew America* asks us to "imagine a morning in just a decade or so":

> You wake up to a wall-size, high-definition television showing surf off Maui. (This is my favorite island—you can pick your own scene.) You walk or jog or do Stairmaster while catching

> up on the morning news and beginning to review your day's schedule. Your home office is filled with communications devices, so you can ignore rush-hour traffic. . . . When you are sick, you sit in your diagnostic chair and communicate with the local health clinic. Sensors take your blood pressure, analyze a blood sample, or do throat cultures. The results are quickly relayed to health aides, who make recommendations and prescribe medicine. . . . If you need a specialist, a databank at your fingertips gives you a wide range of choices based on cost, reputation, and outcome patterns. You can choose knowledgeably which risk you want to take and what price you want to pay.

The "diagnostic chair," or "personalized health chair," which could also be programmed to "monitor your diet over time and change recipes to minimize boredom while achieving the desired nutritional effect," appeared first in *Window of Opportunity,* which outlined a future in which we or our descendants would also use computer technology to correct golf swings, provide tax and IRA advice, and provide data on "literally thousands of vacation, recreation, and education opportunities," for example the Ocmulgee Indian Mounds Park in Macon, Georgia, with its "splendid natural walk area, a beautiful collection of ancient Indian ceremonial mounds, and fine museum on the history of the area from 900 A.D. to the present." For any among us whose view of the future might have been somewhat more forbidding or interesting (no

Maui, no Macon, the IRAs all gone bust), Mr. Gingrich would recommend first the reading of science fiction, since "a generation that learns its magic from Tom Swift or Jules Verne has a much more optimistic outlook than one that is constantly being told that the planet is dying and that everything humanity is doing is wrong."

If wishes were horses, beggars would ride, as they said in the generation that learned its magic from Tom Swift and Jules Verne. To know that large numbers of Americans are concerned about getting adequate medical care is one thing; to give them the willies by talking about their "health chairs" is quite another, suggesting not the future but the past, the drone of the small-town autodidact, the garrulous bore in the courthouse square. There is about these dismal reductions something disarming and poignant, a solitary neediness, a dogged determination to shine in public that leads Mr. Gingrich to reveal to us, again and again, what his own interests dictate that we should not see. He concludes *To Renew America* with a "personalization" of his concern for voter concerns, an account of how he and his second wife, Marianne, spent the Christmas before he became Speaker in Leetonia, Ohio, "a wonderful small town that is like a scene from a Norman Rockwell *Saturday Evening Post* cover."

For much of this account Mr. Gingrich remains well within the secured territory of H.R. 0003–95 and H.R. 0006–95, the Taking Back Our Streets and American Dream Restoration Acts. He expresses concern for Marianne's eighty-year-old mother, who "worked and saved all her life" but now worries about "the reports that Medicare will go bankrupt by 2002." He worries that his eight-year-old nephew, Sean, "cannot walk around Youngstown the way I once wandered the streets of Harrisburg." He wonders how Marianne's sister and her husband will manage putting their boys, Jon and Mark, through college. Then, midway through this tuned and calculated Christmas reverie, Mr. Gingrich drops, abruptly and inexplicably, through the ice, off message: "At heart," he dismayingly confides, "I am still a happy four-year-old who gets up every morning hoping to find a cookie that friends or relatives may have left for me somewhere." This cookie is worrisome: Was it forgotten? Hidden? Why would they hide it? Where are they? Are they asleep, out, absentee friends, deadbeat relatives? The cookie was the treat and leaving is the trick? What we get from these problematic detours and revelations, from the cookies and the health chairs and the high-resolution views of Maui, from the Ten Steps and the Five Pillars and the thirty gigabytes to an improved golf swing, is a shadow of something unexplained, a scent of failure, which remains one reason why, in a country made even more uncomfortable by losers than Mr. Gingrich claims to be, personal popularity among large numbers of voters may continue to elude him.

Political Pornography

September 19, 1996

On the morning of Sunday, June 23, 1996, the day the pre-publication embargo on Bob Woodward's *The Choice* was lifted, *The Washington Post,* the paper for which Mr. Woodward has so famously been, since 1971, first a reporter and then an editor, published on the front page of its "A" section two stories detailing what its editors believed most newsworthy in *The Choice.* In columns one through four, directly under the banner and carrying the legend *The Choice—Inside the Clinton and Dole Campaigns,* there appeared passages from the book itself, edited into a narrative describing the meetings Hillary Clinton had from 1994 to 1996 with Jean Houston, who was characterized in the *Post* as "a believer in spirits, mythic and other connections to history and other worlds" and as "the most dramatic" of Mrs. Clinton's "10 to 11 confidants," a group that included her mother.

This account of Mrs. Clinton's not entirely remarkable and in any case private conversations with Jean Houston appeared under the apparently accurate if unsurprising headline "At a Difficult Time, First Lady Reaches Out, Looks Within," occupied one-hundred and fifty-four column inches, was followed by a six-column-inch box explaining the rules under which Mr. Woodward conducted his interviews, and included among similar revelations the news that, according to an unidentified source (Mr. Woodward tells us that some of his interviews were on the record, others "conducted under journalistic ground rules of 'background' or 'deep background,' meaning the information could be used but the sources of the information would not be identified"), Mrs. Clinton had at an unspecified point in 1995 disclosed to Jean Houston ("Dialogue and quotations come from at least one participant, from memos or from contemporaneous notes or diaries of a participant in the discussion") that "she was sure that good habits were the key to survival."

The remaining front-page columns above the fold in that Sunday's *Post* were given over to a news story based on *The Choice,* written by Dan Balz, running seventy-nine column inches and headlined "Dole Seeks 'a 10' Among List of 15: Running Mate Must Not Anger Right, Book Says." Mr. Woodward, according to this story, "quotes Dole as saying he wants a running mate who will be 'a 10' in the eyes of the public, with the candidate telling the head of his search team, Robert F. Ellsworth, 'Don't give me someone who would send up [anger] the conservatives.'" Those *Post* readers sufficiently surprised by this disclosure to continue reading learned that "at the top of the list of 15 names, assembled in the late spring by Ellsworth and Dole's campaign manager, Scott Reed, was Colin L. Powell." When I read this in the *Post* I assumed that I would find some discussion of how or whether the vice-presidential search team had managed to construe their number-one choice of Colin L. Powell as consistent with the mandate "Don't give me someone who would send up the conservatives," but there was no such discussion to be found, neither in the *Post* nor in *The Choice* itself.

Mr. Woodward's aversion to engaging the ramifications of what people say to him has been generally understood as an admirable quality, at best a mandarin modesty, at worst a kind of executive big-picture focus, the entirely justifiable oversight of someone with a more important game to play. Yet what we see in *The Choice* is something more than a matter of an occasional inconsistency left unexplored in the rush of the breaking story, a stray ball or two left unfielded in the heat of the opportunity, as Mr. Woodward describes his role, "to sit with many of the candidates and key players and ask about the questions of the day as the campaign unfolded." What seems most remarkable in this Woodward book is exactly what seemed remarkable in the previous Woodward books, each of which was presented as the insiders' inside story and each of which went on to become a number-one bestseller: these are books in which measurable cerebral activity is virtually absent.

The author himself disclaims "the perspective of history." His preferred approach has been one in which "issues could be examined before the possible outcome or meaning was at all clear or the possible consequences were weighed." The refusal to consider outcome or meaning or consequence has, as a way of writing a book, a certain Zen purity, but tends toward a process in which no research method is so commonplace as to go unexplained ("The record will show how I was able to gain information from records or interviews. . . . I could then talk with other sources and return to most of them again and again as necessary"), no product of that research so predictable as to go unrecorded. The world rendered is an Erewhon in which not only inductive reasoning but ordinary reliance on context clues appear to have vanished. Any reader who wonders what Vice President Gore thought about Whitewater could turn to page 418 of *The Choice* and find that he believed the matter "small and unfair," but was sometimes concerned that "the Republicans and the scandal machinery in Washington" could keep it front and center. Any reader unwilling to hazard a guess about what Dick Morris's polling data told him about Medicare could turn to page 235 of *The Choice* and find that "voters liked Medicare, trusted it and felt it was the one federal program that worked."

This tabula rasa typing requires rather persistent attention on the part of the reader, since its very presence on the page works to suggest that significant and heretofore unrevealed information must have just been revealed by a reporter who left no stone unturned to obtain it. The weekly lunch shared by President Clinton and Vice President Gore, we learn in *The Choice,* "sometimes did not start until 3 P.M. because of other business." The president, "who had a notorious appetite, tried to eat lighter food." The reader attuned to the conventions of narrative might be led by the presentation of these quotidian details into thinking that a dramatic moment is about to occur, but the crux of the four-page prologue having to do with the weekly lunches turns out to be this: the president, according to Mr. Woodward, "thought a lot of the criticism he received was unfair." The vice president, he reveals, "had some advice. Clinton always had found excess reserve within himself. He would just have to find more, Gore said."

What Mr. Woodward chooses to leave unrecorded, or what he apparently does not think to elicit, is in many ways more instructive than what he commits to paper. "The accounts I have compiled may, at times, be more comprehensive than what a future historian, who has to rely on a single memo, letter, or recollection of what happened, might be able to piece together," he noted in the introduction to *The Agenda,* an account of certain events in the first years of the Clinton administration in which he endeavored, to cryogenic effect, "to give every key participant in these events an opportunity to offer his or her recollections and views." The "future historian" who might be interested in piecing together the details of how the Clinton administration arrived at its program for health care reform, however, will find, despite a promising page of index references, that none of the key participants interviewed for *The Agenda* apparently thought to discuss what might have seemed the central curiosity in that process, which was by what political miscalculation a plan initially meant to remove third-party profit from the health care equation (or to "take on the insurance industry," as *Putting People First,* the manifesto of the 1992 Clinton-Gore campaign, had phrased it) would become one distrusted by large numbers of Americans precisely because it seemed to enlarge and further entrench the role of the insurance industry.

This disinclination of Mr. Woodward's to exert cognitive energy on what he is told reaches critical mass in *The Choice,* where not much said to the author by a candidate or potential candidate appears to have been deemed too insignificant for inclusion, too casual for documentation. ("Most of them permitted me to tape-record the interviews; otherwise I took detailed notes.") President Clinton declined to be interviewed directly for this book, but Senator Dole "was interviewed for more than

12 hours and the typed transcripts run over 200 pages." Accounts of these interviews, typically including date, time, venue, weather, and apparel details (for one Saturday interview in his office the candidate was "dressed casually in a handsome green wool shirt") can be found, according to the index of *The Choice* ("Dole, Robert J. 'Bob,' interviews by author with"), on pages 87–89, 183, 214–215, 338, 345–348, 378, 414, and 423.

Study of these pages suggests the deferential spirit of the enterprise. In the course of the Saturday interview for which Senator Dole selected the "handsome green wool shirt," a ninety-minute session which took place on February 4, 1995, in Dole's office in the Hart Senate Office Building ("My tape recorder sat on the arm of his chair, and his press secretary, Clarkson Hine, took copious notes"), Mr. Woodward asked Dole if he had thought, in 1988, that he was the best candidate. He reports Dole's answer: "Thought I was." This gave Mr. Woodward the opportunity to ask what he had previously (and rather mystifyingly, since little else in *The Choice* tends to this point) defined for the reader as "an important question for my book": "You weren't elected," he reminded Senator Dole, "so you have to come out of that period feeling the system doesn't elect the best?"

Senator Dole, not unexpectedly, answered agreeably: "I think it's true. I think Elizabeth raises that a lot, whether it's president, or Senate or whatever, that a lot of the best—somebody people would describe [as] the best—doesn't make it. That's the way the system works. You also come out of that, even if you lose, if you still have enough confidence in yourself, that you didn't lose because you weren't the best candidate. You lost for other reasons. You can always rationalize these things."

On Saturday, July 1, 1995, again in Dole's Hart office (Senator Dole in "casual khaki pants, a blue dress shirt with cufflinks, and purple Nike tennis shoes"), Mr. Woodward elicited, in the course of a two-and-a-half-hour interview, these reflections from the candidate:

> *On his schedule:* "We're trying to pace ourselves. It's like today I'm not traveling, which is hard to believe. Tomorrow we go to Iowa, get back at 1 A.M. We're off all day Monday. Then we go to New Hampshire."
>
> *On his speechwriters:* "You can't just read something that somebody's written and say 'Oh, boy, this is dynamite.' You've got to have a feel for it and you've got to think, Jimminy, this might work. And this is the message. And I think we're still testing it, and I think you can't say that if I said this on day one, it's going to be written in stone forever."
>
> *On the message, in response to Mr. Woodward's suggestion that "there's something people are waiting for somebody to say that no one has said yet":* "Right. I think you're right."
>
> *On his strategy:* "As long as we're on target, on message, and got money in the bank, and people

are signing up, we're mostly doing the right thing. But I also have been around long enough to know that somebody can make a mistake and it'll be all over, too."

On the Senate: "Somebody has to manage it. And it may not be manageable. It isn't, you know, it's a frustrating place sometimes but generally it works out."

"I was not out of questions," Mr. Woodward concludes, "but I too was growing tired, and it seemed time to stand up and thank him."

Mr. Woodward dutifully tries, in the note that prefaces *The Choice,* to provide the "why" paragraph, the "billboard," the sentence or sentences that explain to the reader why the book was written and what it is about. That these are questions with which he experiences considerable discomfort seems clear:

> Presidential elections are defining moments that go way beyond legislative programs or the role of the government. They are measuring points for the country that call forth a range of questions which every candidate must try to address. Who are we? What matters? Where are we going? In the private and public actions of the candidates are embedded their best answers. Action is character, I believe, and when all is said and sifted, character is what matters most.

This *quo vadis,* or valedictory, mode is one in which Mr. Woodward, faced with the question of what his books are about, has crashed repeatedly, as if his programming did not extend to this point. The "human story is the core" was his somewhat more perfunctory stab at explaining what he was up to in *The Commanders.* For *Wired,* his 1984 book about the life and death of the comic John Belushi, Mr. Woodward spoke to 217 people on the record and obtained access to "appointment calendars, diaries, telephone records, credit card receipts, medical records, handwritten notes, letters, photographs, newspaper and magazine articles, stacks of accountants' records covering the last several years of Belushi's life, daily movie production reports, contracts, hotel records, travel records, taxi receipts, limousine bills and Belushi's monthly cash disbursement records," only to arrive, not unlike HAL in *2001,* at these questions: "Why? What happened? Who was responsible, if anyone? Could it have been different or better? Those were the questions raised by his family, friends and associates. Could success have been something other than a failure? The questions persist. Nonetheless, his best and most definitive legacy is his work. He made us laugh, and now he can make us think."

In any real sense, these books are "about" nothing but the author's own method, which is not, on the face of it, markedly different from other people's. Mr. Woodward interviews people, he tapes or takes notes ("detailed" notes) on what they say. He takes "great care to compare and verify various sources' accounts of the same events." He obtains documents, he reads them, he files them: for *The Brethren,* the book he wrote with Scott Armstrong about the Supreme Court, the documents filled "eight file drawers." He consults *The Almanac of American Politics* ("the bible, and I relied on it"), he reads what others have written on the subject. "In preparation for my own reporting," he tells us about *The Choice,* "I and my assistant, Karen Alexander, read and often studied hundreds of newspaper and magazine articles."

Should the information he requires necessitate travel, he goes the extra mile: "I traveled from coast to coast many times, visiting everyone possible and everywhere possible," he tells us about the research for *Wired.* Since John Belushi worked in the motion-picture industry and died at the Chateau Marmont in Los Angeles, these coast-to-coast trips might have seemed to represent the minimum in dogged fact-gathering, but never mind: the author had even then, in 1984, transcended method and entered the heady ether of methodology, a discipline in which the reason for writing a book could be the sheer fact of being there. "I would like to know more and *Newsweek* magazine was saying that maybe that is the thing I should look at next," he allowed when a caller on *Larry King Live* asked if he might not want to write about Whitewater. "I don't know. I do not know about Whitewater and what it really means. I am waiting—if I can say this—for the call from somebody on the inside saying 'I want to talk.'"

Here is where we reach the single unique element in the method, and also the problem. As any prosecutor and surely Mr. Woodward knows, the person on the inside who calls and says "I want to talk" is an informant, or snitch, and is generally looking to bargain a deal, to improve his or her own situation, to place the blame on someone else in return for being allowed to plead down or out certain charges. Because the story told by a criminal or civil informant is understood to be colored by self-interest, the informant knows that his or her testimony will be unrespected, even reviled, subjected to rigorous examination and often rejection. The informant who talks to Mr. Woodward, on the other hand, knows that his or her testimony will be not only respected but burnished into the inside story, which is why so many people on the inside, notably those who consider themselves the professionals or managers of the process—assistant secretaries, deputy advisers, players of the game, aides who intend to survive past the tenure of the patron they are prepared to portray as hapless—do want to talk to him. Many Dole campaign aides did want to talk, for *The Choice,* about the herculean efforts and adroit strategy required to keep the candidate with whom they were saddled even marginally on message, on the program:

> Dole offered a number of additional references to the past, how it had been done before, and Reed

> [Dole campaign manager Scott Reed] countered with his own ideas about how he would handle similar situations. A sense of diffusion and randomness wouldn't work. Making seat-of-the-pants, airborne decisions was not the way he operated. . . . Dole needed a coherent and understandable message on which to run, Reed said. Deep down, he added, he knew Dole knew what he wanted to say, but he probably needed some help putting it together and delivering it. . . . Reed felt he had hit the right weaknesses.

Similarly, many Clinton foreign policy advisers did want to talk, again for *The Choice,* about the equally herculean efforts and strategy required to guide the president, on the question of Bosnia, from one of his "celebrated rages" ("I'm getting creamed!" Clinton, "unleashing his frustration" and "spewing forth profanity," is reported to have said on being told of the fall of Srebrenica) to a more nuanced appreciation of the policy options on which his aides—Deputy National Security Adviser Sandy Berger, say, and National Security Adviser Anthony Lake—had been laboring unappreciated. "Berger reminded him," Woodward tells us, "that Lake was trying to develop an Endgame Strategy." At a meeting a few days later in the Oval Office, when Vice President Gore mentioned a photograph in *The Washington Post* of a refugee from Srebrenica who had hanged herself from a tree, the adroit guidance continued:

"My 21-year-old daughter asked about that picture," Gore said. "What am I supposed to tell her? Why is this happening and we're not doing anything?"

It was a chilling moment. The vice president was directly confronting and criticizing the president. Gore believed he understood his role. He couldn't push the president too far, but they had built a good relationship and he felt he had to play his card when he felt strongly. He couldn't know precisely what going too far meant unless he occasionally did it.

"My daughter is surprised the world is allowing this to happen," Gore said carefully. "I am too."

Clinton said they were going to do something.

This is a cartoon, but not a cartoon in which anyone who spoke to the author will appear to have taken any but the highest ground. Asked, in the same appearance on *Larry King Live,* why he thought people talked to him, Mr. Woodward responded:

> Only because I get good information and I talk to people at the middle level, lower level, try to talk to the people at the top. They know that I am going to reflect their point of view. One of my earlier books, somebody called me who was in it and said "How am I going to come out?" and I said "Well, essentially, I write self-portraits."... They really are self-portraits, because I go to people and I double-check them but—but who are you?

> What are you doing? Where do you fit in? What did you say? What did you feel?

Those who talk to Mr. Woodward, in other words, can be confident that he will be civil ("I too was growing tired, and it seemed time to stand up and thank him"), that he will not feel impelled to make connections between what he is told and what is already known, that he will treat even the most patently self-serving account as if untainted by hindsight (that of Richard Darman, say, who in 1992 presented himself to Mr. Woodward, who in turn presented him to America, as the helpless Cassandra of the 1990 Bush budget deal); that he will be, above all, and herein can be found both Mr. Woodward's compass and the means by which he is set adrift, "fair."

I once heard a group of reporters agree that there were at most twenty people who run any story. What they meant by "running the story" was setting the terms, setting the pace, deciding the agenda, determining when and where the story exists, and shaping what the story will be. There were certain people who ran the story in Vietnam, there were certain people in Central America, there were certain people in Washington. An American presidential campaign is a Washington story, which means that the handful of people who run the story in Washington—the people who write the most influential columns, the people who conduct the

Sunday shows on which Washington talks to itself—will also run the campaign. Bob Woodward, who is unusual in that he is not a regular participant in the television dialogue and appears in print, outside his books, only infrequently, is one of the people who run the story in Washington.

In this business of running the story, in fact in the business of news itself, certain conventions are seen as beyond debate. "Opinion" will be so labeled, and confined to the op-ed page or the television talk shows. "News analysis" will be so labeled, and will appear in a subordinate position to the "news" story it accompanies. In the rest of the paper as on the evening news, the story will be reported "impartially," the story will be "evenhanded," the story will be "fair." "Fairness" is a quality Mr. Woodward seems particularly to prize ("I learned a long time ago," he told Larry King, "you take your opinions and your attitudes, your predispositions—get them in your back pocket, because they are only going to get in the way of doing your job"), and mentions repeatedly in his thanks to his assistants.

It was "Karen Alexander, a 1993 graduate of Yale University," who "brought unmatched intellect, grace and doggedness and an ingrained sense of fairness" to *The Choice*. On *The Agenda,* it was "David Greenberg, a 1990 graduate of Yale University," who "repeatedly worked to bring greater balance, fairness, and clarity to our reporting and writing." It was "Marc E. Solomon, a 1989 Yale graduate," who "brought a sense of fairness and balance" to *The Commanders*. On *The Veil,* it was

"Barbara Feinman, a 1982 graduate of the University of California at Berkeley," whose "friendship and sense of fairness guided the daily enterprise." For *The Brethren,* Mr. Woodward and his coauthor, Scott Armstrong, thank "Al Kamen, a former reporter for the *Rocky Mountain News,*" for his "thoroughness, skepticism, and sense of fairness."

The genuflection toward "fairness" is a familiar newsroom piety, in practice the excuse for a good deal of autopilot reporting and lazy thinking but in theory a benign ideal. In Washington, however, a community in which the management of news has become the single overriding preoccupation of the core industry, what "fairness" has often come to mean is a scrupulous passivity, an agreement to cover the story not as it is occurring but as it is presented, which is to say as it is manufactured. Such institutionalized events as a congressional hearing or a presidential trip will be covered with due diligence, but the story will vanish the moment the gavel falls, the hour Air Force One returns to Andrews. "Iran-contra" referred exclusively, for many Washington reporters, to the hearings. The sequence of events that came to be known as "the S&L crisis," which was actually less a "crisis" than the structural malfunction that triggered an uncontrolled meltdown in middle-class confidence, existed as a "story" only on those occasions (hearings, indictments) when it showed promise of rising to its "crisis" slug. Similarly, "Whitewater" (as in "I do not know about Whitewater and what it really means") survived as a story only to the extent that it allowed those who covered it to calibrate the waxing or waning possibility of a "smoking gun," or "evidence."

"If there is evidence it should be pursued," Mr. Woodward told Larry King to this point. "In fairness to the Clintons. And it's—it—you know, we all in the news business, and in politics have to be very sensitive to the unfair smear. . . . It's not fair and again it goes back to what's the evidence?" Yet the actual interest of Whitewater lies in what has already been documented: it is "about" the S&L crisis, and thereby offers a detailed and specific look at the kinds of political and financial dealing that resulted in the meltdown in middle-class confidence. What Whitewater "really means" or offers, then, is an understanding of that meltdown, which has been reported as if it existed in a vacuum, an inexplicable phenomenon weirdly detached from the periodic growth figures produced in Washington. This could be a valuable story, but it is not one that will be put together by waiting for the call from somebody on the inside saying "I want to talk."

Every reporter, in the development of a story, depends on and coddles, or protects, his or her sources. Only when the protection of the source gets in the way of telling the story does the reporter face a professional, even a moral, choice: he can blow the source and move to another beat or he can roll over, shape the story to continue serving the source. The necessity for making this choice between the source and the story seems not to have come up in the course of writing Mr. Woodward's books, for good reason: since he proceeds from a position in which the very impulse to sort through the evidence and reach a conclusion is seen as suspect, something to be avoided in the higher interest of fairness, he has been able, consistently and conveniently, to define the story as that which the source tells him.

This fidelity to the source, whoever the source might be, leads Mr. Woodward down avenues that might at first seem dead-end. On page 16 of *The Choice* we have President Clinton, presumably on the word of a White House source, "thunderstruck" that Senator Dole, on the morning after Clinton's mother died in early 1994, should have described Whitewater on the network news shows as "unbelievable," "mind-boggling," "big, big news" that "cries out more than ever now for an independent counsel." On page 346 of *The Choice* we have Senator Dole, on December 27, 1995, telling Mr. Woodward "that he had never used Whitewater to attack the president personally," to which Mr. Woodward responds only: "What would be your criteria for picking a vice-president?" On page 423 of *The Choice* we have Mr. Woodward, on April 20, 1996, by which date he had apparently remembered what he said on page 16 that Senator Dole said, although not what he said on page 346 that Senator Dole said, advising Senator Dole that the president had resented his "aggressive call for a Whitewater independent counsel back in early 1994, the day Clinton's mother had died."

Only now do we arrive at what seems to be for Mr. Woodward the point, and it has to do with his own role as honest broker, or conscience to the candidates. He reports that Senator Dole was "troubled" by this disclosure, even "haunted by what he might have done," so much so that he was moved to write Clinton a letter of apology:

> Later that week, Dole was at the White House for an anti-terrorism bill signing ceremony. Clinton took him aside into a corridor so they could speak alone. The president thanked him for the letter. He said he had read it twice. He was touched and appreciated it very much.
>
> "Mothers are important," Dole said.
>
> Emotion rose up in both men. They looked at each other for an instant, then moved back to business. Soon they agreed on a budget for the rest of the year. It was not the comprehensive seven-year deal both had envisioned and worked on for months. But it was a start.

"This human story is the core," as Mr. Woodward said of *The Commanders.* To believe that this moment in the White House corridor occurred is not difficult: we know it occurred, precisely because whether or not it occurred makes no difference, has no significance, appears at first to tell us, like the famous moment described in *Veil,* the exchange between the author and William

Casey in Room C6316 at Georgetown Hospital, nothing. "You knew, didn't you," Mr. Woodward thought to ask Casey on that occasion.

> The contra diversion had to be the first question: you knew all along.
>
> His head jerked up hard. He stared, and finally nodded yes.
>
> Why? I asked.
>
> "I believed."
>
> What?
>
> "I believed."
>
> Then he was asleep, and I didn't get to ask another question.

This account provoked, in the immediate wake of *Veil*'s 1987 publication, considerable talk-show and dinner-table controversy (was Mr. Woodward actually in the room, did Mr. Casey actually nod, where were the nurses, what happened to the CIA security detail), including, rather astonishingly, spirited discussion of whether or not the hospital visit could be "corroborated." In fact there was so markedly little reason to think the account inauthentic that the very question seemed to obscure, as the account itself had seemed to obscure, the actual problem with the scene in Room C6316 at Georgetown Hospital, which had to do with timing, or with what did Mr. Woodward know and when did he know it.

The hospital visit took place, according to *Veil,* "several days" after Mr. Casey's resignation, which occurred on January 29, 1987. This was almost four months after the crash of the Hasenfus plane in Nicaragua, more than two months after the Justice Department disclosure that the United States had been selling arms to Iran in order to divert the profits to the contras, and a full month after both the House and Senate Permanent Subcommittees on Intelligence had completed reports on their investigations into the diversion. The inquiries of the two congressional investigating committees established in the first week of January 1987, the Senate Select Committee on Secret Military Assistance to Iran and the Nicaraguan Opposition and the House Select Committee to Investigate Covert Arms Transactions with Iran, were already underway. The report of the Tower Commission would be released in three weeks.

Against this background and this amount of accumulated information, the question of whether the director of Central Intelligence "knew" about the diversion was, at the time Mr. Woodward made his hospital visit and even more conclusively at the time he committed his account of the visit to paper, no longer at issue, no longer relevant, no longer a question. The hospital interview, then, exists on the page only as a prurient distraction from the real questions raised by the diversion, only as a dramatization of the preferred Washington view that Iran-contra reflected not a structural problem but a "human story," a tale of how one man's hubris could have shaken the basically solid foundations of the established order, a disruption of the stable status quo that could be seen to end, satisfyingly, with that man's death.

Washington, as rendered by Mr. Woodward, is by definition basically solid, a diorama of decent intentions in which wise if misunderstood and occasionally misled stewards will reliably prevail. Its military chiefs will be pictured, as Colin Powell was in *The Commanders,* thinking on the eve of battle exclusively of their troops, the "kids," the "teenagers": a human story. The clerks of the Supreme Court will be pictured, as the clerks of the Burger court were in *The Brethren,* offering astute guidance as their justices negotiate the shoals of ideological error: a human story. The more available members of its foreign diplomatic corps will be pictured, as Saudi ambassador Prince Bandar bin Sultan was in *The Commanders* and *Veil,* gaining access to the councils of power not just because they have the oil but because of their "backslapping irreverence," their "directness," their exemplification of "the new breed of ambassador—activist, charming, profane": yet another human story. Its opposing leaders will be pictured, as President Clinton and Senator Dole are in *The Choice,* finding common ground on the importance of mothers: the ultimate human story.

That this crude personalization works to narrow the focus, to circumscribe the range of possible discussion or speculation, is, for the people who find it useful to talk to Mr. Woodward, its point. What they have in Mr. Woodward is a widely trusted reporter, even an American icon, who can be relied upon to present a Washington in which problematic or questionable matters will be definitively resolved by the discovery, or by the demonstration that there can be no discovery, of "the smoking gun," "the evidence." Should such narrowly defined "evidence" be found, he can then be relied upon to demonstrate, "fairly," that the only fingerprints on the smoking gun are those of the one bad apple in the barrel, the single rogue agent in the tapestry of good intentions.

"I kept coming back to the question of personal responsibility, Casey's responsibility," Mr. Woodward reports having mused (apparently for once prepared, at the moment when he is about to visit a source on his deathbed, to question the veracity of what he has been told) before his last visit to Room C6316 at Georgetown Hospital. "For a moment, I hoped he would take himself off the hook. The only way was an admission of some kind or an apology to his colleagues or an expression of new understanding. Under the last question on 'Key unanswered questions for Casey,' I wrote: 'Do you see now that it was wrong?'" To commit such Rosebud moments to paper is what it means to tell "the human story at the core," and it is also what it means to write political pornography.

Clinton Agonistes

September 22, 1998

1.

No one who ever passed through an American public high school could have watched William Jefferson Clinton running for office in 1992 and failed to recognize the familiar predatory sexuality of the provincial adolescent. The man was, Jesse Jackson said that year to another point, "nothing but an appetite." No one who followed his appearances on *The Road to the White House* on C-SPAN could have missed the reservoir of self-pity, the quickness to blame, the narrowing of the eyes, as in a wildlife documentary, when things did not go his way: a response so reliable that aides on Jerry Brown's 1992 campaign looked for situations in which it could be provoked.

The famous tendency of the candidate to take a less than forthcoming approach to embarrassing questions had already been documented and discussed, most exhaustively in the matter of his 1969 draft status, and he remained the front-runner. The persistent but initially unpublished rumors about extramarital rovings had been, once Gennifer Flowers told her story to the *Star,* published and acknowledged, and he remained on his feet. "I have acknowledged wrongdoing," he had told America during his and his wife's rather premonitory *60 Minutes* appearances on Super Bowl Sunday of that year. "I have acknowledged causing pain in my marriage. I think most Americans who are watching this tonight, they'll know what we're saying, they'll get it, and they'll feel that we have been more than candid. And I think what the press has to decide is, are we going to engage in a game of gotcha?"

Nothing that is now known about the forty-second president of the United States, in other words, was not known before the New Hampshire primary in 1992. The implicit message in his August 1998 testimony to the Office of the Independent Counsel was not different in kind from that made explicit in January 1992: *I think most Americans who are watching this . . . they'll know what we're saying, they'll get it, and they'll feel that we have been more than candid.* By the time of the 1992 general election, the candidate was before us as he appears today: a more detailed and realized character than that presented in the Office of the Independent Counsel's oddly novelistic *Referral to the United States House of Representatives* but recognizably drawn to similar risk, voraciously needy, deeply fractured, and yet there, a force to contend with, a possessor of whatever manna accrues to those who have fought themselves and survived. The flaws already apparent in 1992 were by no means unreported, but neither, particularly in those parts of the country recently neutralized by their enshrinement as "the heartland," were they seized as occasions for rhetorical outrage. "With 16 million Americans unemployed, 40 million Americans without health care and 3 million Americans homeless, here's what we have to say about presidential aspirant Bill Clinton's alleged previous marital infidelity," the *Peoria Journal-Star* declared on its editorial page at the time of the *60 Minutes* appearance. "So what? And that's all."

There were those for whom the candidate's clear personal volatility suggested the possibility of a similar evanescence on matters of ideology or policy, but even the coastal opinion leaders seemed willing to grant him a *laissez-passer* on this question of sex: "To what degree, if any, is the private action relevant to the duties of the public office?" *The Los Angeles Times* asked on its editorial page in January 1992. "Shouldn't our right to know about a candidate's sex life be confined . . . to offenses such as rape, harassment, or sex discrimination?" *The New York Times* report on the *60 Minutes* interview, which appeared on page A14 and was headlined

"Clinton Defends His Privacy and Says the Press Intruded," was followed the next day by an editorial ("Leers, Smears and Governor Clinton") not only commending the candidate for having drawn a line "between idle curiosity and responsible attention" but noting that "he won't provide details and he need not, unless it develops that his private conduct arguably touches his public performance or fitness for office." The same day, January 28, 1992, A. M. Rosenthal wrote in the *Times* that Governor and Mrs. Clinton had "presented to the American public a gift and a lasting opportunity":

> The gift is that they treated us as adults. The opportunity is for us to act that way. . . . We can at least treasure the hope that Americans would be fed up with the slavering inquisition on politicians' sexual history and say to hell with that and the torturers. That would be a thank-you card worthy of the gift from the Clinton couple—the presumption that Americans have achieved adulthood, at last.

Few in the mainstream press, in 1992, demanded a demonstration of "contrition" from the candidate. Few, in 1992, demanded "full remorse," a doubtful concept even in those venues, courtrooms in which criminal trials have reached the penalty phase, where "remorse" is most routinely invoked. Few, in 1992, spoke of the United States as so infantilized as to require a president above the possibility of personal reproach. That so few did this then, and so many have done this since, has been construed by some as evidence that the interests and priorities of the press have changed. In fact the interests and priorities of the press have remained reliably the same: then as now, the press could be relied upon to report a rumor or a hint down to the ground (tree it, bag it, defoliate the forest for it, destroy the village for it), but only insofar as that rumor or hint gave promise of advancing the story of the day, the shared narrative, the broad line of whatever story was at the given moment commanding the full resources of the reporters covering it and the columnists commenting on it and the on-tap experts analyzing it on the talk shows. (The 1998 *Yearbook of Experts, Authorities & Spokespersons* tellingly provides, for producers with underdeveloped Rolodexes of their own, 1,477 telephone numbers to call for those guests "who will drive the news issues in the next year.") In *Spin Cycle,* a book in which Howard Kurtz of *The Washington Post* endeavored to show the skill of the "Clinton propaganda machine" (similarly described by Joe Klein, despite what might seem impressive evidence to the contrary, as "the most sophisticated communications apparatus in the history of American politics") at setting the agenda for the press, there appears this apparently ingenuous description of how the press itself sets its agenda:

> A front-page exclusive would ripple through the rest of the press corps, dominate the briefing,

> and most likely end up on the network news. The newsmagazine reporters were not quite as influential as in years past, but they could still change the dialogue or cement the conventional wisdom with a cover story or a behind-the-scenes report. Two vital groups of reinforcements backed up the White House regulars. . . . One was the columnists and opinion-mongers—Jonathan Alter at *Newsweek,* Joe Klein at *The New Yorker,* William Safire and Maureen Dowd at *The New York Times,* E. J. Dionne and Richard Cohen at *The Washington Post*—who could quickly change the zeitgeist. . . . the other was the dogged band of investigative reporters—Jeff Gerth at the *Times,* Bob Woodward at the *Post,* Glenn Simpson at *The Wall Street Journal,* Alan Miller at *The Los Angeles Times.*

Once the "zeitgeist" has been agreed upon by this quite small group of people, any unrelated event, whatever its actual significance, becomes either non-news or, if sufficiently urgent, a news brief. An example of the relegation to non-news would be this: Robert Scheer, in his *Los Angeles Times* review of *Spin Cycle,* noted that its index included eighteen references to Paula Jones and sixteen to John Huang, but none to Saddam Hussein. An example of the relegation to news brief would be this: on August 16, 1998, after hearing flash updates on the Omagh bombing in Northern Ireland ("worst attack in almost thirty years of violence . . . latest figures as we have it are 28 people dead . . . 220 people injured . . . 103 still in hospital") and on the American embassy bombings in East Africa, Wolf Blitzer, on a two-hour *Late Edition with Wolf Blitzer* otherwise exclusively devoted to the "legal ramifications, political considerations, and historic consequences" of Monica Lewinsky, said this: "Catherine Bond, reporting live from Nairobi, thanks for joining us. Turning now to the story that has all of Washington holding its breath . . ."

In 1992, as in any election year, the story that had all of Washington holding its breath was the campaign, and since the guardians of the zeitgeist, taking their cue from the political professionals, had early on certified Governor Clinton as the most electable of the Democratic candidates, his personal failings could serve only as a step in his quest, a test of his ability to prevail. Before the New Hampshire primary campaign was even underway, Governor Clinton was reported to be the Democratic candidate with "centrist credentials," the Democratic candidate who "offered an assessment of the state of the American economy that borrows as much from Republicans like Jack Kemp as it does from liberals," the Democratic candidate who could go to California and win support from "top Republican fundraisers," the candidate, in short, who "scored well with party officials and strategists." A survey of Democratic National Committee members had shown Clinton in the lead. The late Ronald H. Brown, at the time chairman of the

Democratic Party, had been reported, still before a single vote was cast in New Hampshire, to have pressured Mario Cuomo to remove his name from the New York primary ballot, so that a divisive favorite-son candidacy would not impede the chosen front-runner.

By the morning of January 26, 1992, the Sunday of the *60 Minutes* appearance and shortly after the candidate sealed his centrist credentials by allowing the execution of the brain-damaged Rickey Ray Rector to proceed in Arkansas, William Schneider, in *The Los Angeles Times,* was awarding Governor Clinton the coveted "Big Mo," noting that "the Democratic Party establishment is falling in line behind Clinton." In a party that reserves a significant percentage of its convention votes (eighteen percent in 1996) for "superdelegates," the seven-hundred-some elected and party officials not bound by any popular vote, the message sent by this early understanding among the professionals was clear, as it had been when the professionals settled on Michael Dukakis in 1988: the train was now leaving the station, and, since the campaign, as "story," requires that the chosen candidates be seen as contenders who will go the distance, all inconvenient baggage, including "the character issue," would be left on the platform. What would go on the train was what Joe Klein, echoing the note of romantic credulity in his own 1992 coverage of the candidate Bill Clinton (that was before the zeitgeist moved on), recalled in 1998 in *The New Yorker* as the "precocious fizz" of the War Room, "the all-nighters . . . about policy or philosophy," the candidate who "loved to talk about serious things" and "seems to be up on every social program in America."

2.

It was January 16, 1998, when Kenneth W. Starr obtained authorization, by means of a court order opaquely titled "*In re* Madison Guaranty Savings & Loan Association," to extend his languishing Whitewater inquiry to the matter of Monica Lewinsky. It was also January 16 when Monica Lewinsky was detained for eleven hours and twenty-five minutes in Room 1016 of the Ritz-Carlton Hotel in Pentagon City, Virginia, where, according to the independent counsel's log of the "meeting," the FBI agent who undertook to read Miss Lewinsky "her rights as found on the form FD-395, Interrogation, Advice of Rights" was, for reasons the log does not explain, "unable to finish reading the FD-395." Miss Lewinsky herself testified:

> Then Jackie Bennett [of the Office of the Independent Counsel] came in and there was a whole bunch of other people and the room was crowded and he was saying to me, you know, you have to make a decision. I had wanted to call my mom, they weren't going to let me call my attorney, so I just—I just wanted to call my mom and they—Then Jackie Bennett said, "You're 24, you're

smart, you're old enough, you don't need to call your mommy."

It was January 17 when President Clinton, in the course of giving his deposition in the civil suit brought against him by Paula Corbin Jones, either did or did not spring the perjury trap that Kenneth Starr either had or had not set. By the morning of January 21, when both Susan Schmidt in *The Washington Post* and ABC News correspondent Jackie Judd on *Good Morning America* jumped the stakes by quoting "sources" saying that Monica Lewinsky was on tape with statements that the president and Vernon Jordan had told her to lie, the "character issue" had gone from idle to full throttle, with Sam Donaldson and George Stephanopoulos and Jonathan Alter already on air talking about "impeachment proceedings."

In most discussions of how and why this matter came so incongruously to escalate, the press of course was criticized, and was in turn quick to criticize itself (or, in the phrasing preferred by many, since it suggested that any objection rested on hairsplitting, to "flagellate" itself), citing excessive and in some cases erroneous coverage. Perhaps because not all of the experts, authorities, and spokespersons driving this news had extensive experience with the kind of city-side beat on which it is taken for granted that the D.A.'s office will leak the cases they doubt they can make, selective prosecutorial hints had become embedded in the ongoing story as fact. "Loose attribution of sources abounded," Jules

Witcover wrote in the March/April 1998 *Columbia Journalism Review,* although, since he tended to attribute the most egregious examples to "journalistic amateurs" and "journalistic pretenders" (Arianna Huffington and Matt Drudge), he could still express "hope," based on what he discerned two months into the story as "a tapering off of the mad frenzy of the first week or so," that, among "established, proven professional practitioners," any slip had been "a mere lapse of standards in the heat of a fast-breaking, incredibly competitive story of major significance."

For the same *CJR,* the cover line of which was "Where We Went Wrong . . . and What We Do Now," a number of other reporters, editors, and news executives were queried, and expressed similar hopes. The possibility of viewer confusion between entertainment and news shows was mentioned. The necessity for more careful differentiation among different kinds of leaks was mentioned. The "new technology" and "hypercompetition" and "the speed of news cycles these days" were mentioned, references to the way in which the Internet and the multiplication of cable channels had collapsed the traditional cyclical presentation of news into a twenty-four-hour stream of provisional raw takes. "We're in a new world in terms of the way information flows to the nation," James O'Shea, deputy managing editor for news of the *Chicago Tribune,* said. (The Lewinsky story had in fact first broken not in the traditional media but on the Internet, in a 1:11 A.M. January 18, 1998, posting on the *Drudge Report.*) "The days when you can decide not to print a story because it's not well enough sourced are long gone. When a story gets into the public realm, as it did with the *Drudge Report,* then you have to characterize it, you have to tell your readers, 'This is out there, you've probably been hearing about it on TV and the Internet. We have been unable to substantiate it independently.' And then give them enough information to judge the validity of it."

That the "story" itself might in this case be anything other than (in Witcover's words) "a fast-breaking, incredibly competitive story of major significance" was questioned by only one panelist, Anthony Lewis of *The New York Times,* who characterized "the obsession of the press with sex and public officials" as "crazy," but allowed that "after Linda Tripp went to the prosecutor, it became hard to say we shouldn't be covering this." The more general attitude seemed to be that there might have been an excess here or an error there, but the story itself was important by definition, significant because it was commanding the full resources of everyone on it—not unlike a campaign, which this story, in that it offered a particularly colorful version of the personalized "horse race" narrative that has become the model for most American political reporting, in fact resembled. "This is a very valid story of a strong-willed prosecutor and a president whose actions have been legitimately questioned," Walter Isaacson of *Time* said. "A case involving sex can be a very legitimate story, but we can't let our journalistic standards lapse simply because the sexual element makes everyone over-excited."

This, then, was a story "involving sex," a story in which there was a "sexual element," but, as we so frequently heard, it was not about sex, just as Whitewater, in the words of one of the several score editorials to this point published over the years by *The Wall Street Journal,* was "not merely about a land deal." What both stories were about, of course (although in the absence of both sex and evidence against the president one of them had proved a harder sell), was which of the contenders, the "strong-willed prosecutor" or his high-placed target, would go the distance, win the race. "The next forty-eight to seventy-two hours are critical," Tim Russert was saying on January 21, 1998, on MSNBC, where the daily recalibration of such sudden-death scenarios would by August raise the cable's Nielsen households from 49,000 a year before to 197,000. "I think his presidency is numbered in days," Sam Donaldson was saying by Sunday of the same week.

"On the high-status but low-interest White House beat, there is no story as exciting as that of the fall of a president," Jacob Weisberg observed in *Slate* in March. The president, everyone by then agreed, was "toast." The president "had to go," or "needed to go." The reasons the president needed to go had seemed, those last days in January and into February, crisp, easy to explain, grounded as they were in the galvanizing felony prospects set adrift without attribution by the Office of the Independent Counsel: obstruction of justice, subornation of perjury. Then, as questions threatened to slow the story (Would it not be unusual to prosecute someone for perjury in a civil suit? Did the chronology present a circumstantial case for, or actually against, obstruction? If someone lied in a deposition about a matter later ruled not essential to and so inadmissable in the case at hand, as Lewinsky had been ruled in *Jones v. Clinton,* was it in fact perjury?), the reasons the president "needed to go" became less crisp, more subjective, more a matter of "the mood here in the capital," and so, by definition, less open to argument from those not there in the capital.

This story was definitely moving, as they kept saying on MSNBC. By April 1, 1998, when U.S. District Court Judge Susan Webber Wright rendered the possibility of any felony technically remote by dismissing *Jones v. Clinton* altogether, the story had already rolled past its inconvenient legal (or "legalistic," a much-used word by then) limitations: ten weeks after America first heard the name Monica Lewinsky and still in the absence of any allegation bearing on the president's performance of his duties, the reasons the president needed to go were that he had been "weakened," that he would be "unable to function." The president's own former chief of staff, Leon Panetta, had expressed concern about "the slow drip-drip process and the price he's paying in terms of his ability to lead the country."

When congressional staff members were asked in late March 1998 where they believed the situation was leading, twenty-one percent of Democratic staff members (forty-three percent of Republican) had foreseen, in the absence of resignation, impeachment proceedings.

The story was positioned, in short, for the satisfying long haul. By August 17, 1998, when the president confirmed the essential fact in the testimony Monica Lewinsky had given the grand jury eleven days before, virtually every "news analyst" on the eastern seaboard was on air (we saw the interiors of many attractive summer houses) talking about "the president's credibility," about "can he lead" or "still govern in any reasonably effective manner," questions most cogently raised that week by Garry Wills in *Time* and, to a different point, by Thomas L. Friedman in *The New York Times.* Proceeding from a belief both in President Clinton's underlying honor and in the redemptive power, if he was to be faced by crippling harassment, of the "principled resignation," Wills had tried to locate the homiletic possibilities in the dilemma, the opportunities for spiritual growth that could accrue to the country and to the president through resignation. The divergence between this argument and that made by Friedman was instructive. Friedman had seemed to be offering "can he lead" mainly as a strategy, an argument with which the professionals of the political process, who were increasingly bewildered by the public's apparent disinclination to join the rush to judgment by then general in the columns and talk shows, might most adroitly re-educate that "substantial majority" who "still feel that Mr. Clinton should remain in office."

In other words we had arrived at a dispiriting and familiar point, and would be fated to remain there even as telephone logs and Epass Access Control Reports and pages of grand-jury testimony floated down around us: "the disconnect," as it was now called, between what the professionals—those who held public office, those who worked for them, and those who wrote about them—believed to be self-evident and what a majority of Americans believed to be self-evident. John Kennedy and Warren Harding had both conducted affairs in the Oval Office (more recently known as "the workplace," or "under the same roof where his daughter lay sleeping"), and these affairs were by no means the largest part of what Americans thought about either of them. "If you step back a bit, it still doesn't look like a constitutional crisis," former federal prosecutor E. Lawrence Barcella told *The Los Angeles Times* to this point. "This is still a case about whether the President had sex with someone half his age. The American people have understood—certainly better than politicians, lawyers, and the press—that if this is ultimately about sex, it's really no one else's business. There are acceptable lies and unacceptable lies, and lying about someone's sex life is one of those tolerated lies."

Ten days after the president's August 17 admission to the nation, or ten days into the endless tape loop explicating the inadequacies of that admission, Mr. Clinton's own polls, according to *The Washington Post,* showed pretty much what everyone else's polls showed and would continue to show, notwithstanding the release first of Kenneth Starr's "narrative" and "grounds for impeachment" and then of Mr. Clinton's videotaped testimony and 3,183 pages of "supporting documents": that a majority of the public had believed all along that the president had some kind of involvement with Monica Lewinsky ("Cheat once, cheat twice, there's probably a whole line of them," a thirty-four-year-old woman told Democratic pollster Peter Hart in a focus session attended by *The Los Angeles Times*), continued to see it as a private rather than a political matter, believed Kenneth Starr to be the kind of sanctimonious hall monitor with sex on the brain they had avoided in their formative years (as in the jump-rope rhyme *Rooty-toot-toot! Rooty-toot-toot! / There go the boys from the Institute! / They don't smoke and they don't chew / And they don't go with the girls who do*), and, even as they acknowledged the gravity of lying under oath, did not wish to see the president removed from office.

The charge that he tried to conceal a personally embarrassing but not illegal liaison had not, it seemed, impressed most Americans as serious. Whether or not he had ever asked Vernon Jordan to call Ron Perelman and whether Vernon Jordan had in fact done so before or after the subpoena was issued to Monica Lewinsky had not, it seemed, much mattered to these citizens. Outside the capital, there had seemed to be a general recognition that the entire "crisis," although mildly entertaining, represented politics as usual, particularly since it had evolved from a case, the 1994 *Jones v. Clinton,* that would probably never have been brought and certainly never been funded had Mr. Clinton not been elected president. For Thomas L. Friedman, then, the way around this was to produce more desirable polling results by refocusing the question, steering the issue safely past the shoals of "should he be president," which was the essence of what the research was asking. "What might influence the public most," Friedman wrote, "is the question of 'can' Mr. Clinton still govern in any reasonably effective manner."

Since taking this argument to its logical conclusion raised, for a public demonstrably impatient with what it had come to see as a self-interested political class, certain other questions (If the president couldn't govern, who wouldn't let him? Was it likely that they would have let a lame duck govern anyway? What in fact was "governing," and did we want it?), most professionals fell back to a less vulnerable version of what the story was: a story so simple, so sentimental, as to brook no argument, no talking back from "the American people," who were increasingly seen as recalcitrant children, fecklessly resistant to responsible guidance. The story, William J. Bennett told us on *Meet the Press,* was about the "moral and intellectual disarmament" that befalls a nation when its president is not "being a decent example" and "teaching the kids the difference between right and wrong." The story, Cokie Roberts told us in the *New York Daily News,* was about reinforcing the lesson "that people who act immorally and lie get punished." The story, William Kristol told us on *This Week,* was about the president's "defiance," his "contempt," his "refusal to acknowledge some standards of public morality."

Certain pieties were repeated to the point where they could be referred to in shorthand. Although most Americans had an instinctive sense that Monica Lewinsky could well have been, as the *Referral* would later reveal her to have been, a less than entirely passive participant in whatever happened, we heard about the situational inviolability of interns (interns were "given into our care," interns were "lent to us by their parents") until Cokie Roberts's censorious cry to an insufficiently outraged congresswoman ("But with an *intern?*") could stand alone, a verdict that required no judge or jury. We heard repeatedly about "our children," or "our kids," who were, as presented, avid consumers of the *Nightly News* in whose presence sex had never before been mentioned and discussions of the presidency were routine. "I'd like to be able to tell my children, 'You should tell the truth,'" Stuart Taylor of the *National Journal* told us on *Meet the Press.* "I'd like to be able to tell them, 'You should respect the president.' And I'd like to be able to tell them both things at the same time." Jonathan Alter, in

Newsweek, spoke of the president as someone "who has made it virtually impossible to talk to your kids about the American presidency or let them watch the news."

"I approach this as a mother," Cokie Roberts said on *This Week.* "We have a right to say to this president, 'What you have done is an example to our children that's a disgrace,'" William J. Bennett said on *Meet the Press.* The apparent inability of the public to grasp this *Kinder-Kirche* point (perhaps because not all Americans could afford the luxury of idealizing their own children) had itself become an occasion for outrage and scorn: the public was too "complacent," or too "prosperous," or too "fixed on the Dow Jones." The public in fact became the unindicted coconspirator: "This ought to be something that outrages us, makes us ashamed of him," Mona Charen complained on *Late Edition with Wolf Blitzer.* "This casts shame on the entire country because he behaved that way and all of the nation seems to be complicit now because they aren't rising up in righteous indignation."

This was the impasse (or, as it turned out, the box canyon) that led many into a scenario destined to prove wishful at best: "The American people," we heard repeatedly, would cast off their complicity when they were actually forced by the report of the independent counsel to turn their attention from the Dow and face what Thomas L. Friedman, in the *Times,* called "the sordid details that will come out from Ken Starr's investigation." "People are not as sophisticated as this appears to be," William

Kristol had said hopefully the day before the president's televised address. "We all know, inside the Beltway, what's in that report," Republican strategist Mary Matalin said. "And I don't think . . . the country needs to hear any more about tissue, dresses, cigars, ties, anything else." George Will, on *This Week,* assured his co-panelists that support for the president would evaporate in the face of the *Referral.* "Because Ken Starr must—the president has forced his hand—must detail graphically the sexual activity that demonstrates his perjury. Once that report is written and published, Congress will be dragged along in the wake of the public. . . . Once the dress comes in, and some of the details come in from the Ken Starr report, people—there's going to be a critical mass, the yuck factor—where people say, 'I don't want him in my living room any more.'"

The person most people seemed not to want in their living rooms any more was "Ken" (as he was now called by those with an interest in protecting his story), but this itself was construed as evidence of satanic spin on the part of the White House. "The president's men," William J. Bennett cautioned in *The Death of Outrage: Bill Clinton and the Assault on American Ideals,* ". . . attempt relentlessly to portray their opposition as bigoted and intolerant fanatics who have no respect for privacy." He continued:

> At the same time they offer a temptation to their supporters: the temptation to see themselves as realists, worldly-wise, sophisticated: in a word,

> European. This temptation should be resisted by the rest of us. In America, morality is central to our politics and attitudes in a way that is not the case in Europe, and precisely this moral streak is what is best about us. . . . Europeans may have something to teach us about, say, wine or haute couture. But on the matter of morality in politics, America has much to teach Europe.

American innocence itself, then, was now seen to hang on the revealed word of the *Referral.* The report, Fox News promised, would detail "activities that most Americans would describe as unusual." These details, *Newsweek* promised, would make Americans "want to throw up." "Specifics about a half-dozen sex acts," *Newsday* promised, had been provided "during an unusual two-hour session August 26 in which Lewinsky gave sworn testimony in Starr's downtown office, not before the grand jury."

This is arresting, and not to be brushed over. On August 6, Monica Lewinsky had told the grand jury that sexual acts had occurred. On August 17, the president had tacitly confirmed this in both his testimony to the grand jury and his televised address to the nation. Given this sequence, the "unusual two-hour session August 26" might have seemed, to some, unnecessary, even excessive, not least because of the way in which, despite the full knowledge of the prosecutors that the details elicited in this session would be disseminated to the world in two weeks under the *Referral* headings

"November 15 Sexual Encounter," "November 17 Sexual Encounter," "December 31 Sexual Encounter," "January 7 Sexual Encounter," "January 21 Sexual Encounter," "February 4 Sexual Encounter and Subsequent Phone Calls," "March 31 Sexual Encounter," "Easter Telephone Conversations and Sexual Encounter," "February 28 Sexual Encounter," and "March 29 Sexual Encounter," certain peculiar and warped proprieties had been so pruriently observed. "In deference to Lewinsky and the explicit nature of her testimony," *Newsday* reported, "all the prosecutors, defense lawyers and stenographers in the room during the session were women."

Since the "explicit nature of the testimony," the "unusual activity," the "throw-up details" everyone seemed to know about (presumably because they had been leaked by the Office of the Independent Counsel) turned out to involve masturbation, it was hard not to wonder if those in the know might not be experiencing some sort of rhetorical autointoxication, a kind of rapture of the feed. The average age of first sexual intercourse in this country has been for some years sixteen, and is younger in many venues. Since the average age of first marriage in this country is twenty-five for women and twenty-seven for men, sexual activity outside marriage occurs among Americans for an average of nine to eleven years. Six out of ten marriages in this country are likely to end in divorce, a significant percentage of those who divorce doing so after engaging in extramarital sexual activity. As of the date of the 1990 census, there were in this country 4.1 million households headed by unmarried couples. More than thirty-five percent of these households included children. Seventh-graders in some schools in this country were as early as the late 1970s reading the Boston Women's Health Book Collective's *Our Bodies, Ourselves,* which explained the role of masturbation in sexuality and the use of foreign objects in masturbation. The notion that Americans apparently willing to overlook a dalliance in the Oval Office would go pale at its rather commonplace details seemed puzzling in the extreme, as did the professed inability to understand why these Americans might favor the person who had engaged in a common sexual act over the person who had elicited the details of that act as evidence for a public stoning.

But of course these members of what Howard Fineman recently defined on MSNBC as "the national political class," the people "who read the *Hotline* or watch cable television political shows such as this one," were not talking about Americans at large. They did not know Americans at large. They occasionally heard from one, in a focus group or during the Q&A after a lecture date, but their attention, since it was focused on the political process, which had come to represent the concerns not of the country at large but of the organized pressure groups that increasingly controlled it, remained remote. When Howard Fineman, during the same MSNBC appearance, spoke of "the full-scale panic" that he detected "both here in Washington and out around the country," he was referring to calls he had made to "a lot of Democratic consultants, pollsters, media people and so forth," as well as to candidates: "For example one in Wisconsin, a woman running for the Democratic seat up there, she said she's beginning to get calls and questions from average folks wanting to know what her view of Bill Clinton is."

"Average folks," however, do not call their elected representatives, nor do they attend the events where the funds get raised and the questions asked. The citizens who do are the citizens with access, the citizens with an investment, the citizens who have a special interest. When Representative Tom Coburn (R-Okla.) reported to *The Washington Post* that during three days in September 1998 he received five hundred phone calls and 850 e-mails on the question of impeachment, he would appear to have been reporting, for the most part, less on "average folks" than on constituents who already knew, or had been provided, his telephone number or e-mail address; reporting, in other words, on an organized blitz campaign. When Gary Bauer of the Family Research Council seized the moment by test-running a drive for the presidency with a series of Iowa television spots demanding Mr. Clinton's resignation, he would appear to have been interested less in reaching out to "average folks" than in galvanizing certain caucus voters, the very caucus voters who might be expected to have already called or e-mailed Washington on the question of impeachment.

When these people on the political talk shows spoke about the inability of Americans to stomach "the details," then, they were speaking, in code, about a certain kind of American, a minority of the population but the minority to whom recent campaigns have been increasingly pitched. They were talking politics. They were talking about the "values" voter, the "pro-family" voter, and so complete by now was their isolation from the country in which they lived that they seemed willing to reserve its franchise for, in other words give it over to, that key core vote.

3.

The cost of producing a television show on which Wolf Blitzer or John Gibson referees an argument between an unpaid "former federal prosecutor" and an unpaid "legal scholar" is significantly lower than that of producing conventional programming. This is, as they say, the "end of the day," or the bottom-line fact. The explosion of "news comment" programming occasioned by this fact requires, if viewers are to be kept from tuning out, nonstop breaking stories on which the stakes can be raised hourly. The Gulf War made CNN, but it was the trial of O. J. Simpson that taught the entire broadcast industry how to perfect the pushing of the stakes. The crisis that led to the Clinton impeachment began as and remained a situation in which a handful of people, each of whom believed that he or she had something to gain (a book contract, a scoop, a sinecure as a network "analyst," contested ground in the culture wars, or, in the case of Starr, the justification of his failure to get either of the Clintons on Whitewater), managed to harness this phenomenon and ride it. This was not an unpredictable occurrence, nor was it unpredictable that the rather impoverished but generally unremarkable transgressions in question would come in this instance to be inflated by the rhetoric of moral rearmament.

"You cannot defile the temple of justice," Kenneth Starr told reporters during his many front-lawn and driveway appearances. "There's no room for white lies. There's no room for shading. There's only room for truth. . . . Our job is to determine whether crimes were committed." This was the authentic if lonely voice of the last American wilderness, the voice of the son of a Texas preacher in a fundamentalist denomination (the Churches of Christ) so focused on the punitive that it forbade even the use of instrumental music in church. This was the voice of a man who himself knew a good deal about risk-taking, an Ahab who had been mortified by his great Whitewater whale and so in his pursuit of what Melville called "the highest truth" would submit to the House, despite repeated warnings from his own supporters (most visibly on the editorial page of *The Wall Street Journal*) not to do so, a report in which his attempt to take down the government was based in its entirety on ten occasions of backseat intimacy as detailed by an eager but unstable participant who appeared to have memorialized the events on her hard drive.

This was a curious document. It was reported by *The New York Times,* on the day after its initial and partial release, to have been written in part by Stephen Bates, identified as a "part-time employee of the independent counsel's office and the part-time literary editor of *The Wilson Quarterly,*" an apparent polymath who after his 1987 graduation from Harvard Law School "wrote for publications as diverse as *The Nation, The Weekly Standard, Playboy,* and *The New Republic.*" According to the *Times,* Mr. Bates and Mr. Starr had together written a proposal for a book about a high school student in Omaha barred by her school from forming a Bible study group. The proposed book, which did not find a publisher, was to be titled *Bridget's Story.* This is interesting, since the "narrative" section of the *Referral,* including as it does a wealth of nonrelevant or "story" details (for example the threatening letter from Miss Lewinsky to the president which the president said he had not read, although "Ms. Lewinsky suspected that he had actually read the whole thing"), seems very much framed as "Monica's Story." We repeatedly share her "feelings," just as we might have shared Bridget's: "I left that day sort of emotionally stunned," Miss Lewinsky is said to have testified at one point, for "I just knew he was in love with me."

Consider this. The day in question, July 4, 1997, was six weeks after the most recent of the president's attempts to break off their relationship. The previous day, after weeks of barraging members of the White House staff with messages and calls detailing her frustration at being unable to reach the president, her conviction that he owed her a job, and her dramatically good intentions ("I know that in your eyes I am just a hindrance—a woman who doesn't have a certain someone's best interests at heart, but please trust me when I say I do"), Miss Lewinsky had dispatched a letter that "obliquely," as the narrative has it, "threatened to disclose their relationship." On this day, July 4, the president has at last agreed to see her. He accuses her of threatening him. She accuses him of failing to secure for her an appropriate job, which in fact she would define in a later communiqué as including "anything at *George* magazine." "The most important things to me," she would then specify, "are that I am engaged and interested in my work, I am *not* someone's administrative/executive assistant, and my salary can provide me a comfortable living in NY."

At this point she cried. He "praised her intellect and beauty," according to the narrative. He said, according to Miss Lewinsky, "he wished he had more time for me." She left the Oval Office, "emotionally stunned," convinced "he was in love with me." The "narrative," in other words, offers what is known among students of fiction as an unreliable first-person narrator, a classic literary device whereby the reader is made to realize that the situation, and indeed the narrator, are other than what the narrator says they are. It cannot have been the intention of the authors to present their witness as the victimizer and the president her hapless victim, and yet there it was, for all the world to read. That the authors of the *Referral* should have fallen into this basic craft error suggests the extent to which, by the time the *Referral* was submitted, the righteous voice of the grand inquisitor had isolated itself from the more wary voices of his cannier allies.

That the voice of the inquisitor was not one to which large numbers of Americans would respond had always been, for these allies, beside the point: what it offered, and what less authentic voices obligingly amplified, was a platform for the reintroduction of fundamentalism, or "values issues," into the general discourse. "Most politicians miss the heart and soul of this concern," Ralph Reed wrote in 1996, having previously defined "the culture, the family, a loss of values, a decline in civility, and the destruction of our children" as the chief concerns of the Christian Coalition, which in 1996 claimed to have between a quarter and a third of its membership among registered Democrats. Despite two decades during which the promotion of the "values" agenda had been the common cause of both the "religious" (or Christian) and the neoconservative right, too many politicians, Reed believed, still "debate issues like accountants." John Podhoretz, calling on Republicans in 1996 to resist the efforts of

Robert Dole and Newt Gingrich to "de-ideologize" the Republican Party, had echoed, somewhat less forthrightly, Reed's complaint about the stress on economic issues. "They do not answer questions about the spiritual health of the nation," he wrote. "They do not address the ominous sense we all have that Americans are, with every intake of breath, unconsciously inhaling a philosophy that stresses individual pleasure over individual responsibility; that our capacity to be our best selves is weakening."

That "all" of us did not actually share this "ominous sense" was, again, beside the point, since neither Reed nor Podhoretz was talking about all of us. Less than fifty percent of the voting-age population in this country actually voted (for anyone) for president in 1996. The figures in the previous five presidential-year elections ranged from fifty to fifty-five percent. Only between thirty-three and thirty-eight percent voted in any midterm election since 1974. The figures for those who vote in primary elections, where the terms on which the campaign will be waged are determined, drop even further, in some cases into the single digits. Ralph Reed and John Podhoretz had been talking in 1996, as William Kristol and Mary Matalin would be talking in 1998, about that small group of citizens for whom "the spiritual health of the nation" would serve as the stalking horse for a variety of "social," or control-and-respect, issues. They were talking, in other words, about that narrow subsection of the electorate known in American politics as most-likely-to-vote.

What the Christian Coalition and *The Weekly*

Standard were asking the Republican Party and (by logical extension) its opponents to do in 1996 was to further narrow most-likely-to-vote, by removing from debate those issues that concerned the country at large. This might have seemed, at the time, a ticket only to marginalization. It might have seemed, as recently as 1996, a rather vain hope that the nation's opinion leaders would soon reach general agreement that the rearming of the citizenry's moral life required that three centuries of legal precedent and even constitutional protections be overridden in the higher interest of demonstrating the presence of moral error, or "determining whether a crime has been committed," as Kenneth Starr put it in the brief he submitted to the Supreme Court in the matter of whether Vincent Foster's lawyer could be compelled to turn over notes on conversations he had with Foster before his death. Yet by August 1998, here were two of those opinion leaders, George Will and Cokie Roberts, stiffening the spines of those members of Congress who might be tempted to share the inclination of their constituents to distinguish between mortal and venial sins:

> *G.W.:* Cokie, the metastasizing corruption spread by this man [the president] is apparent now. And the corruption of the very idea of what it means to be a representative. We hear people in Congress saying, "Our job is solely to read the public opinion polls and conform thereto. Well, if so, that's not intellectually complicated, it's not morally demanding. But it makes a farce of being a . . .

C.R.: No, at that point, we should just go for direct democracy.

G.W.: Exactly. Get them out of here and let's plug computers in. . . .

C.R.: . . . I must say I think that letting the [impeachment] process work makes a lot of sense because it brings—then people can lead public opinion rather than just follow it through the process.

G.W.: What a concept.

C.R.: But we will see.

To talk about the failure of Congress to sufficiently isolate itself from the opinion of the electorate as a "corruption of the very idea of what it means to be a representative" is to talk (another kind of "end of the day," or bottom-line fact) about disenfranchising America. "The public was fine, the elites were not," an unnamed White House adviser had told *The Washington Post* about the difference of opinion, on the matter of the president's "apology" or "nonapology," between the political professionals and what had until recently been deferred to, if only pro forma, as the electorate. "You've got to let the elites win one."

No one should have doubted that the elites would in fact win this one, since, even before the somewhat dampening polling on the Starr report and on the president's videotaped testimony, the enterprise had achieved the perfect circularity toward which it had long been tending. "I want to find out who else in the political class thinks the way Mr. Clinton does about what is acceptable behavior," George Will had said in August, explaining why he favored impeachment proceedings over a resignation. "Let's smoke them out." That a majority of Americans seemed capable of separating Mr. Clinton's behavior in this matter from his performance as president had become, by that point, irrelevant, as had the ultimate outcome of the congressional deliberation. What was going to happen had already happened: since future elections could now be focused on the entirely spurious issue of correct sexual, or "moral," behavior, those elections would be increasingly decided by that committed and well-organized minority brought most reliably to the polls by "pro-family," or "values," issues. The fact that an election between two candidates arguing which has the more correct "values" left most voters with no reason to come to the polls had even come to be spoken about, by less wary professionals, as the beauty part, the bonus that would render the process finally and perpetually impenetrable. "Who cares what every adult thinks?" a Republican strategist asked *The Washington Post* to this point in early September 1998. "It's totally not germane to this election."

Vichy Washington

June 24, 1999

I.

On an evening late in April 1999, some 350 survivors of what they saw as a fight for the soul of the republic gathered at the Mayflower Hotel in Washington to honor Representative Henry J. Hyde and the twelve House managers who, under his leadership, had carried the charges of impeachment to the floor of the Senate. C-SPAN caught the distinctive, familial fervor of the event, which was organized to benefit the Independent Women's Forum, an organization funded in part by Richard Mellon Scaife and the "women's group" in the name of which Kenneth Starr volunteered in 1994 to file an amicus curiae brief arguing that *Jones v. Clinton* should go forward.

Live from the Mayflower, there on-screen were the familiar faces from the year-long entertainment that had preceded the impeachment, working the room amid the sedate din and the tinkling of glasses. There were the pretty women in country-club dinner dresses, laughing appreciatively at the bon mots of their table partners. There was the black-tie quartet, harmonizing on "Vive la, vive la, vive l'amour" and "Goodbye My Coney Island Baby" as Henry Hyde doggedly continued to spoon up his dessert, chocolate meeting mouth with metronomic regularity, his perseverance undeflected even by Bob Barr, leaning in to make a point.

The word "courage" was repeatedly invoked. Midge Decter, a director of the Independent Women's Forum, praised Henry Hyde's "manliness," and the way in which watching "him and his merry hand" on television during the impeachment trial had caused her to recall "whole chunks" of Rudyard Kipling's "If." Robert L. Bartley, the editor of *The Wall Street Journal,* had found similar inspiration in the way in which the managers had "exposed truths to the American people, and they did this in the face of all the polls and focus groups, and they were obviously doing an unpopular thing, and I think that is why they deserve our greatest credit." The words of Henry V before the Battle of Agincourt were recalled by Michael Novak, as they had been by Henry Hyde in his closing statement during the Senate impeachment trial, but for this occasion adapted to "our Prince Hal, our own King Henry": "He that outlives this day, and comes safe home, will stand at tiptoe when this day is named. . . . Then shall our names, familiar in his mouth as household words, Henry the King, Rogan and Hutchinson, Canady, Cannon, McCollum, Lindsey Graham, Gekas, Chabot, Bryant, Buyer, Barr, and Sensenbrenner."

This evening could have seemed, for those who still misunderstood the Reagan mandate to have been based on what are now called "social" issues, the last redoubt. Familiar themes were sounded, favorite notes struck. Even the most glancing reference to the depredations of "the Sixties" (". . . according to Sean Wilentz, a scholar who exemplifies all the intellectual virtues and glories of the Sixties . . .") proved a reliable crowd-pleaser. In deference to the man who had not only sponsored the Hyde Amendment (banning Medicaid payments for abortions) but who had a year before testified as a character witness for a defendant accused of illegally blockading abortion clinics ("He's a hero to me," Hyde had said. "He has the guts I wish more of us had"), the "unborn" were characterized as "the stranger, the other, the unwanted, the inconvenient."

Mentions of "Maxine Waters" were cues for derision. "Barney Frank" was a laugh line that required no explication. The loneliness of the shared position was assumed, and proudly stressed. Yet the mood of the evening was less elegiac than triumphal, less rueful than rededicated, as if there in a ballroom at the Mayflower was the means by which the American political dialogue could be finally reconfigured: on the sacrificial altar of the failed impeachment, in the memory of the martyred managers, the message of moral rearmament that has driven the conservative movement to what had seemed no avail might at last have met its moment. "As we were coming in," William J. Bennett told the guests that night, "I said to my friend Dan Oliver, I said 'Good group.' Dan said, 'Good group? This is it, pal. This is the army. This is all of it.'"

The notion that a failed attempt to impeach the president might nonetheless have accomplished exactly what it was meant to accomplish, that the desired phoenix might even then be rising from the ashes of acquittal, might have seemed to many, in the immediate wake of the November 1998 elections, when the disinclination of the American people to see the president impeached translated into the loss of five Republican congressional seats, wishful. "It's pretty clear that impeachment dropped off the public's radar screen," Henry Hyde said to a *Los Angeles Times* reporter as he realized on election night that he was losing not only his anticipated mandate but five of his votes. The next morning, in the O'Hare Hilton, he told three aides that his Judiciary Committee inquiry, which party leaders had inexplicably construed as so in tune with public sentiment as to promise a gain of twenty seats, would have to be telescoped, and impeachment delivered out of the House while his lame ducks could still vote.

Over the next several weeks, as they contemplated the unexpected hit they had taken by feeding the greed of their conservative base for impeachment, Republicans would float many fanciful scenarios by which the party could be extricated from its own device. Senator Arlen Specter of Pennsylvania argued on the op-ed page of *The New York Times* for "abandoning impeachment," in effect handing off this suddenly sticky wicket to the courts, where, since not many lawyers saw a makeable case for perjury, it could conveniently dematerialize. Robert Dole laid out a plan based on the distinctly improbable agreement of the president in his own censure. Even Henry Hyde saw a way for the president to save the day, by resigning: "I think he could be really heroic if he did that. He would be the savior of his party. . . . It would be a way of going out with honor." By mid-December 1998, former Senator Alan K. Simpson was expressing what had become by default the last-ditch position of most Republicans, which was that any hemorrhaging they were suffering outside their conservative base could be contained before 2000 by the putative inability of these less ideological voters to remember that long. "The attention span of Americans," Simpson said, "is 'which movie is coming out next month?' and whether the quarterly report on their stock will change."

This casual contempt for the electorate at large was by then sufficiently general to pass largely unremarked upon. A good deal of what seemed at the time opaque in the firestorm that consumed the attention of the United States from January 1998 until the spring of 1999 has since been illuminated, but what remains novel, and unexplained, was the increasingly histrionic insistence of the political establishment that it stood apart from, and indeed above, the country that had until recently been considered its validation. Under the lights at CNN and MSNBC and the Sunday shows, it became routine to declare oneself remote from "them," or "out there." The rhetorical expression of outrage, or "speaking out," became in itself a moral position, even when the reasons for having spoken out could not be recalled. ". . . Whether or not it happens," Robert H. Bork said to *The Washington Post* in December 1998 about impeachment, which he favored, "I will still think I was right. . . . I just spoke out. I think on a television show, maybe Larry King. I wish I could recall what I was concerned with, but I can't at the moment."

The electorate, as anyone who had turned on a television set since the spring of 1998 had heard repeatedly, was "complicit" in the "corruption" of the president, or of the administration, or of the country itself, which was therefore in need of the "purging" to be effected, as in myth, by the removal of the most visible figure on the landscape. "It would be an enormous emetic—culturally, politically, morally—for us to have an impeachment," the Reverend John Neuhaus, editor of the conservative monthly *First Things,* told Michael Powell of *The Washington Post.* "It would purge us." The reason the public was "complicit," and the country in need of "purging," was that the public was "materialistic," interested only in "the Dow," or, later, "their pension funds." The reason the public was "materialistic" was that the public had, well, no morals. "My wife likes to say they must be polling people coming out of Hooters on Saturday night," Senator Robert C. Smith of New Hampshire said at the time he was announcing his bid for the presidency. "I will not defend the public," William J. Bennett told *The New York Times* in February 1999, after Paul M. Weyrich had written to supporters of his Free Congress Foundation that since the nation was in the grip of an "alien ideology" they should abandon the idea that a moral majority existed and take steps to "quarantine" their families. "Absolutely not. If people want to pander to the public and say they're right they can. But they're not right on this one."

"What's popular isn't always what's right," Representative J. C. Watts of Oklahoma said, arguing in the House for impeachment. "Polls would have rejected the Ten Commandments. Polls would have embraced slavery and ridiculed women's rights." On the weekend in January 1999 when the "favorable" rating of the Republican Party dropped to thirty-six percent, the lowest point since Watergate, Senator Phil Gramm said on *Meet the Press* that the people of Texas "didn't elect me to read those polls." Not even when the bumper stickers of the John Birch Society were common road sightings had we been so insistently reminded that this was not a democracy but a republic, or a "representative form of government." For the more inductive strategists in the movement, the next logical step was obvious: since a republic depended by definition on an electorate, and since the electorate at hand had proved itself "complicit," the republic itself could be increasingly viewed as doubtful, open for rethinking. "The Clinton affair and its aftermath will, I think, turn out to be a defining moment that exposed the rot in the institutions of American republican government," Charles Murray wrote in *The Weekly Standard* in February 1999. "Whether the response will be to shore up the structure or abandon it remains an open question."

2.

On the morning of February 11, 1994, Michael Isikoff, at that time a reporter for *The Washington Post* and later the author of *Uncovering Clinton: A Reporter's Story,* received, from the conservative strategist Craig Shirley, a heads-up on what would be said that afternoon at the Conservative Political Action Conference at the Hotel Omni Shoreham, where a woman brought to Washington by Cliff Jackson, the Hot Springs lawyer who orchestrated Troopergate, was scheduled to give a press conference. Isikoff went over to the Shoreham, witnessed what would turn out to be the debut performance of Paula Jones, and the next morning conducted a three-hour interview with her, in a suite at the Shoreham where she was flanked by her husband and her then lawyer, Danny Traylor. Isikoff asked Paula Jones about her eighteen-month-old son, Madison, and told her about his own baby daughter. He asked her whether her parents had been Democrats or Republicans, a point about which she was uncertain. "I guess any man probably would be more [interested in politics] than a woman," she said. "That's just not my interest in life." Isikoff tells us that he questioned Traylor and Jackson independently about their initial involvement, and reports that the answers they gave "point toward an innocent explanation." If Isikoff did indeed choose to ask Paula Jones herself why, given her lack of interest in politics, her lawyer had hooked her up with Cliff Jackson and Craig Shirley and the Conservative Political Action Conference, he chose not to record her answer, although he renders certain details from that initial interview with some avidity:

> *Paula Jones:* "He had boxer shorts and everything and he exposed hisself [sic] with an erection . . . holding it . . . fiddling it or whatever. And he asked me to—I don't know his exact word—give him a blow job or—I know you gotta know his exact words."
>
> *Isikoff:* "Exact words."
>
> *Paula Jones:* "He asked me to do something. I know that. I'll tell you, I was so shocked. I think

> he wanted me to kiss it. . . . And he was saying it in a very disgusting way, just a horny-ass way . . ."
>
> *Isikoff:* "What do you mean in a very disgusting way?"
>
> *Paula Jones:* "Disgusting way, he just, it was *please, I want it so bad*—just that type of way, like he was wanting it bad, you know."

Over the next several years, first on the Paula Jones story for the *Post* and then on the Paula Jones and the Kathleen Willey and the Monica Lewinsky stories for *Newsweek,* Isikoff would encounter a number of such choices, moments in which a less single-minded reporter might well have let attention stray to the distinctly peculiar way the story was unfolding itself, the way in which corroborating witnesses and incriminating interviews would magically materialize, but Isikoff kept his eye on the ball, his story, which was, exactly, "uncovering" Clinton. There was for example the moment when Joe Cammarata, one of the lawyers chosen by those working behind the scenes on the Jones case to replace Danny Traylor, had accommodated Isikoff's need to find "evidence that Clinton did this to other women" by recalling a "mysterious phone call" he had received from a woman who would not give her name but said that "a similar thing" had happened to her when she was working in the White House. "This was weird, I thought," Isikoff recalls. "The caller had imparted a hell of a lot of detail. Cammarata, for his part, was more than happy to let me figure it out. If I could track this woman down, he reasoned, I'd probably pass it along to him. Then he could subpoena her. As he saw it, I would save him some legwork."

Examine this. Isikoff thought the call was "weird," but any suspicions this aroused seem not to have suggested to him that the Jones defense team, or someone working through the Jones defense team, might be planting a story. As might have been predicted, this tip led Isikoff to Kathleen Willey, at which point we enter another reportorial twilight zone. "A journalistic dance between aggressive reporter and reluctant source began," Isikoff writes, "a dance that was to continue for months." In the average reporting experience, reluctant sources hang up, or say no comment, then screen their calls, leave town. This "reluctant source," however, having extracted the promise that Isikoff would not publish her story "until she gave the green light," allowed herself to be interviewed for more than two hours, telling her story "in gripping and microscopic detail."

Asked by the "aggressive reporter" if anyone could corroborate her story, another point at which, if she did not want the story out, she could have recouped her losses by saying no, Kathleen Willey obligingly named two women. One of the women she named was Julie Hiatt Steele, to whom, on the spot, she placed a call, arranging a meeting later that day between Steele and Isikoff. The second woman was Linda Tripp, then at the Pentagon. Dutifully, a relentless op on the case, Isikoff followed up his conveniently arranged meeting with Julie Hiatt Steele by tagging along with a *Newsweek* reporter who had access to the Pentagon. There, in a cubicle in the basement, Isikoff confronted Linda Tripp, who, within minutes, although "alarmed" by his visit, delivered the story's next reveal: "'There's something here, but the story's not what you think it is,' she said cryptically. 'You're barking up the wrong tree.'"

Note "cryptically." That was in March 1997. By April, Linda Tripp had delivered considerably more ("twenty-three-year-old former White House intern," got her job through "a wealthy campaign contributor," a "big insurance executive," "thrown out of the White House," "had gotten her a job at another federal agency," "hideaway off the Oval Office," "oral sex"), and had even let Isikoff listen in on a phone call from the former intern, "an excited and somewhat whiny young woman complaining about another woman named 'Marsha.'" Marsha, Linda Tripp explained, was Marsha Scott, the president's personnel aide. Marsha was supposed to have brought the young woman back to the White House after the 1996 election. Marsha had not. Marsha was giving the young woman the runaround.

No matter how many clues the remarkably patient Tripp provided, the story remained, Isikoff tells us, presenting himself as an impartial fact-gatherer to whom speculative connections were anathema, in the cryptic range. "I'm a reporter, not a voyeur," he tells us, appropriating the high-road benefit, and, also, "Tripp wouldn't give me the ex-intern's name or the agency she worked for." And there was something else: "Tripp was certain the relationship was entirely consensual. . . . That, it seemed to me, placed it outside the scope of the Paula Jones lawsuit—my main justification for proceeding down this path."

But wait, he surely said to himself at this point, or perhaps not. You got to Tripp via Willey. You got to Willey via the Jones defense team. Who gains here? Who wants what out? Why? Four months later, Isikoff was still refusing to acknowledge the possibility of connections. In August 1997, in a CNBC green room, he happened to be discussing legal strategy on the Jones case with Ann Coulter, one of the "movement," or conservative, lawyers who had become a fixture on the news-comment shows. According to Isikoff, he remarked to Coulter that she seemed to have inside knowledge of *Jones v. Clinton,* and she laughed. "Oh, yes," he reports her responding. "There are lots of us busy elves working away in Santa's workshop." "Busy elves?" Isikoff recalls having thought, and then: "I remembered something about George Conway in New York. Now Coulter. Who else? And what were they doing?"

Some might have seen this as a line of inquiry worth pursuing, but Isikoff, after a call to Conway's office at Wachtell, Lipton, Rosen & Katz in New

York ("Conway and Coulter were fast friends" who "bonded over their common disdain for Clinton, and they loved nothing more than to gossip into the night about the latest developments in the Jones lawsuit"), seems to have satisfied himself that Conway and the other ardently conservative lawyers with whom Conway was in touch might be useful sources, but not themselves the story. Not until October 1997, when Linda Tripp summoned him to a meeting with Lucianne Goldberg and provided him with a beer, a bowl of pistachio nuts, and the name Monica Lewinsky, did his reporter's instincts briefly revive: "I stopped eating the nuts and started taking notes." There were, Linda Tripp said, tapes, and she was prepared to play them, but Isikoff, who "had been invited to appear on a CNBC talk show, *Hardball,*" and so was "a bit pressed for time," refused, famously, to listen:

> It's an interesting journalistic issue. My hesitation was instinctive—but rooted in principles I had drummed into me when I first started as a young reporter at the *Post.* We don't tape without permission, the late Howard Simons, then the paper's managing editor, had decreed.... We reporters shouldn't deceive our sources, any more than we should deceive the public. Or so Simons—a wise and revered editor—had taught me.
>
> Of course, I wasn't being asked by Tripp to tape anybody secretly. But the distinction was a bit fuzzy. Tripp's taping of Lewinsky was ongoing. If

> I started to listen in on her conversations as she was taping them—as opposed to when she was finished—then I inevitably would have become part of the process. . . . And I was in a bit of a hurry to make it to *Hardball.*

"What do you do when you find yourself sucked into the story?" Isikoff asks rhetorically toward the end of *Uncovering Clinton,* the part in which he says mea culpa but not quite. "What happens when you become beholden to sources with an agenda? There are no easy answers here." Much that he learned later, he tells us, "cast a somewhat different light" on events. He was, for example, "chagrined to discover" that Linda Tripp and Lucianne Goldberg "had been talking about a book deal from the start." But what could there have been, in that, to "discover"? If Isikoff was, as he presents himself here, "an aggressive reporter" still unaware that there was more in this than met the eye, would not "a book deal" have been his first assumption? During his first meetings with Tripp, Isikoff had read part of her proposal for a book to be called *The President's Women.* He knew Lucianne Goldberg to be a literary agent. The idea of a book was nonetheless, Isikoff tells us, "well off my radar screen; indeed, it seemed a bit counterintuitive. Why were they wasting their time sharing information with me, if that was their purpose?"

If Isikoff asked himself this question, he seems to have adroitly avoided the answer, which might have led him to another aspect of the story that he was managing to keep well off his radar screen. What there was to "discover," of course, he already knew: by the time Linda Tripp and Lucianne Goldberg gave him Monica Lewinsky's name, any idea of "a book deal" would have been, as Lucianne Goldberg noted in her review of *Uncovering Clinton* in *Slate,* "a moot point that I can safely say faded to the vanishing point." The reason the point was moot was that, even by Isikoff's own account, Lucianne Goldberg was by then operating less as a lone agent than as a kind of useful front, a cutout for those unable to reveal themselves as running the same move: a cutout for Linda Tripp, a cutout for the ardent young movement lawyers (the "busy elves" Ann Coulter had mentioned) who made up the shadow legal team for *Jones v. Clinton,* and a cutout ultimately for the Office of the Independent Counsel.

"I had relied on the elves for information at critical junctures," Isikoff tells us on page 357 of *Uncovering Clinton,* still in his modified mea culpa mode, "even while they concealed from me their role in bringing the Lewinsky allegations to the Jones lawyers and later to Ken Starr." Among the "elves," whose contributions to *Jones v. Clinton* included writing briefs and arranging a moot court at which the nominal Jones lawyers were prepped for their argument before the Supreme Court by Robert H. Bork, the most frequently named were Jerome M. Marcus, an associate at Berger & Montague in Philadelphia, George T. Conway III at Wachtell

Lipton in New York, and Richard W. Porter, a Chicago partner, as Kenneth Starr was a Washington partner, at Kirkland & Ellis. Jerome Marcus and Richard Porter had been classmates at the University of Chicago, as had Paul Rosenzweig, who was approached to work on *Jones v. Clinton* in 1994, decided against it, and in 1997 joined the Office of the Independent Counsel.

Review Isikoff's admission of imperfect prescience, the reporter's dilemma for which there were "no easy answers." The elves, he told us on page 357, had "concealed" from him their role in bringing the Lewinsky allegations to the Jones lawyers and later to Ken Starr. Go back to page 182 of *Uncovering Clinton,* the CNBC green room: when Ann Coulter said to Isikoff that there were "lots of us busy elves working away in Santa's workshop," was this not said to have been a response to his remark that she seemed to have "inside knowledge" of *Jones v. Clinton?* Or go back to page 135, where Isikoff gives a quite detailed account of what Linda Tripp told him during their early meetings, when she was not yet telling him the name of the intern. Linda Tripp told him, he reports, that "she herself had been asked by her White House–provided lawyer not to volunteer information about a memo she had seen about the White House travel office that implicated First Lady Hillary Rodham Clinton." Travel office? Travelgate? White House–provided lawyer? Did this not suggest a prior relationship with the Office of the Independent Counsel?

Given the players and the relationships already in place, would it not have been, as Isikoff said about the red herring that was the book deal, "counterintuitive" not to suspect that a certain amount of information was passing between the Jones team and the Office of the Independent Counsel and Linda Tripp? Did he not suspect it? If he suspected it, why did he not pursue it? Could it have been because he already knew it? This is an area that *Uncovering Clinton* was cannily designed, by virtue of the way its author chose to present himself, to leave safely uncharted. "As a reporter," the author tells us, "I don't think ideologically." And then, about his primary sources, Linda Tripp and Lucianne Goldberg: "I could not have cared less about their motives or their ultimate goal. My interest in them was quite simple and fairly well focused: Was the stuff they were telling me true? Could it be corroborated? Would it make a story for *Newsweek*?"

3.

When Paula Jones was brought to the 1994 Conservative Political Action Conference to air her charge against the president, Ralph Reed, under whose leadership the Christian Coalition had grown from fewer than five thousand members to a potent political force and whose presence might have lent the fateful press conference at the Shoreham a degree of legitimacy, was asked to participate. For what he seems to have seen as pragmatic reasons, he declined. As he explained in his 1996 *Active Faith: How Christians Are Changing the Soul of American Politics,* Reed considered it a mistake for conservatives to build their case against Clinton around Paula Jones: "When one of the nation's leading evangelical preachers suggests that the President may be a murderer, when a pro-life leader says that to vote for Clinton is to sin against God, and when conservative talk-show hosts lampoon the sexual behavior of the leader of the free world, the manner of their speech reflects poorly on the gospel and on our faith."

This was at a time when Jerry Falwell, on his *Old Time Gospel Hour,* was marketing *The Clinton Chronicles,* a forty-dollar video asserting that Clinton had ordered the murders of Arkansas opponents and governed the state "hooked on cocaine." A second video, *Circle of Power,* was suggesting that "countless people" who "had some connection to Bill Clinton" had "mysteriously died," and that "this is going on today." Even well in from the ideological frontiers of telemarketing, "impeachment" was already the word of the hour: a contributor to *The Weekly Standard,* Gary Schmitt, was calling for Clinton's impeachment on the grounds that the president had told Jim Lehrer during a PBS interview that he believed Kenneth Starr's Whitewater investigation to be a partisan effort and so would not rule out the possibility of presidential pardons for those convicted in connection with that investigation. Reed, in his 1996 book, recalled attending a conservative dinner where the speaker had called for Clinton's impeachment and imprisonment on the grounds that he was "the most criminal president in our history."

Reed saw the feeding of this particular fire as a strategy only for self-immolation. "Like an army that overwhelms its enemies but leaves the land uninhabitable, some religious conservatives have come dangerously close to defining themselves in purely anti-Clinton terms," he wrote. "Those who are identified as followers of Christ should temper their disagreements with Clinton with civility and the grace of God, avoiding the temptation to personalize issues or demonize their opponents. This is critical to remember if our movement is to avoid the fate of its predecessors." Some of the harshest attacks on Clinton, Reed noted, had their origins in the "Christian nation" or "Reconstructionist" movement, the more unyielding proponents of which advocated "legislating the ancient Jewish law laid out in the Old Testament: stoning adulterers, executing homosexuals, even mandating dietary laws":

> There are historical precedents for Reconstructionist ideas stretching back to the millenialistic strains of Puritan thinking, American Revolutionary ideology, and even the anti-slavery movement. But those currents did not reflect the mainstream of Christian thinking then, and they certainly do not today. Reconstructionism is an authoritarian

> ideology that threatens the most basic civil liberties of a free and democratic society. If the pro-family movement hopes to realize its goals of relimiting government and reinstilling traditional values in our culture and in public policy, it must unequivocally dissociate itself from Reconstructionism and other efforts to use the government to impose biblical law through direct political action. It must firmly and openly exclude the triumphalist and authoritarian elements. . . .

That the fire had already jumped this break should have been, in retrospect, clear, since, even then, the word "authoritarian" no longer carried the exact freight it carried for Reed. The problem with rock music, Robert H. Bork told us in his 1996 *Slouching Towards Gomorrah,* was that it had encouraged the "subversion of authority," which in turn was the problem with the "baby boomers," who were already, principally because Clinton could be shoehorned into their number, a target of choice for the derision and excoriation engaged in even by many who were themselves members of the same generation. As this view took hold, the word "authority" was frequently preceded, as in William J. Bennett's *The Death of Outrage,* by the word "moral," "moral authority" being the manna allegedly possessed by all American presidents before William Clinton. Clinton, according to David S. Broder and Richard Morin of *The Washington Post,* confronted "his fellow citizens with choices between deeply held moral standards and an abhorrence of judging others' behavior, a conflict the baby boomers have stirred all their adult lives."

These "boomers," who had "no respect for authority," or who "flouted established moral standards," made increasingly frequent appearances. "The battle to dethrone Bill Clinton takes its place in the ongoing Boomer War, a three-decade struggle to define our culture and control our history and symbols," Michael Powell wrote in *The Washington Post,* citing Robert Bork, who had suggested in defense of Kenneth Starr that his was a useful effort to "kill off the lax moral spirit of the Sixties." The pollster Daniel Yankelovich, whose 1981 *New Rules* and later opinion surveys for the Democratic Leadership Council inspired the 1992 Clinton-Gore campaign's *Putting People First,* was quoted by Broder and Morin as having said that "we are beginning to measure a shift back toward absolute as opposed to relative values." The "shift back" was to a period before the mid-sixties, which had been marked, according to Yankelovich, by a "radical extension of individualism."

Reenter Robert Bork, who in *Slouching Towards Gomorrah* identified "radical individualism," or "the drastic reduction of limits to personal gratification," as one of the two "defining characteristics of modern liberalism" (the other being "radical egalitarianism") and, as such, a root cause of "Western decline." That Bork has tended to support his arguments with something other than a full deck of facts (as evidence of "Western decline," he asked us in 1996 to consider "the latest homicide figures for New York City, Los Angeles, or the District of Columbia," as well as "the rising rate of illegitimate births," both of which were dropping steadily during the 1990s) has never deflected his enthusiasm for taking positions, since facts seemed to exist for him in the same mutable state positions did, unfixed weapons to be deployed as needed in that day's sortie against the "leftist dream world."

Bork is worth some study, since it is to him that we owe the most forthright statements of what might be required to effect "a moral and spiritual regeneration," the necessity for which has since entered the talk-show and op-ed ether. Such a regeneration could be produced, Bork speculated in *Slouching Towards Gomorrah,* by one of four events: "a religious revival; the revival of public discourse about morality; a cataclysmic war; or a deep economic depression." As for the first of these options, Bork saw possibilities in "the rise of an energetic, optimistic, and politically sophisticated religious conservatism," but not in the "mainline churches," which no longer posited "a demanding God . . . who dictates how one should live and puts a great many bodily and psychological pleasures off limits." "The carrot alone has never been a wholly adequate incentive to desired behavior," Bork wrote. "It is not helpful that the ideas of salvation and damnation, of sin and virtue, which once played major roles in Christian belief, are now almost never heard of in the mainline churches."

It is of course not true that ideas of salvation and damnation or sin and virtue are "now almost never heard of in the mainline churches." Anyone who repeats the responses in the Episcopal litany asks for deliverance "from all evil and wickedness, from sin, from the crafts and assaults of the devil, from thy wrath and from everlasting damnation," and the Catholic baptismal sponsor swears in the name of the child to "reject Satan, father of sin and prince of darkness." Nor is it true, as Bork also wrote, that "the intellectual classes" view religion as "primitive superstition," or believe either that "science has left atheism as the only respectable intellectual stance" or that the question of faith was definitely answered by "Freud, Marx, and Darwin." These "atheists" and "mainline churches" that had abandoned sin and virtue had nonetheless become fixed stations in the conservative canon, recognizable cues, along with "Freud, Marx, and Darwin" and "the ACLU" and all the other calculated outrages; what John J. DiIulio Jr. described in *The Weekly Standard* as "the radical-feminist faithful, the non-judgmental clergy, the Hollywood crowd, and the abortion-on-demand minions."

The literal "truth" or "untruth" of what Bork wrote or said was, then, beside the point, since this was metaphor, and was so understood within the movement: polemic, political litany, a rhetorical incitement to the legislation of "desired behavior," which was to say the scourging of "immoral" behavior. That Bork himself understood this seems clear enough, since he seems to believe that

Thomas Jefferson had some kind of similar intention—*this will raise the rabble*—when he wrote the Declaration of Independence. "It was indeed stirring rhetoric," Bork allows,

> entirely appropriate for the purpose of rallying the colonists and justifying their rebellion to the world. But some caution is in order. The ringing phrases are hardly useful, indeed may be pernicious, if taken, as they commonly are, as a guide to action, governmental or private. Then the words press inevitably towards extremes of liberty and the pursuit of happiness that court personal license and social disorder.

The extent to which "personal license" might be sought out for punishment was suggested by Bork in his earlier *The Tempting of America: The Political Seduction of the Law:* "Moral outrage is a sufficient ground for prohibitory legislation," he wrote. "Knowledge that an activity is taking place is a harm to those who find it profoundly immoral."

4.

"The Republican right wing in this country doesn't like it when we say coup d'etat, so I'll make it easier for them," Representative Jose E. Serrano (D-N.Y.) said on the floor of the House the day the impeachment vote was taken. "*Golpe de estado.* That's Spanish for overthrowing a government." The word "coup," which had begun to surface in the dialogue as the more ambiguous aspects of the Starr investigation became known, had predictably provoked impassioned objections, some of them reasoned (impeachment was a legitimate constitutional process, a conviction by the Senate on the impeachment charges brought by the House would result in the removal of the president but not of the political party holding the presidency) and others less reasoned (Hillary Rodham Clinton had said that there was a "vast right-wing conspiracy" to get her husband, ergo, there was not, or, alternately, it was not "vast," or it was not a "conspiracy"); and yet there were, in the sequence of events that culminated in impeachment, certain factors that seemed distinctly exotic to the politics of the United States.

There was, first of all, the sense of a "movement," an unchartered sodality that was dedicated to the "remoralization" (William Kristol's word) of the nation and that, for a variety of reasons (judicial activism, feminism, "nonjudgmentalism," what Bork called "the pernicious effects of our passion for equality"), believed itself inadequately represented in the nation's conventional electoral process. There was the reliance, as in the more authoritarian Latin American structures, on *orejas,* "ears," tale-tellers like Linda Tripp, citizens encouraged, whether directly or through the rhetoric of the movement, to obtain evidence against those perceived as enemies of the movement. There was the aid from the private sector, the dependence on such rich sympathizers as Richard Mellon Scaife and John Whitehead and the Chicago investment banker Peter W. Smith. There was the way in which it was seen as possible that the electoral process could be bypassed, that the desired change in the government could be effected by a handful of unseen individuals, like George Conway and Jerome Marcus and Richard Porter, working in concert.

There was the shared conviction of urgency, of mission, of an end so crucial to the fate of the republic as to sweep away possible reservations about means. If the Office of the Independent Counsel was violating Justice Department prosecutorial guidelines by prosecuting its case in the press, this had been justified, Kenneth Starr told Steven Brill, because it was "a situation where what we are doing is countering misinformation that is being spread about our investigation in order to discredit our office and our dedicated career prosecutors." If the treatment of Monica Lewinsky had seemed to some to violate her legal rights, this too had been justified by the imperative of the "prosecution," the "investigation." "When you're asked to cooperate in an investigation of this kind it's going to be hellish no matter how nice you are to her," Michael Emmick of the Office of the Independent Counsel told members of the American Bar Association in February 1999. "That's one of the ugly truths about law enforcement. It's very ugly at times. We tried to make it as undifficult as we could." Since the moral necessity and therefore the absolute priority of the "investigation" were assumed, any assertion of the right of the accused to defend himself could be construed only as prima facie evidence of guilt, which is what people meant when they condemned the president's defense as "legalistic."

In fact we had seen this willingness to sacrifice means to ends before, in the late 1980s, when it had seemed equally exotic. "Sometimes you have to go above the written law," Fawn Hall had testified on behalf of Lieutenant Colonel Oliver North, expressing a view shared, in that instance, by most conservatives. Representative Henry J. Hyde, for example, had argued that Fawn Hall was echoing Thomas Jefferson, who had written in an 1810 letter to John Colvin that to insist on "a strict observance of the written law" over "the laws of necessity, of self-preservation, of saving our country when in danger" would be "absurdly sacrificing the end to the means." "All of us," Hyde wrote in the "Supplemental Views" he attached to the 1987 *Report of the Congressional Committees Investigating the Iran-Contra Affair,* "at some time confront conflicts between rights and duties, between choices that are evil and less evil, and one hardly exhausts moral imagination by labeling every untruth and deception an outrage." Hyde continued:

> We have had a disconcerting and distasteful whiff of moralism and institutional self-righteousness in these hearings. . . . It has seemed to me that the Congress is usually more eager to assert authority than to accept responsibility, more ready to criti-

> cize than to constructively propose, more comfortable in the public relations limelight than in the murkier greyness of the real world, where choices must often be made, not between relative goods, but between bad and worse. . . .

The "less evil" choice at hand, of course, had been the covert support of the Nicaraguan contras, or "freedom fighters," who were for the conservative movement in the 1980s what the shifting cast of starring (Paula Jones, Monica Lewinsky) and day players (the Arkansas state troopers, Kathleen Willey, Dolly Kyle Browning, Juanita Broaddrick) who "proved" the moral perfidy of William Jefferson Clinton would become in the 1990s: flags around which the troops could be mobilized and an entire complex of "movement values" attached. For these symbolic purposes, the contras had proved the less fragile standard, since their support involved issues that could be sufficiently inflated to launch the entire matter into the ozone of "national security." Unlike "covert support for the freedom fighters," "Monica Lewinsky" remained resistant to inflation: no matter how many mentions of "perjury" and "rule of law" and "constitutional obligation" got pumped into the noise, the possibility of dallying and lying about it continued to be understood by, and regarded as irrelevant to the survival of the nation by, a majority of the nation's citizens.

This presented a problem. On a broad range of loosely cultural issues (the balanced budget, welfare reform, the death penalty), the positions shared by the president and the citizens in question could by no alchemy be presented as the products of "left-liberal ideology," which had been firmly established in the litany of the movement as the root cause of the nation's moral crisis. "For the model of cultural collapse to work," Andrew Sullivan observed in October 1998 in an analysis of the conservative dilemma in *The New York Times Magazine,* "Clinton must represent its nadir." It was the solution to this problem, the naming of the citizens themselves as co-conspirators in the nation's moral degradation, that remains the most strikingly exotic aspect of the events that came to dominate the late 1990s. "No analysis can absolve the people themselves of responsibility for the quandary we appear to be in," Don Eberly, director of the Civil Society Project in Harrisburg, Pennsylvania, told David S. Broder and Richard Morin of *The Washington Post.* "Non-judgmentalism, the trump card of moral debate, seems to have gained strength among the people, especially in the sexual realm, and this clearly does not bode well for America."

The citizens, it seemed, were running behind the zeitgeist, incapable of understanding momentous events. "The objection that the American people are opposed to impeachment ignores culture lags of historical frequency, including general opposition to the liberation of the slaves," William F. Buckley Jr. told *The New York Times.* The citizens were incapable of understanding momentous events because they had succumbed to the lures of hedonism, materialism, false modernity, "radical individualism" itself. "A certain portion of the American public is cowed by popular culture," Craig Shirley, the conservative strategist who gave Michael Isikoff the heads-up on the unveiling of Paula Jones at the 1994 Conservative Political Action Conference, told the *Times.* "They do not want to be thought of as not being modern or sophisticated." "Given their obstinate lack of interest in the subject, asking a group of average Americans about politics is like asking a group of stevedores to solve a problem in astrophysics," a senior editor of *The Weekly Standard,* Andrew Ferguson, had written in 1996. "Before long they're explaining, not merely that the moon is made of cheese, but what kind of cheese it is, and whether it is properly aged, and how it would taste on a Triscuit."

Within the movement, then, this censorious approach to the electorate was not entirely recent. What was recent was the extent to which the movement crusade to save America from its citizens would come to be acquiesced in by, which is to say aided and abetted by, that small but highly visible group of people who, day by day and through administration after administration, relay Washington to the world, tell its story, agree among themselves upon and then disseminate its narrative. They report the stories. They write the op-ed pieces. They appear on the talk shows. They consult, they advise, they swap jobs, they travel with unmarked passports between the public and the private, the West Wing and the green room. They make up the nation's permanent professional political class, and they are for the most part people who would say of themselves, as Michael Isikoff said of himself, that they "don't think ideologically."

And yet this was an instance in which the narrative they agreed upon, that the president's behavior had degraded and crippled the presidency and the government and the nation itself, worked at every point to obscure, in some cases by omission and in other cases through dismissal as "White House spin," what we now know to have been going on. It would have been possible to read the reports from Washington in four or five daily newspapers and still not know, until it was detailed by Renata Adler in *The Los Angeles Times Book Review* on March 14, 1999, that by the time Linda Tripp surfaced on the national screen as Monica Lewinsky's confidante she had already testified in four previous Office of the Independent Counsel investigations: Filegate, Travelgate, the Vincent Foster suicide, and Whitewater.

In the face of even this single piece of information, a good many of the attitudes struck during the past year might have seemed, if not deliberate obfuscation, at best perplexing digressions. "I couldn't buy the party line that this was more about Clinton's accusers than his own actions," George Stephanopoulous told us in his own mea culpa but not quite, *All Too Human.* On the first Sunday in February 1999, when it seemed clear that there were not enough votes for conviction in the Senate, Cokie Roberts was still on air calling for a censure vote, "a Democratic vote saying what he did was wrong." Otherwise, she said, "the way it will be written for history is that this was a partisan witch hunt, that it was an illegitimate process," and "the spinners could certainly win if you do it that way."

These people lived in a small world. Consider again the sentence that appears on page 357 of *Uncovering Clinton,* particularly its second clause: "*I had relied on the elves for information at critical junctures—even while they concealed from me their role in bringing the Lewinsky allegations to the Jones lawyers and later to Ken Starr.*" What we now know occurred was, in other words, a covert effort to advance a particular agenda by bringing down a president. We know that this covert effort culminated in the kind of sting operation that reliably creates a crime where a crime may or may not have otherwise existed. We knew all along that the "independence" of the independent prosecutor could have been, or should have been, open to some question, since, before his appointment as independent prosecutor, Kenneth Starr had consulted with the Jones legal team on the projected amicus curiae brief to be filed on behalf of the Independent Women's Forum arguing that *Jones v. Clinton* should go forward. This had been reported, but was allowed to pass unremarked upon in what passed for the dialogue on the case. The Jones lawyer with whom Starr consulted, Isikoff tells us, was Gil Davis, whose billing records showed that the conversations with Starr covered four and a half hours, for which Davis billed Paula Jones $775.

The clues were always there, as they had been for Isikoff. There was always in the tale of the foolish intern and her disloyal friend a synchronicity that did not quite convince. There was from the outset the occasional odd reference in a news story, the name here or there that did not quite belong in the story, the chronology that did not quite tally, the curiously inexorable escalation of *Jones v. Clinton.* At least some of this, in other words, would appear to have been knowable, but it remained unacknowledged in the narrative that was the official story. "What drives Ken Starr onward?" Michael Winerip asked in *The New York Times Magazine* in September 1998. "Who is this minister's son in such relentless pursuit that he forced the president to admit his sins on national television?"

> Everyone has a theory on Starr. After the Lewinsky affair broke, Hillary Clinton called Starr "a politically motivated prosecutor who is allied with the right-wing opponents of my husband." Harold Ickes, the former Clinton aide, says he sees Starr as a dangerous moralist who views the Clintons "like Sodom and Gomorrah and is hell-bent on running them out of Washington."
>
> Even Starr's best friends don't know what to make of it all. They were caught off guard when he took the independent counsel's job in 1994 and are not sure why he wanted it. "I have no idea,"

> says Theodore Olson, a prominent Washington lawyer. "He never asked me. I was shocked when I heard the news."

"I was shocked when I heard the news." This was the same small world. Theodore Olson, whose wife, Barbara Olson, was a member of the National Advisory Board of the Independent Women's Forum, the group for which Kenneth Starr was to have written the amicus curiae brief urging that *Jones v. Clinton* go forward, was a Washington partner of the Los Angeles–based Gibson, Dunn & Crutcher. Gibson, Dunn had also been the firm of William French Smith, attorney general during the Reagan administration. Kenneth Starr had been William French Smith's chief of staff at the Justice Department, and it was William French Smith who in 1983 arranged Starr's appointment to the U.S. Circuit Court of Appeals for the District of Columbia, where he served with, and often voted with, Robert H. Bork. Olson was one of the lawyers, along with Robert Bork, enlisted by George Conway to prepare the Jones lawyers for the Supreme Court arguments that led to the Court's 9–0 decision denying a sitting president immunity from civil suits. The preparation took place at the Army-Navy Club in Washington. At a point after Christmas 1997, concerned about the ideological reliability of Linda Tripp's lawyer and under pressure to find a replacement before the cards started falling into place, Jerome Marcus and Richard Porter approached Theodore Olson about

taking on Tripp's legal representation. Olson could not.

Ann Coulter, via George Conway, then suggested James Moody, who could, and did. James Moody was a Washington lawyer and a member, along with George Conway and Robert H. Bork and Kenneth Starr and Theodore and Barbara Olson, of the Federalist Society, an organization of conservative legal scholars and students that became influential during the Reagan administration and had been the recipient, according to *The Washington Post,* of at least $1.5 million from Richard Mellon Scaife's foundations and trusts. Moody was also an admirer of the Grateful Dead, and, with Ann Coulter, had flown to San Francisco for the memorial concert that followed the 1995 death of Jerry Garcia. James Moody and Ann Coulter called themselves, according to Isikoff, "the only two right-wing Deadheads in Washington."

"Even Starr's best friends don't know what to make of it all." Nor did we, since this was the tone in which the nation's permanent professional political class had chosen to tell us the story. To suggest that the investigation might be politically motivated, we were told repeatedly, was to misrepresent "Ken" Starr, whose own tendency to encourage this reading was understood in Washington as a badge of scholarly innocence, a "clumsiness," at worst an "amateurishness" (that was the editorial page of *The Washington Post*), the endearing "tin ear," not important. "What's important," the *Post* declared in a February 1999 editorial calling for a bipartisan censure, "is to have a clear record and a clear statement of the standard of conduct—the expectations—that this president has violated by the lying to escape being held to account that is a hallmark of his career." In the absence of censure, the *Post* warned: "The president and his people will end up portraying this sorry episode as mostly a partisan proceeding, an effort by his enemies to win through entrapment and impeachment what they could not at the polls. Mr. Clinton will be the victim in this telling, not a president who dishonored the office but one who was caught up in a politics of personal destruction."

This merits study. The word "partisan," as in "partisan proceeding," suggests, in the United States, a traditional process, "taking sides," "knows how to count," Democrats, Republicans, the ballot box. The word "partisan," then, worked to contain the suggestion that anything outside that tradition was at work here. Both the "president who dishonored the office" and the "one who was caught up in a politics of personal destruction" further trivialized what had taken place, reducing it to the "personal," to a parable about the "character" of either the president or his attackers. By reducing the matter to the personal as by labeling it "partisan" or "bipartisan," it was possible to divest what had taken place of its potentially disruptive gravity, possible to avoid all consideration of whether or not a move on the presidency had been covertly run, of whether or not the intent of such a move had been to legitimize a minority ideological agenda, and of whether or not—most disruptive of all—such a move was ongoing.

On November 2, 1998, the day before the midterm elections, *The Washington Post* published a much-discussed piece by Sally Quinn, a *Post* writer and the wife of former *Post* executive editor Benjamin Bradlee. Whether or not this piece should have been published became a matter of momentary controversy within the Washington establishment, precisely because it reported so accurately the collegial, even collaborative approach the establishment was taking toward the matter at hand, the unwillingness to consider the ramifications of the refusal to conjugate the verb *to conspire,* the way in which an institutional forgetfulness was serving to preserve the sanctity of the Washington status quo. "Privately," Quinn wrote, "many in Establishment Washington would like to see Bill Clinton resign and spare the country, the presidency, and the city any more humiliation."

In 1972, when word reached the *Post* that there had been a break-in at the Watergate office of the Democratic National Committee, those assigned to work the story were Metro reporters, Bob Woodward and Carl Bernstein. Woodward, Benjamin Bradlee wrote in his autobiography, *A Good Life,* was then "one of the new kids on the staff," and Bernstein "the Peck's Bad Boy of the Metro staff." Woodward and Bernstein, in other words, were at that time Washington outsiders, and it was to their status as Washington outsiders that their ability to get "the real story" was commonly attributed. Those to whom Quinn spoke, on the other hand, seemed to believe that it was their own status as Washington insiders that gave them unique knowledge of the "real story" behind the drive for impeachment, which came down to what they saw as the president's betrayal, by his failure to tell the truth, of the community and the country.

Those to whom Quinn spoke also seemed to believe that, despite their best efforts to disseminate it, this unique knowledge remained unshared by and unappreciated by the rest of the country. "Clinton's behavior is unacceptable," the pollster Geoff Garin told her. "If they did this at the local Elks Club hall in some other community it would be a big cause for concern." "He came in here and he trashed the place, and it's not his place," David Broder of the *Post* said. "It's a canard to say this is a private matter," the *Wall Street Journal* columnist Albert R. Hunt said. "It's had a profound effect on governance." "There's no way any president going through this process can be able to focus, whether on Kosovo or the economic crisis," the NBC correspondent Andrea Mitchell said. "It's just a tragedy for everyone."

But not necessarily for everyone in Washington. The president would soon be, as David Broder would write in the *Post,* "disgraced and enfeebled." The time would soon come for the president, as Broder would also write, to "step aside for the man he clearly believes is well qualified to be his successor, Vice-President Gore." Since the matter had been so firmly established as "personal," there would be no need to pursue the possibility that the "process," or the "tragedy," or the "profound effect on governance," had been initiated by someone other than the president. In fact such a possibility need not even enter the picture, for this was a view from inside Washington, where those who did not "think ideologically" appreciated the drift, the climate, the wheeling of the ideological seasons, and also their access to whoever turns the wheel. As Quinn explained, "Starr is a Washington insider too."

God's Country

October 5, 2000

I.

The words "compassionate conservatism" sound like and have often been dismissed as political rhetoric, a construction without intrinsic meaning, George W. Bush's adroit way of pitching the center, allowing middle-class voters to feel good about themselves while voting their interests. Former governor Lamar Alexander of Tennessee called them "weasel words." Joe Andrews, the national chairman of the Democratic National Committee, called them "a contrived copout." "You can't have these massive tax cuts and at the same time . . . be a compassionate conservative," Senator Paul Wellstone of Minnesota told *The New York Times.* To the extent that the words were construed to mean anything at all, then, they were misunderstood to suggest a warmer, more generous, more ameliorative kind of conservative. "I'm a conservative, and proud of it, but I'm a compassionate conservative," Senator Orrin Hatch told Judith Miller of *The New York Times* in March 1981. "I'm not some kind of ultra-right-wing maniac." Former governor Pete Wilson of California offered a still more centrist reading: compassionate conservatism, he was quoted as saying by *The Washington Post,* is "old-fashioned budget-balancing with spending for preventive health measures and protection of the environment, and a strong pro-choice position on abortion."

This suggests a pragmatic but still traditional economic conservatism into which many Americans could comfortably buy. Yet the phrase "compassionate conservatism" describes a specific and deeply radical experiment in social rearrangement, the aim of which was defined by Governor Bush, in his acceptance speech at the Republican convention in Philadelphia, with sufficient vagueness to signal the troops without alerting the less committed: what he meant by compassionate conservatism, he said, was "to put conservative values and conservative ideas into the thick of the fight for justice and opportunity." Marvin Olasky, the journalism professor at the University of Texas who became a Bush adviser in 1993 and is the author of the seminal work on the subject, *The Tragedy of American Compassion* (this was the 1992 book that Newt Gingrich received as a Christmas present from William

J. Bennett in 1994 and promptly recommended to all Republican members of Congress), and of the more recent *Compassionate Conservatism,* has been more forthright. "Compassionate conservatism is neither an easy slogan nor one immune from vehement attack," he advises readers on page 1 of *Compassionate Conservatism:*

> It is a full-fledged program with a carefully considered philosophy. It will face in the twenty-first century not easy acceptance but dug-in opposition. It will have to cross a river of suspicion concerning the role of religion in American society. It will have to get past numerous ideological machine-gun nests. Only political courage will enable compassionate conservatism to carry the day and transform America.

The source of this "river of suspicion" and these "ideological machine-gun nests" becomes clear on reading the text, which is largely devoted to detailing a 1999 road trip during which Olasky, who before "God found me and changed me when I was twenty-six," had wrestled first with atheism ("I was bar mitzvahed at thirteen and an atheist by fourteen") and then with the Communist Party U.S.A. ("What if Lenin is wrong? What if there is a God?"), introduced his fourteen-year-old son, Daniel, to anti-poverty programs in Texas, the Midwest, and the Northeast. The drift soon emerges. "God's in charge," a couple who run a community center in South Dallas tell Olasky and Daniel. "I had to learn that God's in charge," they are told by a former user of heroin and cocaine who now runs the day-to-day operation of a recovery center in Minneapolis. A teacher at an evangelical summer school in Dallas explains how "curriculum is cleverly tied" to a pending mountain field trip, for example by assigning "Bible passages concerning mountains, eagles, and hawks."

Outside Houston, they visit "Youth-Reach Houston" and its founder, "Curt Williams, forty, who wears his long black hair pulled back in a pony tail" and who in 1984 "followed a pretty girl into a church and found welcome there. . . . Having hit bottom, he went to church and felt spiritually compelled to throw away his drugs and pornography." In Indianapolis, they meet with Mayor Stephen Goldsmith, chief domestic policy adviser to the Bush campaign and a civic leader who had studied "the negatives (high taxes, red tape, bad schools) that drive middle-class people away from the city" and found the answer in "using his bully pulpit to promote Catholic schools," since, as he tells Olasky and Daniel, "only hardened skeptics have trouble accepting that widespread belief in a Supreme Being improves the strength and health of our communities."

Again and again, Olasky and Daniel learn of successful recoveries effected in one or another "have-not" program, which is to say a program prevented from receiving the funding it deserves for the sole reason, Olasky suggests, that it is "faith-based." Again and again, they hear the same language ("hitting bottom," "putting God in charge," "changing one life at a time"), which is, not coincidentally, that of the faith-based twelve-step movement, from which a good deal of the "new thinking" on welfare derives. (Alcoholics Anonymous, according to James Q. Wilson, is "the single most important organized example of personal transformation we have.") Visiting a faith-based prison program outside Houston, they meet Donnie Gilmore, who was "pushing thirty with a resume of breaking into houses and stealing cars" when "his four-year-old daughter asked him about Jesus, and he realized he had never opened a Bible."

Gilmore then joined the "InnerChange" program ("Texas Governor George W. Bush gave the program a try, and state officials kept the American Civil Liberties Union at bay . . .") developed by Prison Fellowship Ministries, which is the organization founded by Charles ("Chuck") Colson after his release from the Maxwell Federal Prison Camp in Alabama and in which "the keys to success" are "God's grace and man's mentoring." "I have a couple of editions of the Bible with me," Colson reportedly said on the day he left for Maxwell to serve seven months of a one-to-three-year sentence for obstruction of justice in the prosecution of Daniel Ellsberg. "That's all."

"Repeatedly," Olasky notes with approval, "Daniel and I had found that the impetus for a compassionate conservative program came out of a

Bible study or some other church or synagogue function." Both father and son are made "uneasy" by more secular programs, for example KIPP (Knowledge Is Power Program) Academy, a charter school in Houston, where, despite the fact that it seemed "excellent," its public nature meant that "students miss out on that added dimension," i.e., prayer and Bible study. Similarly, in Minneapolis, they visit a Goodwill program that seemed to be successfully introducing women to the basic workplace manners (be on time, answer the phone politely) needed to make the transition from welfare to work. "All of this was impressive," Olasky allows, and yet, "as Daniel noted in comparing this helpful program to the faith-based equivalents we were seeing elsewhere, 'The absence of interest in God is glaring.'"

This use of "faith-based" is artful, and worth study. Goodwill was founded by a Methodist minister and run during its early years out of the Morgan Memorial Chapel in Boston, which would seem to qualify it as based in faith, although not, in the sense that Olasky apparently construes the phrase, as "faith-based." "Faith-based," then, is, as Olasky uses it, a phrase with a special meaning, a code phrase, employed to suggest that certain worthy organizations have been prevented from receiving government funding solely by virtue of their religious affiliation. This is misleading, since "religiously affiliated" organizations (for example

Catholic Charities) can and do receive such funding. The organizations that have not are those deemed "pervasively sectarian," a judgment based on the extent to which they proselytize, or make religious worship or instruction a condition of receiving aid. This, the Supreme Court has to date maintained, would violate the establishment clause of the First Amendment, the original intent of which Olasky believes to have been warped. "Daniel and I spent some time talking about what happened 210 years ago," he wrote. "There's nothing about 'separation of church and state.' That was Thomas Jefferson's personal expression in a letter written over a decade after the amendment was adopted. . . . The founding fathers would be aghast at court rulings that make our part of the world safe for moral anarchy."

Olasky is insistent that the faith propagated by these "faith-based" organizations need by no means be exclusively Christian, and here we enter another area of artful presentation. "My tendency is to be inclusive," he told *The Los Angeles Times.* "That can include Wiccans and Scientologists. If people are going to get mad at me, then so be it." The goal of compassionate conservatism, he has written repeatedly, is "faith-based diversity," a system in which the government would offer those in need of aid a choice of programs: "Protestant, Catholic, Jewish, Islamic, Buddhist, atheist." Perhaps because the theological imperative to convert nonbelievers runs with considerably more force among evangelical Christians than among Buddhists or atheists, most of the programs described in *Compassionate Conservatism* are nonetheless Christian, and, to one degree or another, evangelical. "All organizations, religious or atheistic, [had] the opportunity to propose values-based pre-release programs," Olasky notes by way of explaining how Texas state officials "kept the American Civil Liberties Union at bay" on behalf of Prison Fellowship, "but only Prison Fellowship went all the way."

In Philadelphia, Olasky and Daniel visit Deliverance Evangelistic, where John J. DiIulio Jr. "took his first steps toward faith in Christ" and where the pastor speaks of how "the ACLU is using and abusing" the First Amendment. They also visit the Bethel Community Bible Church, where they meet a paraplegic weight lifter who "sold drugs and saw no meaning to life until God grabbed him twelve years ago." Now he runs the Bethel weight room, which is "used by forty men each week, with no payment or conditions for use except one: the men need to attend church, Bible study, or church counseling at least once per week." Some of the programs Olasky describes refuse to compromise their evangelical mission by accepting government funding ("the reason we're here is that kids need to come to Christ"); others take the money, and devise ways of nominally separating it from the teaching mission.

Olasky and Daniel for example visit "the praying tailback," Herb Lusk, "the first National Football League player to use the end zone as the pulpit by crouching prayerfully following a touchdown." As pastor of the Greater Exodus Baptist Church in

Philadelphia, Lusk does accept government funding for the church's welfare-to-work program, but works around it: "No, we don't talk about Christ during the training, but we promote our offer of a free lunch for participants, with Bible teaching during it." "Evangelism is central to everything we do," Olasky is told by a Dallas woman, Kathy Dudley, who left her suburban home for the inner city, where she defines her mission as "discipleship." "Early in the 1990s," Olasky reports, "one official offered her a $170,000 grant, but she asked, 'If I take this money and hire a housing director, I will hire a Christian and expect a certain standard of behavior. If the director has sex outside of marriage, I will fire him immediately. Do you have a problem with this?' Yes, the official told her. She spurned the grant."

2.

In addition to teaching at Austin, Marvin Olasky has written a number of books, none of which tapped into the national moment with the exact force that *The Tragedy of American Compassion* did but the range of which suggests the dexterity with which the excitable mind can divine the sermon in every stone. There was *Prodigal Press: The Anti-Christian Bias of the American News Media*. There was *Telling the Truth: How to Revitalize Christian Journalism*. There was *Corporate Public Relations: A*

New Historical Perspective, drawn from five years Olasky spent writing speeches in the public affairs office at DuPont, an experience that led him to the Manichean conclusion that corporations were engaged in a liberal conspiracy to eliminate competition by supporting government regulation. "I wanted to work at DuPont because I was on the side of free enterprise," he told Michael King of *The Texas Observer.* "But I found out . . . you were largely lobbying government officials and others so that when they do the next set of regs—say environmental regs—that they write the regs in such a way that benefits you and hurts your smaller competitor."

There was *Fighting for Liberty and Virtue: Political and Cultural Wars in Eighteenth-Century America.* There was *The American Leadership Tradition: Moral Vision from Washington to Clinton,* which locates the "moral vision" of American presidents in their "religious beliefs and sexual morality" and offers a foreword by former Nixon aide Charles Colson, he of the career-making seven months at Maxwell, who speaks of "dedicated Olaskyites" and suggests that "a generation or two hence, historians will look back at this era and put Marvin Olasky among the pantheon of seminal thinkers who have changed the way people and societies think."

From Austin, communicating largely by e-mail, Olasky also manages to both edit and write a column for every issue of a weekly magazine, *World,* which is published out of Asheville, North Carolina, and has as its national editor Bob Jones IV, the great-grandson of the founder and son of the current president of Bob Jones University. The "mission statement" of *World,* until it was edited into a slightly more elliptical version in February 1999, read this way:

> To help Christians apply the Bible to their understanding of and response to everyday current events. To achieve this by reporting the news on a weekly basis in an interesting, accurate, and arresting fashion. To accompany reporting with practical commentary on current events and issues from a perspective committed to the final authority of the Bible as the inerrant written Word of God. To assist in developing a Christian understanding of the world, rather than accepting existing secular ideologies.

Ninety-five percent of *World*'s 103,000 subscribers, according to its own 1999 survey, identify themselves as Caucasian. Ninety-eight percent attend church "usually every week." Twenty-two percent are Baptist, seventeen percent are Presbyterian or Reformed, twelve percent members of the Presbyterian Church in America (a fundamentalist breakaway from the mainline Presbyterian Church U.S.A. and the denomination to which Olasky himself belongs), and eleven percent pentecostal or charismatic. Forty-five percent of those with children "homeschool," or teach at least one child at home. Asked to rate twenty-six individuals and movements named by *World,* these readers think most highly of James Dobson (who as head of

Focus on the Family threatened to leave the Republican Party if Bush chose a pro-choice running mate), of "crisis pregnancy centers," and of Charles Colson. They think least highly of President William Clinton, of the National Organization for Women, and of "the religious left."

Since *World* largely reflects or encourages these predispositions, its coverage tends to the predictable. *"Homosexuals take the offensive,"* a 1999 cover line read. Onward *World* went, marching as to war through 1999 and into 2000: *"A teenage martyr: The funeral of Cassie Bernall." "Battling the cultural menace." "Abortion Speech Police." "An inside look at the scary summer gathering of a fading feminist organization,"* i.e., the National Organization for Women. *"Armey: End Christian bashing." "Texas students fight for pre-game prayers." "Darwinists circle wagons against science teacher."* Some stories are, for the general reader, more arresting, involving as they do people or issues or points of view somewhat outside the general discourse. This is a community of readers to whom a call to counter a "gay activist campaign" against "Dr. Laura" Schlessinger, the Orthodox Jewish talk-show host who referred to homosexuality as a "biological error," can serve as a summons to the barricades, in this case the main gate of Paramount Pictures. This is a community to which a "Pandora's box of controversies" can be opened by the question of whether Christians should continue to buy CDs featuring divorced Christian singers, or "fallen stars." "How credible can evangelicals be in condemning such sins as homosexuality and extramarital sex," *World* asked, "when many seem so tolerant of the sin of divorce?"

Olasky himself is divorced from his first wife. "I've been married since 1976, and in the early 1970s had a brief marriage followed by divorce," is the way he put it in a letter to *The New York Times Magazine* objecting to a piece that suggested he had "hidden his divorce from the press." He met his second wife, Susan, at the University of Michigan, where she was an undergraduate and he a graduate student in the throes of abandoning communism. "When I met him, he was definitely an anti-Communist, but I wouldn't say he was a Christian, at that point," Susan Olasky later told *The Texas Observer.* She said that Whittaker Chambers's *Witness,* which Olasky had recommended that she read, "described where he was then." After their arrival in Austin, Susan Olasky founded the Austin Crisis Pregnancy Center, the purpose for which Olasky believes "God brought about" the move. Charles Colson is also divorced from his first wife, which would not be worth mentioning had he not in summer 2000 called upon Charles Stanley, a fellow Christian broadcaster whose wife had recently divorced him, to resign as pastor of the thirteen-thousand-member First Baptist Church of Atlanta. "Given the already high divorce rate among Baptists," Colson declared (the highest 1998 divorce rates in the United States, according to the U.S. Census Bureau, were, outside Nevada, in the heavily Baptist states of Tennessee, Arkansas, Alabama, and Oklahoma), "the last thing we need to do is to give one of our own leaders a pass, no matter how much we may respect him." What Charles Stanley needed, Colson said, was "a time for personal repentance and healing."

Olasky, having had this time, now seems sufficiently cleansed of the sin of which too many evangelicals are tolerant to write frequently and enthusiastically about marriage, both his own and in general, as well as about the correct relative roles of men and women. "God does not forbid women to be leaders in society, generally speaking," he explained in a 1998 issue of the evangelical *Journal for Biblical Manhood and Womanhood,* "but when that occurs it's usually because of the abdication of men. . . . There's a certain shame attached. Why don't you have a man who's able to step forward?" An entire May 2000 issue of *World* was devoted to marriage and the family, with special emphasis on what remains a lively issue among evangelicals, this "headship and submission" question, which has to do with whether the language in Ephesians 5:22 and 5:23 commanding wives to "be subject" to their husbands "for the husband is the head of the wife as Christ is the head of the church" should be understood strictly or placed in the context of other biblical teachings. In the course of arguing for the latter position and against the extremity of the first ("The Bible advocates neither feminism nor sexual segregation"), Olasky inadvertently opened a window on a view of women not far from that of the Taliban:

> The Bible clearly shows the error both of feminists who claim no differences between men and women, and of sexual segregationists who argue that women are to be concerned "only" with marriage and motherhood. . . . Men go wrong, biblically, by either abdicating or waxing arrogant, either by running from God-given functions or refusing to hear what women have to say. In 1 Samuel 25, Abigail knows that her husband, Nabal, is a fool; when she acts to save her whole household, David tells her, "May you be blessed for your good judgment." I know that my wife often has better judgment than I, and that if I am not to be Nabal Olasky I should listen. And so should we all. Today, some Christian men believe women should be co-leaders in everything. That leaves many men feeling emasculated and many women wishing that guys would step up and make a decision, already. Other Christian men go to the opposite extreme and assert that married women should not even be studying the Bible by themselves or in groups with other women; they should be taught only by their husbands.

3.

The intention that led Olasky to write *The Tragedy of American Compassion* ("I hoped to see welfare transformed, as much as possible, from government monopoly to faith-based diversity") might have well been dismissed as the evangelical impulse of someone operating at a considerable remove from the centrist American political tradition. Yet the book had a certain think-tank imprimatur that caused it to begin percolating through neoconservative circles. *The Tragedy of American Compassion* had been largely written during a year, 1990, that Olasky spent in Washington as a fellow at the Heritage Foundation. The book's central notions bore a reassuring resemblance to arguments already so much a part of the discourse that they had two years before inspired Peggy Noonan to incorporate the "thousand points of light" into the acceptance speech delivered by Governor Bush's father at the 1988 Republican convention. Alfred Regnery, who ultimately published the book, appeared in the acknowledgments, as did Patricia Bozell. Charles Murray, who was at the time writing *The Bell Curve* with Richard J. Herrnstein as a fellow at the American Enterprise Institute, wrote the preface.

The Tragedy of American Compassion was published in 1992, a year when certain key rhetorical assumptions, those having to do with the "moral depredations" of the 1960s and the "moral squalor" of American life since, were already in place. Robert H. Bork, having been sanctified as one of the two living martyrs of the judicial confirmation process, was already handing down the dicta that would shape his 1996 *Slouching Towards Gomorrah: Modern Liberalism and American Decline.* William J. Bennett was about to publish his first book of moral teachings, *The Book of Virtues,* with *The Moral*

Compass and *The Death of Outrage* still in the pipeline. This was a febrile moment, and the characteristically schematic ideas that emerged from it often seemed specifically crafted to support the mood of moral rearmament that was coming to dominate the dialogue. In January 1995, on C-SPAN, Marvin Olasky gave Brian Lamb an instructive precis of the process by which this moment had come to pass: "John Fund of *The Wall Street Journal* read it [*The Tragedy of American Compassion*] and wrote about it and liked it and talked about it with others. Bill Bennett read it and was talking about it. Some other people were, and then it got to the Speaker and he got excited about it and has been talking about it."

"Our models are Alexis de Tocqueville and Marvin Olasky," Newt Gingrich had just told the nation in his first 1995 address as Speaker of the House, apparently having already incorporated into his program the Christmas present William J. Bennett had given him a few weeks before. The "most important book on welfare and social policy in a decade," Bennett himself said about Olasky's book. Three years after the largely unnoticed initial publication of *The Tragedy of American Compassion,* then, its reductive and rather spookily utilitarian thesis, that the government should fund the faithful because faith "works," had become the idea whose time had come, the ultimate weapon in the "values" wars, a super stealth missile with first-strike capability, precisely aimed to simultaneously get welfare out of the system and get religion into it.

By his own account, Olasky wrote the book after comparing the evangelism of nineteenth-century philanthropy to secular welfare efforts, which he believed to be rendered useless by their lack of emphasis on personal responsibility. This belief was confirmed, he wrote, by taking "a first-hand look at contemporary compassion toward the poor" during two days he spent disguised as a beggar in order to visit Washington soup kitchens: "I put on three used T-shirts and two dirty sweaters, equipped myself with a stocking cap and a plastic bag, removed my wedding ring, got lots of dirt on my hands, and walked with the slow shuffle that characterizes the forty-year-old white homeless male of the streets." During his two days (no nights) as a street person, he was offered, he reported (and here we reach the germ of the experiment), "lots of food, lots of pills of various kinds, and lots of offers of clothing and shelter," but never a Bible.

There could never have been much doubt that the parable of the white homeless male in search of a Bible would resonate with George W. Bush. This was a man who not only grew up in Texas and did business in Texas but managed a Texas sports franchise, pretty much rendering him a market-maker in the secular God business. This was a man who, in the course of a primary-season debate, would famously name Jesus Christ as the "political philosopher" he most admires. This was a man who, when the Texas economy went belly-up in the mid-1980s, joined a group of Midland businessmen who met once a week under the guidance of a national group called Community Bible Study, the class format of which includes the twelve-step technique of personal testimony, in this case "seeing the truths of the Bible lived out in the lives of leaders and class members." The participants in Bush's class were "baby boomers, men with young families," a former member told Hanna Rosin of *The Washington Post*. "And we suddenly found ourselves in free fall. So we began to search for an explanation. Maybe we had been too involved with money. Maybe we needed to look inwardly and find new meaning in life."

It was 1993 when Marvin Olasky was first called to meet with Bush, who was at the time shopping for issues with which to defeat the incumbent governor of Texas, Ann Richards. Olasky and Bush, along with Bush adviser Karl Rove, talked for an hour, during which, according to Olasky, Bush "asked questions that went to the heart of issues involving children born out of wedlock and men slowly dying from drug abuse on the streets." Bush did not have occasion to call again on Olasky until 1995, when, as governor, he saw the political potential in taking up the side of a Christian drug program called Teen Challenge, which state regulators had tried to shut down because it refused to comply with certain state regulations, including one that required drug counselors to be trained in conventional anti-addiction techniques. (Conventional anti-addiction techniques in this country are largely based on the twelve-step regime, which carefully refers to an unspecified "Higher Power," or "God as we understand Him." The anti-addiction technique of choice at Teen Challenge was, in the words of its executive director, "Jesus Christ.") Over his next few years as governor, Bush not only made Texas the first state to sanction the redirection of state funds into faith-based programs but virtually dismantled state regulation of such programs, accruing, in the course of this pioneering endeavor, considerable political capital from the religious right. "An opportunity arose for a far-sighted governor to take the lead" is how Olasky describes this. "George W. Bush was a natural, both because of his father's earlier interest in the 'thousand points of light' and his own personal, faith-based change in 1986 from heavy drinking at times to abstinence from alcohol."

Olasky was never a full-time Bush adviser, yet his involvement would seem to have been something more than "maybe they met once or twice," the version preferred by those Bush aides made nervous by the enthusiasm with which Olasky airs his less marketable positions, on the role of women, say, or on the necessity of conversion. T. Christian Miller of *The New York Times,* reporting in July 2000 on the campaign's "pattern of distancing Bush from the controversies that have dogged Olasky," quoted a Bush spokesman saying that the two had met only twice, once in 1996 and once in 1999, although the 1993 and 1995 meetings have been extensively documented. "Marvin is an evangelical Christian, and Bush is an evangelical Christian," John J. DiIulio Jr., a Bush adviser, told David Grann by way of suggesting the philosophical distance. "But Bush does not believe that every faith-based program is about religious conversion."

Olasky does believe this, and, on the basis of what Governor Bush himself has said, it would be hard to argue that Bush did not at some level, however unexamined, agree. "When asked why some faith-based groups succeed where secular organizations fail," Olasky wrote of Bush, "he praised programs that help to 'change the person's heart.'" "A person with a changed heart," Olasky quotes Bush as having told him, "is less likely to be addicted to drugs and alcohol. . . . I've had some personal experience with this. As has been reported, I quit drinking. The main reason I quit was because I accepted Jesus Christ into my life in 1986." To accept Jesus Christ as personal savior is pretty much the heart and soul of evangelical conversion (or of being "born again," which both Governor Bush and Vice President Gore claim to be), and incurs the obligation, for evangelical Christians who want to be saved, of converting others, which is to say, in Bush's words, changing the person's heart. The evangelical obligation to convert, the biblical basis for which is Matthew 28:19 ("Go therefore and make disciples of all nations, baptizing them in the name of the Father and of the Son and of the Holy Spirit"), rests on the belief that Bush notoriously expressed to a reporter for the

Austin American-Statesman in 1993, that those who do not believe in Christ will go to hell. "Bush was giving the orthodox biblical answer," Marvin Olasky later explained to *Salon* on this point. "On the face of it, you have to believe in Christ to go to heaven; Jews don't believe in Christ; therefore, Jews don't go to heaven. So of course there was an uproar."

Olasky was made the head of Bush's policy subcommittee on religion in February 1999, after the two met for a four-hour session during which they and Bush aides hammered out policy with John J. DiIulio Jr., James Q. Wilson, and Robert L. Woodson Sr., the founder of the National Center for Neighborhood Enterprise and one of the people Olasky cites as a formative influence. In an October 1999 *World* column urging conservative Christians not to abandon the political process, Olasky himself described his role as "trying to walk the above talk by giving informal advice to one of the contenders for the G.O.P. nomination," a circumstance that had led him, he explained, to recuse himself from editing *World*'s campaign coverage. By the end of March 2000, however, in the wake of a small media storm over a column he had written for the *Austin American-Statesman* accusing three political commentators who happened to be Jews (David Brooks, William Kristol, and Frank Rich) of favoring John McCain because he lacked Bush's "Christian albatross" and so afforded them "a post-Clinton glow without pushing them to confront their own lives," Olasky downgraded his involvement to "my very minor Bush advising role last year" and declared that, since this involvement was no longer an issue and since Christian conservatives would "clearly favor the Bush position," he was now free to comment on the campaign.

However casually or occasionally delivered, Olasky's message demonstrably locked into certain of the candidate's established preferences, notably those for spinning off the government to the private sector and for taking a firm line with its less productive citizens. "Marvin offers not just a blueprint for government," Bush declared in the foreword he provided for *Compassionate Conservatism,* "but also an inspiring picture of the great resources of decency, caring, and commitment to one another that Americans share." Just how closely Olasky's "blueprint for government" would be followed was made clear on July 22, 1999, when Bush delivered, in Indianapolis, the speech that Olasky describes as the culmination of a process that began with the four-hour February meeting. "First, the ivy cabinet of policy conceptualizers came up with ideas and proposals," he wrote. "Second, Bush's kitchen cabinet of Austin advisers reviewed the proposals and tried to meld them. Third, Governor Bush decided which ones to run with and which to table."

"In every instance where my administration sees a responsibility to help people," Bush promised that day in Indianapolis, "we will look first to faith-based organizations, charities, and community groups that have shown their ability to save and change lives. . . . We will change the laws and regulations that hamper the cooperation of government and private institutions." The stories told that day as illustration of this "ability to save and change lives" now seem familiar, not only because they were so often repeated during the campaign but because they are identical in tone and venue to those told by Marvin Olasky. Bush for example cited the case in Texas of "a young man named James Peterson, who'd embezzled his way into a prison term" and who, as the time approached for his parole hearing, joined InnerChange, the faith-based program through which Olasky and Daniel met the similarly converted "Donnie Gilmore." Offered parole, "James" turned it down, electing to stay in prison "to finish the InnerChange course," a version of whatever happened that Bush seemed both to believe and to construe as a happy ending. "As James put it, 'There is nothing I want more than to be back in the outside world with my daughter Lucy, [but] I realized that this was an opportunity to become a living [witness] for my brothers [in prison] and to the world. I want to stay in prison to complete the transformation [God] has begun in me.' "

Among those present that day in Indianapolis were political reporters from America's three major newspapers, Adam Clymer for *The New York Times,* Terry M. Neal for *The Washington Post,* and Ronald Brownstein from *The Los Angeles Times.* "First major policy speech," their stories would read the next morning. "Most elaborate definition to date of his 'compassionate conservatism' credo." They would have heard the candidate say that federal money should be "devolved," not just to states but to "charities and neighborhood healers." They would have heard the candidate promise that his administration would expand the "role and reach" of such organizations "without changing them or corrupting them": a significant victory for Olasky, since the phrase would open the door to what he calls "theological conservatives," i.e., those whose aim is conversion. They would have heard the candidate, by way of forestalling any possible concern that an "unchanged" (or "uncorrupted") "neighborhood healer" might render "faith" the ultimate means test, offer the by now familiar but empirically ambiguous utilitarian argument. "It works," the candidate had said, and then: "Sometimes our greatest hope is not found in reform. It is found in redemption." That a mainstream American political candidate should make these remarkable statements might have seemed worth reporting, but did not: talk of "redemption" as a political platform had by July 1999 become sufficiently commonplace that neither the word "redemption" nor the words "without changing them or corrupting them" appeared the next day in any of the three major papers.

4.

Jeff Flock, CNN Correspondent: Well, Kyra, we've got our ear to the ground here in Wisconsin, this is Port

Washington, north of Milwaukee, as you point out. We are inside the Allen-Edmonds shoe manufacturing plant . . . trying to get a sense [from] undecided voters if they made up their mind based on what they saw yesterday. . . . First of all is . . . the COO of Allen-Edmonds, I have got to ask you, you're on the fence. Have you made up your mind as a result of what you saw last night?

Unidentified Male: Well, I'm still undecided . . .

Flock: Now you tend to the Republican and vote Republican, but at this point, you are still undecided. Al Gore could get your vote.

Unidentified Male: Possibly, yes. . . . Certainly I'm going to listen to the next two debates, and I think not only are the issues important, but also the sincerity of the candidates. . . . Just a whole lot of honesty needs to be brought back into the candidacy.

— CNN *Early Edition,* OCTOBER 4, 2000

This question of the "undecided," or "swing," voter, about whom we have heard so much in recent elections, is interesting. "Scientific" political forecasting, that done not by professional pollsters but by a handful of political scientists around the country, for some months prior to the November 2000 election showed Vice President Gore the probable winner. In May 2000, when Robert G. Kaiser of *The Washington Post* reported on this academic forecasting, the only disagreement among the political scientists to whom he spoke had to do with the point spread by which Gore would win. Thomas M. Holbrook of the University of Wisconsin at Milwaukee gave Gore 59.6 percent, Christopher Wlezien of the University of Houston 56.1 percent, Alan I. Abramowitz of Emory University 53 or 54 percent, and Michael Lewis-Beck of the University of Iowa 56.2 percent. By the end of August 2000, when seven of these academic forecasters (including Robert S. Erickson of Columbia University, James E. Campbell of the University of Buffalo, and Helmut Norpoth of the State University of New York at Stony Brook) presented their forecasts at the annual meeting of the American Political Science Association in Washington, six of the seven had somewhat narrowed but not significantly changed the Gore lead, their August forecasts ranging from a 52.3 to a 55.4 Gore victory. The seventh, Holbrook, citing the record number of Americans who reported themselves satisfied with their personal financial situation, had slightly increased the Gore lead, to 60.3 percent.

This kind of forecasting, which was based on analyzing mathematical models of the thirteen presidential elections since 1948 and of the state of the economy (both actual and perceived) during each of these elections, had in the past proved remarkably accurate. Wlezien's early forecasts were accurate within six-tenths of one percent in 1988 and one-tenth of one percent in 1996. Lewis-Beck's early call on the 1996 election (in collaboration with Charles Tien of Hunter College) was, according to *The Washington Post,* not only closer to the ultimate result than polls conducted immediately before the election (Lewis-Beck and Tien gave Clinton 54.8 percent, the eventual recorded result was 54.7) but also closer, by almost three percentage points, than exit polls conducted while the election was actually in progress. "The outcome of a presidential election can be accurately predicted based on factors that are known well before the official campaign gets underway," Abramowitz told the *Post.* "Despite the time, effort and money devoted to campaigning, there is very little that the candidates can do during September and October to alter the eventual outcome of a presidential election."

Political reporters and operatives are nonetheless dismissive of this academic forecasting, since the models on which it is based, focusing as they do on economic indicators, relentlessly exclude the questions of personality or "positioning" that are seen as key to the "undecided" vote and so dominate discussion of presidential elections. The models largely discount the number of "undecided" answers that are elicited by polling, since, as James E. Campbell noted in *Before the Vote: Forecasting American National Elections,* "the 'socially desirable' answer . . . may be a late decision, both out of a sense of open-mindedness and because one may appear more deliberative in obtaining all possible information about the candidate before deciding how to vote." "Character," on which many polls seem to turn, plays no role in these projections. "Values," although much discussed in focus groups, go unmentioned.

Adam Clymer, covering the Washington meeting of the American Political Science Association for *The New York Times,* characterized the forecasters as "seven visitors [i.e., not Washington insiders] seeking to impose a precision and predictability on political life that even those working in its midst [i.e., the insiders the "visitors" will never be] cannot discern." At a time when conventional polling showed Bush running ahead of Gore by double digits, the Bush pollster Fred Steeper told *The Washington Post* that the academic models would necessarily prove wrong, since none factored in the opinion of voters on the question to which the professionals were at that time giving full focus, that of the country's presumed "decline in moral values."

Steeper said this in May 2000. The kind of polling or focus research that elicits opinions about "moral values" (where the "socially desirable" answer is even more clear than in preference polls) would have been, in May, not much more effective at projecting a November outcome than asking a ouija board. Until the final weeks of a presidential campaign, conventional opinion research has been notoriously unreliable. In May 1988, a not atypical *New York Times*/CBS News poll showed Dukakis leading Vice President Bush by ten points. In June 1992, the Field Institute showed Perot and by then President Bush dividing the bulk of the electoral vote, with Clinton "getting so few that he is currently not a factor." To the professionals of the political process, this indicates not an ambiguity in the research but an exciting volatility, the "horse race" construct, in which the election is seen to turn on the skill or lack of skill with which the candidates and their handlers "send signals," or deploy counters derived from the research.

Governor George W. Bush's acceptance speech at the 2000 Republican convention in Philadelphia was a string of such notational counters, each on the face of it deeply meaningless ("When I act, you will know my reasons. . . . When I speak, you will know my heart") but among which could be embedded such signals as "valuing the life of the unborn," or "We must renew our *values* to restore our *country.*" Bush, it was immediately agreed, had sent the right signals, had at once positioned himself to seem, as they were saying on NBC while the confetti was still falling, "a very simple guy—loves his ranch, loves his family" and "also presidential." This instant positive judgment was entirely predictable, a phenomenon that occurs on the last night of every convention, but it was nonetheless seen, by those who made it and by those whose business it was to calibrate it, to significantly change the dynamic of the election. "My view of this process has totally changed," Robert Teeter, the longtime Republican pollster, told *The Washington Post* after the similarly predictable instant positive judgment on the naming of Richard Cheney (Cheney, it was said on CNN, was "one of the governing class") as Governor Bush's running mate. "You used to look for twenty-eight electoral votes or some demographic bloc. Now, the crucial question is how the press and public react in the first forty-eight hours."

That the press and the public might ultimately react in sharply divergent ways seemed not to enter Teeter's analysis, yet we had just lived through a period, that of the events leading up to and following impeachment, during which no political commentator in America failed to express bafflement at the mystery of what was called "the disconnect," which is to say the divergence between what the press thought and what the public thought about President Clinton. "It is impossible to overstate the extent to which the political community felt betrayed by the president and convinced that he would be forced from office," Thomas E. Mann of the Brookings Institution wrote in *Newsday* immediately after the November 1998 congressional elections, the occasion on which the prevailing view of the political community got put to a vote and lost. Mann continued:

> The public, on the other hand, while morally offended by the president's misbehavior and skeptical of the content of his character, has been steadfast in its belief that Clinton's personal failings did not compromise his ability to function successfully as chief executive. Each new public revelation of titillating details served mainly to reinforce their view that the effort to force the president from office was both unwise and, at least in part, politically motivated. This gap between Washington

and public opinion had to close before the president's future could be resolved. Now that the election returns are in, we know how that gap will close. The message from the election is crystal-clear: The Washington community will have to accommodate itself to the views of the country.

In April 1999, two months after the Senate tried and acquitted President Clinton on the articles of impeachment brought by the House and three months before Governor George W. Bush would launch his redemption platform in Indianapolis, I happened to hear several prominent Democratic and Republican pollsters and strategists agree that the 2000 election would necessarily turn, in the absence of hard times, on "values." That these specialists in opinion research were hearing a certain number of Americans express concern about their own future and about the future of America seemed clear. What seemed less clear was the source of this concern, or what inchoate insecurity or nostalgia is actually being voiced when respondents address such questions as whether they fear that "this society will become too accepting of behaviors that are bad for people," say, or believe that "a president should set a moral tone for the country."

On the latter point, a 1998 poll conducted by *The Washington Post* in conjunction with Harvard University and the Kaiser Foundation found that fifty percent of those queried did believe the president should set a moral tone and forty-eight percent did not, a statistically insignificant difference but one cited in a later *Post* story bearing the headline "Polls Suggest Public Seeks Moral Leadership in Wake of White House Scandal." When Americans told researchers that they worried about the future of their family or the country, say, or that they did not believe their fellow citizens to be "as honest or moral as they used to be," what they were actually expressing, according to the *Post,* was their "yearning for a moral compass and virtuous leadership," a notion that tallied with what the nation's opinion leaders had been wishing they yearned for all year. Almost a year before the New Hampshire primary, then, the shape the campaign would take had already been settled upon, and it was not a shape that would require the Washington community to accommodate itself to the views of the country: what was concerning Americans, it had been decided, was the shame they had to date failed to recognize.

5.

More than two-thirds of Americans polled by *The Los Angeles Times* in February 1999, immediately after President Clinton was tried and acquitted by the Senate, said that his misconduct had not caused them to lose respect for the office of the presidency. Sixty-eight percent said that they did not want the issue raised in the 2000 presidential campaign. More than three in five said that Republicans pursued impeachment "primarily because they wanted to hurt President Clinton politically." Only one-third, or a number approximately the size of the Republican base, said that Republicans were motivated by concern about the effect of "Clinton's actions on the legal and moral fabric of the country."

The notional conviction that most Americans felt "revulsion" toward the Clinton administration, and the collateral conviction that this was damaging the Gore candidacy, nonetheless remained general, and, as became clear with the addition of Senator Joseph I. Lieberman to the Democratic ticket, would come to warp Gore's own conduct of his campaign. "The fundamentals are in Gore's favor," the political analyst Allan J. Lichtman acknowledged to *The New York Times* in September 2000. "Peace, prosperity, tranquility at home and a united incumbent party. Why has the race even been close? The Clinton scandals." A Republican pollster, Ed Goeas, suggested that Gore was suffering "the after-effect of impeachment. Voters didn't want Republicans to impeach Clinton because they thought it would rock the boat. Now that that is no longer an issue, they are indulging in a second emotion—they didn't want Clinton impeached, but they think what he did was wrong."

The choice of Senator Lieberman was widely construed as Gore's way of transcending this presumed public sentiment, of "sending a message" to the electorate. The actual message that got sent, however, was not to the electorate but to its political class—to that narrow group of those who wrote and spoke and remained fixed in the belief that "the Clinton scandals" constituted a weight that must be shed. Senator Lieberman, who had previously come to the nation's attention as the hedge player who had briefly seized center stage by managing both to denounce the president for "disgraceful" and "immoral" behavior and to vote against his conviction (similarly, he had in 1991 both voiced support for and voted against the confirmation of Clarence Thomas), was not, except to the press, an immediately engaging personality. There were, in those first wobbly steps as a vice-presidential candidate, the frequent references to "private moments of prayer" and to the "miracle" of his nomination. There were the insistent reminders of his own filial devotion, as displayed to the nation during his "only in America moment" at the Democratic convention: "Mom, thank you, I love you and you and I know how proud Pop would be tonight. Yes we do love you, Mom." There was the unsettling way in which he seemed to patronize his running mate, as if insensitive to the possibility that his unsolicited testimonials to Gore's character ("This is a man of courage! He showed it by picking me to be with him!") could suggest that it would otherwise be seen as doubtful.

His speech patterns, grounded as they were in the burden he bore for the rest of us and the personal rewards he had received from God for bearing it, tended to self-congratulation. In his *In Praise of Public Life,* a modest work in which he peculiarly defends his career as a professional politician, he noted that he must "endure the disdain" of those who distrust politicians, that he risks being "sullied by the fight for election," that winning the fight means only stepping "into yet another arena that has turned uglier than before." After his 1988 election to the Senate, he girded himself for the arena that had turned uglier than before by making "private visits to three religious leaders who meant a lot to me, to ask them for their prayers as I began this new chapter of my life." The religious leaders on whom he chose to call, already exhibiting his preference for hedge betting, were the Catholic archbishop of Hartford, an evangelical Protestant minister in Milford, and the Lubavitch rabbi Menachem Schneerson in Brooklyn.

There was, the reader of *In Praise of Public Life* learns, "no single reason" for the failure after sixteen years of his first marriage, and yet he does give reasons, each of which redounds to his credit. The president may have committed "disgraceful" and "immoral" acts, but Senator Lieberman had not, and the suggestion on a call-in radio show that he might have so upset his ex-wife that she had immediately called the show to say that "she knew I had never committed adultery." There had been instead "the fact that I had become much more religiously observant than I was when we met and married." There had been "the demands my political career put on our private life. That is surely one of the great costs and risks of public life."

There were, in the aftermath of Gore's decision to name Lieberman, many dispiriting reiterations of the benefit that would accrue. "Integrity on the Ticket" was the headline on the *Washington Post*'s lead editorial on the morning after the announcement. "A Gore-Lieberman ticket is not going to be associated with bad behavior," Al From of the Democratic Leadership Council told *The New York Times,* which obtained a similar encomium (to the "credibility" that "Mr. Lieberman brings to everything he touches") from the Reverend Jerry Falwell. Senator Lieberman, it was repeatedly said, gave the ticket "moral authority," the most frequently cited source for which was his having "fearlessly spoken out" or "fearlessly acted on his beliefs" to denounce both Clinton and popular culture. Hollywood, he had asserted, "doesn't understand piety." Although Hollywood, like Clinton at the time of his impeachment, might be considered something less than a moving target, there had been a further "fearless" aspect to Lieberman's crusade: just as he had teamed with Lynne Cheney to denounce "political correctness" (another fairly lethargic target), he had teamed with William J. Bennett to decry "the rising tide of sex and violence in our popular culture." This showed, it was said, Lieberman's "independence," his ability to "follow his conscience," which as presented came to seem a kind of golden retriever bounding ever to the right, determined to outrun his master and his ninety-five percent A.D.A. rating. "On issues that cut very close to the bone," Bennett explained to E. J. Dionne Jr., "he's there."

The rather histrionic humility with which Senator Lieberman accepted this nonpartisan admiration served only to further encourage those who wrote and spoke and offered opinions. "In the choice of a single man," Richard Cohen wrote on the *Washington Post's* op-ed page, ". . . Gore shows he is comfortable with a running mate who was uncomfortable with Clinton's behavior." David Broder mentioned "the moral character he adds. . . . Lieberman embodies and defines the standards by which politicians should be judged." George Will spoke of the "unfeigned revulsion" with which Lieberman had denounced Clinton, and of the way in which that unfeigned revulsion could address "the national longing" to be rid of this president. To the same point, the editorial page of *The New York Times* saw the choice of Lieberman as "a signal that this ticket was moving beyond Mr. Clinton's behavioral—as opposed to his policy—legacy. Mr. Lieberman's authority in this regard derives from his moral bearing, embodied in his criticism of Mr. Clinton's conduct two years ago." Nor was this enthusiasm confined to the editorial and op-ed pages: on page 1 of a single issue, the *Times,* in its own reportorial voice, certified Mr. Lieberman's "moral rectitude," his "seriousness of purpose," his "integrity." He was "untainted." He was "regarded as one of the most upstanding public officials in the nation." He was a "moral compass in the wastelands of politics."

That the ticket would otherwise woefully lack this moral compass, and unless shriven by Senator Lieberman would reap the whirlwind of the assumed national yearning to punish Clinton, was accepted as given, since, for those who wrote and spoke and offered opinions, the furies and yearnings of the nation were necessarily indivisible from the furies and yearnings of its political class. The possibility that the yearnings of the nation might instead be expressed by the occasional actual citizen who managed to penetrate the cloud cover of the coverage seemed not to occur. On the morning of September 4, 2000, in a news-analysis piece headline "Still Riding Wave, a Confident Gore Heads to Florida for Fall Push," Katharine G. Seelye of the *Times,* flying safely within the cloud cover, reminded readers of what was according to the story line the campaign's "central concern": that "while voters appreciate the good times, there is lingering resentment toward Mr. Clinton over his personal behavior, creating a complex web of emotions that still seems to ensnare Mr. Gore." This story appeared on page A14. Also on page A14, the same morning, in a report on a Gore-Lieberman event at a construction site in downtown Philadelphia, Richard Perez-Pena of the *Times* quoted a twenty-one-year-old electrician whom he had interviewed on the site. "Clinton did a real good job with the economy, and Gore was his V.P.," this actual citizen was reported to have said, "so he's the next best thing to Clinton if we can't have Clinton."

6.

Well, there's nothing wrong with candidates indicating what their faith [or] belief is. It's something else when they begin to put it into the public arena in terms of politics. And then what it starts becoming, as we've heard, Governor Bush this week talked about America being God's country. God created it. . . . Vice-Presidential candidate Cheney talked about [how] tolerance in this country should be the way Jesus Christ taught it. Now, that sounds like preaching from a pulpit. What's starting to happen is campaigning and candidates are beginning to outdo each other as [to] how godly they are and how much God has a part in their life. . . . All of a sudden, this new emphasis on faith and religion in—in—in a campaign that should deal with issues may move us off that experience of two hundred years.

—ABRAHAM H. FOXMAN, ON *This Week*, SUNDAY, SEPTEMBER 3, 2000

Bill Clinton lowballed it to the White House with his yeomen telling themselves that "It's the economy, stupid," but the winning party has generally been the one that could claim the high moral ground. That's why Joe Lieberman's talk of God, which helps voters forget Bill Clinton's ungodly activity, has been so fruitful for Al Gore.

—MARVIN OLASKY, IN *World*, SEPTEMBER 23, 2000

This was an election in which there were running for president and vice president on the Democratic ticket two professional politicians, one of whom was born to the game and the other of whom said that he was inspired to play it by the "figures of respect" already on the field, beginning with "the succession of dignified, personable mayors who ran Stamford." There was running for president on the Republican ticket someone whose most successful previous venture was based on his questionable readiness to accept, in the first year of his own father's presidency, a sweetheart ten percent "general partner interest" (aka "promote fee") in the 1989 purchase of the Texas Rangers by a consortium of investors, an $86 million deal in which the candidate's personal investment was only $606,000. There was running for vice president on the Republican ticket someone who had parlayed his Gulf War credits in the Middle East into a $45.5 million stake in Halliburton, and who thought the thing to say when asked why he did not vote in the 2000 presidential primary in Texas (or for that matter in fourteen of the sixteen elections held while he was a resident of Dallas County) was that he had been focused on "global concerns," just as he had been focused on "other priorities" during the Vietnam years he spent failing to get a doctorate at the University of Wisconsin instead of getting drafted.

The grounds on which any one of the four could be construed as a candidate for the "high moral ground" remain obscure, yet their respective claims to this phantom venue, with Governor Bush and Senator Lieberman on point but Vice President Gore and Mr. Cheney not far behind, had come to dominate the campaign. Each had testified to the centrality of "faith" in his life and in that of the nation. Each had declared his intention to install "faith-based organizations" (by this point so obligatory a part of policy discussions that they were referred to by acronym, "FBOs") in the front lines of what had previously been the nation's social support system. "The Constitution guarantees freedom *of* religion, not freedom *from* religion," one or another of them could rather too frequently be heard saying, appropriating as new a line already familiar during the 1950s debate over adding the clause "under God" to the Pledge of Allegiance. ("It's not constitutional, so don't say it," I recall my grandfather instructing me to that point.) "I believe that faith in itself is sometimes essential to spark a personal transformation," Vice President Gore was already saying in May 1999 in Atlanta. By August 2000, Senator Lieberman was saying in Detroit that America was "moving to a new spiritual awakening," requiring only that we its people "reaffirm our faith and renew the dedication of our nation and ourselves to God and God's purpose."

There is a level at which many Americans simply discount what is said during a political campaign, dismiss it as loose talk. When Senator Lieberman tells us "never to indulge the supposition that morality can be maintained without religion," or when Governor Bush says "our nation is chosen by God," or when Vice President Gore talks about What Would Jesus Do or Mr. Cheney appears on a platform in Kansas City with a succession of athletes attesting to the personal role played in their lives by Jesus Christ and the Gospels, what gets said is often understood as no more than a tactical signal, a "message" sent to a certain constituency, a single fleeting moment in a moving campaign; a marker in a game with no causal connection to policy or legislation as it will actually evolve. Evangelical Christians, a spokesman for the National Association of Evangelicals told *The New York Times* in a discussion of Senator Lieberman's religiosity, "are very happy with everything the senator's been saying." They may well have been, and were meant to be, yet the senator had supported neither of two causes, authorization of student-led prayer or the mandatory posting of the Ten Commandments, recently of urgent interest to the evangelical community. Nor, despite what he has called in reference to abortion his "growing personal anxiety that something very wrong is happening in our country," had his votes on abortion legislation, a crucial evangelical concern, been other than generally pro-choice.

The expressed "personal anxiety that something very wrong is happening in our country," then, was exclusively rhetorical, or loose talk. As such, it could be set aside, understood as a nod to those "pro-family" or "values" voters who, although a minority, have been increasingly encouraged, by the way in which both parties have deliberately narrowed campaign dialogue to issues that concern those voters, to decide our elections. There is considerable evidence that this narrowing, which tends to alienate younger voters, has already had a deleterious effect on the electoral process. In the 1996 presidential election, the president of the ACLU Foundation of Southern California pointed out in *The Los Angeles Times,* the number of voters aged eighteen to twenty-one dropped from thirty-eight to thirty-one percent and the number of those aged twenty-one to twenty-four dropped from forty-five to thirty-three percent. In the 1998 congressional elections, the turnout in these age groups was less than seventeen percent, roughly half that of older voters. The competitive pieties of the 2000 campaign are not calibrated to reverse this estrangement of the young: in *What's God Got to Do with the American Experiment?,* a collection of studies and essays compiled under the auspices of the Brookings Institution, Richard N. Ostling noted that members of the generation now approaching voting age, to a greater extent than members of any previous generation, are "thoroughly detached from traditional Christian concepts . . . do not believe Jesus is the unique savior of mankind, do not read the Bible as God's word, and do not accept the idea of moral absolutes."

The September Sunday morning on which Abraham H. Foxman suggested to Cokie Roberts and the Reverend Pat Robertson that an excessive campaign emphasis on faith could "move us off that experience of two hundred years" ("So there's a tiny, tiny minority who consider themselves atheist," Pat Robertson said, "and you can't surrender the deeply held religious beliefs of the entire majority to please some tiny minority") followed several days of op-ed and talk-show debate prompted by the letter, making the same point, that Mr. Foxman had sent to Senator Lieberman after the latter's "new spiritual awakening" event in Detroit. In the course of this debate, the appropriate role of religion in American life had been discussed at some length. It had been widely agreed that the establishment clause of the First Amendment had been, to the extent that it had ensured the disestablishment of the Anglican or Episcopal Church, a good idea. It had also been widely agreed that the aim of the Founders had been not "atheism" (the straw man from the Scopes trial curiously back among us) but "diversity of faith." There had been areas of disagreement, hotly argued but narrow. Some held that one's faith was best practiced in private, others that faith practiced in private was no faith at all; a difference, as differences go, not entirely unlike the 1844 Philadelphia riot in which six people were killed over the issue of which version of the Ten Commandments should be posted in public schools.

Yet virtually all of the many positions and postures taken in this debate rested on a single and largely unchallenged assumption, that religion, whether public or private, was at the heart of the American experience, and that the "experience of two hundred years" to which Mr. Foxman referred had been in fact a record of serial awakenings, the eventual rightful end of which, once the obstructive element increasingly referred to as "the ACLU" had been shown the light, would be what both presidential candidates were now calling the "personal transformation" of the nation's citizens. "I need my civil liberties friends to tell me again the mortal danger of prayer—of religion generally—in public places," William Raspberry wrote in *The Washington Post.* "I keep forgetting it." "Separation between church and state never meant that religion had no place in American life," E. J. Dionne Jr. wrote in the *Post.* "Remember, this is a nation that still stamps 'In God We Trust' on its currency." The fact that the words "In God We Trust" were added to American currency during the same recent period and for the same political reason that the words "under God" were added to the Pledge of Allegiance, home-front ammunition in the Eisenhower administration's cold war arsenal, had vanished (like the fact that the number of Americans who belonged to churches during the American Revolution constituted only seventeen percent of the population) from the collective memory stream. "I confess," Dionne also wrote, "I love what Joe Lieberman is doing to our national debate about religion and public life:"

> Lieberman is not the first politician to say how important faith is to our democracy. President Dwight Eisenhower offered the nation this

> notable sentiment: "Our government makes no sense unless it is founded on a deeply felt religious belief—and I don't care what it is." Today's discussion about religion and politics is much more serious than it was in the "I don't care what it is" past memorialized by Eisenhower. That's what makes so many people uncomfortable.

This was a meaningful shift in the national political dialogue. Politics, it had been until recently understood, is push and pull, give and take, the art of the possible, an essentially pragmatic process by which the differing needs and rights of the nation's citizens get balanced and to some degree met. The insertion into this process of a claim to faith, or to "the high moral ground," it also had been until recently understood, is perilous, permissible if at all only at moments of such urgent gravity as to warrant its inherent danger, which is that the needs and rights of some citizens might be overridden to accommodate the needs and rights of those holding the high ground. This was not such a moment in American life. The nation was not at war. A majority of its citizens seemed to understand that the demonstration of "full remorse" recently demanded of its president would prove less personally meaningful to their families than the skill or lack of skill with which he guided them through the rapids of the global economy.

The possible "legacy" of that president was popularly discussed in negative terms, as the redeeming grail he had hoped for and lost, but on any reasonable scale his legacy was already sizable: the country he would hand over to either Governor Bush or Vice President Gore was one in which median household income had reached an all-time high, the unemployment rate was at its lowest point in three decades, the rate of violent crime was down, and the digital national-debt clock in Manhattan was running, until its creator allowed that the device had outlived its effectiveness and stopped it, backward. It had been Clinton's "legacy," in short, to create the very conditions that had early on led the academic forecasters to call a presidential victory by the incumbent party the most probable outcome of the November 2000 election.

Yet so thin was the air on the high moral ground that none of this was seen as relevant, not even by the candidate who might have seemed poised to benefit from it. What had been for the past several decades the origin myth of the neoconservative right had become, in part because it so uniquely filled the need of the political class to explain its own estrangement from the electorate, the official story, shared by all participants in the process: America, in this apocalyptic telling, had been from its inception until the 1960s a deeply religious nation. During the 1960s, through the efforts of what Robert H. Bork called "the 'intellectual' class and that class's enforcement arm, the judiciary, headed by the Supreme Court of the United States," the nation and its citizens had been inexplicably and destructively "secularized," and were accordingly in need of "transformation," of "moral and intellectual rearmament," of "renewed respect for moral authority." In a country already so increasingly steeped in evangelical teaching that a significant number of its citizens had come to believe that "God created man pretty much in his present form at one time within the last ten thousand years" (forty-seven percent of Americans surveyed by Gallup in 1991 said they believed in such a fell swoop, or "recent special creation"), those who wrote and spoke were arguing about how the nation's political system could best revive those religious values allegedly destroyed (in an interestingly similar fell swoop) during the 1960s.

The delusionary notion that such a revival was now in progress, and would soon prove the correctness of the political class on the Clinton issue, is what lent the 2000 campaign its peculiar, and for the Democratic candidate its dangerous, distance from the electorate. President Clinton may have "escaped conviction," Marvin Olasky wrote in the preface to the most recent edition of *The American Leadership Tradition,* but was nonetheless "convicted in the court of public opinion." The electorate, he wrote, would no longer accept "an anything-goes moral vision." Accordingly, the 2000 election was one in which "the populace seemed to want the next president to be someone who would not disgrace the Oval Office, and that desire gave hope to those who want to revive a tradition of moral leadership."

The logic here, and it was the same logic that surfaced in response to the Lieberman nomination, was that of the origin myth, in which "the populace," once warned, could yet cast out its wicked allegiance to its disgraced leader and be saved before the final Rapture. This fable had been adjusted and trimmed with each retelling, yet one element, the disgraced leader, remained fixed, the rock on which the Bush campaign might have foundered early had the Gore campaign itself, in search of the chimerical "undecided" voter, not rushed to enter the fable's fatal eddy. The distinct possibility that an entire generation of younger voters might see no point in choosing between two candidates retelling the same remote story could benefit only one campaign, the Republican, and the failure of the Democratic campaign to recognize this could yet neutralize the advantage of the legacy it has worked so assiduously to disavow.

ALSO BY JOAN DIDION

AFTER HENRY

In this foray into the American cultural scene, Joan Didion covers ground from Washington to Los Angeles, from a TV producer's gargantuan "manor" to the racial battlefields of New York's criminal courts. A bracing amalgam of skepticism and sympathy, *After Henry* is proof of Didion's infallible radar for the true spirit of our age.

Current Affairs/Literature/0-679-74539-4

MIAMI

It is where Fidel Castro raised money to overthrow Batista and where Castro's enemies have raised armies to overthrow *him*, so far without success. It is where Cuban exile intersects with the cynicism of U.S. foreign policy. It is a city whose skyrocketing murder rate is fueled by the cocaine trade, racial discontent, and an undeclared war on the island ninety miles to the south. *Miami* is a masterly study of immigration and exile, passion, hypocrisy, and political violence.

Current Affairs/Literature/0-679-78180-3

SALVADOR

In 1982, Joan Didion traveled to El Salvador at the ghastly height of its civil war. *Salvador* is an anatomy of that country's particular brand of terror—its mechanisms, rationales, and relationship to the United States. As she travels from battlefields to body dumps, Didion trains a merciless eye not only on the horror but also on the depredations and evasions of her own country's foreign policy.

Current Affairs/Literature/0-679-75183-1

ALSO AVAILABLE:

A Book of Common Prayer, 0-679-75486-5
Democracy, 0-679-75485-7
The Last Thing He Wanted, 0-679-75285-4
Run River, 0-679-75250-1